understanding **german idealis**

Understanding Movements in Modern Thought
Series Editor: Jack Reynolds

This series provides short, accessible and lively introductions to the major schools, movements and traditions in philosophy and the history of ideas since the beginning of the Enlightenment. All books in the series are written for undergraduates meeting the subject for the first time.

Published

Understanding Empiricism
Robert G. Meyers

Understanding Existentialism
Jack Reynolds

Understanding German Idealism
Will Dudley

Understanding Hegelianism
Robert Sinnerbrink

Understanding Hermeneutics
Lawrence K. Schmidt

Understanding Phenomenology
David R. Cerbone

Understanding Poststructuralism
James Williams

Understanding Utilitarianism
Tim Mulgan

Understanding Virtue Ethics
Stan van Hooft

Forthcoming titles include

Understanding Ethics
Tim Chappell

Understanding Feminism
Peta Bowden and Jane Mummery

Understanding Naturalism
Jack Ritchie

Understanding Pragmatism
Axel Mueller

Understanding Psychoanalysis
Joanne Faulkner and
Matthew Sharpe

Understanding Rationalism
Charlie Huenemann

understanding **german idealism**

Will Dudley

ACUMEN

First published in 2007 by Acumen

Acumen Publishing Limited
Stocksfield Hall
Stocksfield
NE43 7TN
www.acumenpublishing.co.uk

ISBN 978-1-84465-095-8 (hardcover)
ISBN 978-1-84465-096-5 (paperback)

British Library Cataloguing-in-Publication Data
A catalogue record for this book is available from the British Library.

Typeset by Graphicraft Limited, Hong Kong.
Printed and bound by Cromwell Press, Trowbridge.

For Janette, who wanted to know, before she agreed to marry me, why German Idealism matters

Contents

Acknowledgements

I am indebted and grateful to many people for their help with my efforts to write an accurate and accessible introduction to German Idealism. The students who took my course on this material in 2005 generously alerted me whenever my explanations were insufficiently clear, and raised excellent questions that indicated where more work needed to be done. The Oakley Center for the Humanities and Social Sciences at Williams College provided funding that supported a reduced teaching load for one semester and hosted a seminar in which a complete draft of my manuscript was read and discussed. The participants in that seminar – Melissa Barry, Stuart Crampton, Joe Cruz, Blake Emerson and Alan White – made innumerable suggestions that led to significant improvements in the text. Earl and Louise Dudley (my parents) and Isaac Dietzel (my former student) also read the entire work and offered many valuable comments. Blake Emerson and Ben Echols served as research assistants during the final push to revise and complete the manuscript.

I also owe a general debt to those who have taught me the most about German Idealism: Alan White, John McCumber, Stephen Houlgate and Robert Pippin. And, finally, I want to thank my family – Janette, Cole, and Ella Dudley – for sustaining me in this project and all else.

Abbreviations

Note: Full details of these works are given in the References.

Fichte
"CC"   "Concerning the Concept of the *Wissenschaftslehre*" (1988)
FNR   *Foundations of Natural Right* (2000)
"R"   "Review of *Aenesidemus*" (2000)
SE   *The System of Ethics* (2005)
SK   *The Science of Knowledge* (1982)

Hegel
D   *The Difference Between Fichte's and Schelling's System of Philosophy* (1977)
E   *The Encyclopedia Logic* (1991)
FK   *Faith and Knowledge* (1977)
ILPR   *Introduction to the Lectures on the History of Philosophy* (1985)
IPH   *Introduction to the Philosophy of History* (1988)
LPR   *Lectures on the Philosophy of Religion*, I (1974); one-volume edition (1988); III (1985)
PhenS   *Phenomenology of Spirit* (1977)
PhilS   *Philosophy of Spirit*. See: *Philosophy of Mind* (1971)
PN   *Philosophy of Nature* (1970)
PR   *Elements of the Philosophy of Right* (1991)

| "S" | "On the Relationship of Skepticism to Philosophy: Exposition of its Different Modifications and Comparison of the Latest Form with the Ancient One" (2000) |
| SL | *Science of Logic* (1989) |

Hume

| THN | *A Treatise of Human Nature* (2000) |

Jacobi

CDS	*Concerning the Doctrine of Spinoza in Letters to Herr Mendelssohn* (1984)
DHF	*David Hume on Faith* (1994)
"OTI"	"On Transcendental Idealism" (1994)

Kant

CPJ	*Critique of the Power of Judgment* (2000)
CPR	*Critique of Pure Reason* (1998)
CPrR	*Critique of Practical Reason* (1996)
G	*Groundwork of the Metaphysics of Morals* (1996)
P	*Prolegomena to Any Future Metaphysics That Will be Able to Come Forward As Science* (2002)

Reinhold

| FPK | *The Foundation of Philosophical Knowledge* (2000) |

Schelling

INHF	*Philosophical Inquiries into the Nature of Human Freedom* (1936)
IPN	*Ideas for a Philosophy of Nature* (1988)
OSPN	*First Outline of a System of Philosophy of Nature* (2004)
"PL"	"Philosophical Letters on Dogmatism and Criticism" (1980)
STI	*System of Transcendental Idealism* (1978)
"UHK"	"Of the I as the Principle of Philosophy, or, On the Unconditional in Human Knowledge" (1980)

Schulze

| A | *Aenesidemus* (2000) |

one

Introduction: modernity, rationality and freedom

German Idealism emerged in 1781, with the publication of Kant's *Critique of Pure Reason*, and ended fifty years later, with Hegel's death. The intervening half-century was without question one of the most important and influential in the history of philosophy. The thinkers of this period, and the themes they developed, revolutionized every area of philosophy, and had an impact that continues to be felt across the humanities and social sciences. Kant, Fichte, Schelling and Hegel – the four most important German Idealists – paved the way for Marx and Kierkegaard, phenomenology and existentialism, critical theory and poststructuralism, and in doing so left a mark that remains highly visible in contemporary social and political theory, religious studies and aesthetics. Reactions to German Idealism, especially those of the neo-Kantians, logical positivists and Bertrand Russell, were also instrumental in the founding of analytic philosophy, which today reveals and benefits from an increasingly sophisticated appreciation of the European philosophical tradition. German Idealism thus lies at the root of both continental and Anglo-American philosophy, and without it there could have been neither the sharp schism between the two that defined the discipline for much of the twentieth century, nor the resources that sustain current hopes of understanding and overcoming this unproductive intellectual sectarianism.

The significance of German Idealism is, unfortunately, matched by its notorious complexity. Its central texts have confounded the most capable and patient interpreters for more than 200 years. Much of this difficulty can be attributed to the challenge the German Idealists faced in trying to find appropriate means of expression for genuinely new ideas. But some of it seems unnecessary, the result of writing that could have been improved, and that deters even intelligent readers with the best of intentions.

Understanding German Idealism is an attempt to convey the significance of this philosophical movement while avoiding its obscurity. Such an effort must be selective in its treatment of thinkers and themes, restricted in scope to only the most important aspects of the most important works of the most important authors. But it is my aim to achieve clarity regarding these essential developments without resorting to oversimplification. If this book is successful, its readers will come away with a sound understanding of the problems that motivated Kant, Fichte, Schelling and Hegel, and of the solutions that they proposed. I hope such readers will be persuaded that the profundity and value of these ideas more than repay the intellectual struggle they require, and that they will be inspired to spend more time working through the details of the original texts on their own.

Modernity, rationality and freedom

The proximate philosophical cause of German Idealism was the scepticism of David Hume (1711–76), which Kant famously described in the *Prolegomena to Any Future Metaphysics That Will Be Able to Come Forward as Science* as "the very thing that ... first interrupted my dogmatic slumber and gave a completely different direction to my researches in the field of speculative philosophy" (*P*: 57). But the larger cultural trend that gave rise to both the *Critique of Pure Reason* and, eight years later, the French Revolution, was the Enlightenment insistence on replacing the premodern acceptance of unjustified authority with the modern demand for rational justification and freedom. The French Revolution promised to supplant inherited monarchy with a truly modern life that would establish and secure freedom for all; Kant promised to supplant inherited dogmatism with a truly modern philosophy that would establish and secure the limits of rational cognition and action.

The modern insistence that belief and action be rationally justified is, in principle if not always in practice, radically egalitarian and radically liberating. If wisdom and power are vested in a special authority, such as a monarch or a priest, ordinary people must defer to that authority for instructions regarding what to think and what to do. But if good reasons are the only legitimate authority, then everyone can lay equal claim to being able to participate in the process of offering and evaluating the arguments that justify our theoretical and practical commitments. And those who do participate in this process achieve emancipation to the extent that their thoughts and actions are no longer determined by external authorities, but rather by themselves. Such modern agents are, in virtue of the exercise of their own rationality, self-determining or free.

The most obvious impediment to replacing the rule of traditional authorities with the liberating self-rule of reason is the authorities themselves, who are rarely inclined to forfeit the power and deference to which they are accustomed. But Kant worries, in a justly famous essay entitled "An Answer to the Question: What is Enlightenment?", that an even more intransigent obstacle is internal: cowardice on the part of those who would be free. He declares the motto of the Enlightenment to be *Sapere aude!* – dare to know! – and he equates this with daring to live up to the nature of *Homo sapiens*.

Freedom requires courage, Kant believes, because it is much easier and more comfortable to rely on others for direction. Rethinking established beliefs is hard work, as is breaking out of established patterns of action. It is less complicated to persist in our old habits, and to allow others to do our thinking for us. Indeed, the tendency to rely on others can itself become habitual, making it even more difficult to abandon the guidance of advisors or purported experts in favour of the free use of our own understanding.

The call to freedom is thus more easily issued than answered. The prospect of throwing off authority is exhilarating, but also frightening. And even those who are brave enough to accept the challenge face a long and arduous task. Liberation cannot be accomplished overnight, but requires an exhaustive and ongoing labour of self-critique. It is this task – the task of examining and re-examining our existing practices and beliefs – to which Kant calls us, in the hope that our response will contribute to human enlightenment and freedom.

Empiricism, scepticism and determinism

If Hume is right, however, Kant's hope is destined to go unfulfilled, for neither courage nor effort can bring about the impossible. Hume contends that the ultimate basis of belief and action is custom or habit, rather than reason, and that our habits are strictly determined by the same natural necessity that governs the entire physical universe. If this is so, then the Enlightenment dream of autonomous subjects forming rationally governed polities is threatened not only by monarchs, priests, cowardice and laziness, but also by inescapable truths of metaphysics and epistemology: human knowledge rests on faith; human behaviour is completely explicable in terms of mechanistic forces; and self-determination is an unattainable fantasy.

Hume's scepticism and determinism are the result of his empiricism, to which he was absolutely committed, and from which he rigorously and relentlessly drew the consequences. Empiricism is founded on the principle that all ideas come from sensory experience, an assumption Hume inherited from his great predecessors, John Locke and George Berkeley. Hume introduces two new distinctions, however, that enable him to take empiricism to its logical conclusion.

Hume first distinguishes between impressions, which are the direct results of sensory experience, and ideas, which are copies of impressions. The feeling I have when I bang my toe on a rock is an impression of pain. My recollection of that feeling the next day is the idea of pain. Hume's version of the empiricist principle states that all ideas come from impressions, either directly or as the result of mental activities that manipulate impressions to form new ideas. The ideas of "horse" and "horn", for example, are copies of our sensory impressions of the corresponding entities. The idea of "unicorn", however, results from our imaginative combination of the ideas of "horse" and "horn", and designates a fictional beast to which no known entity corresponds.

Hume's second novel distinction is that between relations of ideas and matters of fact. Matters of fact are actual states of affairs about which we can learn only through experience of the world. Relations of ideas are definitional truths that can be deduced from the meaning of the terms involved. It is true by definition, and thus a relation of ideas known by every competent speaker of English, that all bachelors are unmarried. Whether or not bachelors need to eat more vegetables, however, is a matter of fact that can be discerned only through a careful study of the relevant population.

Hume claims that matters of fact and relations of ideas exhaust the types of possible objects of knowledge, and he employs this distinction to mount a devastating attack on rationalism. The great rationalists – including Descartes, Spinoza and Leibniz – wary of being deceived by the senses, and impressed by the demonstrable progress in mathematics, attempted to ascertain important truths about the world through the use of reason alone. Spinoza's *Ethics*, modelled explicitly on Euclid's

Geometry, epitomizes this approach: it proceeds from a small set of simple definitions and axioms to deduce a large number of complicated propositions and corollaries. According to Hume's schema, however, Spinoza's work is nothing more than an elaborate investigation of the relations of certain ideas. It may tell us a great deal about the implicit content of Spinoza's definition of "substance", but only empirical investigation can tell us whether such substance exists. Metaphysics, in other words, aspires to inform us about matters of fact, and therefore cannot be done on the model of mathematics, but rather must give way to science.

Having insisted that knowledge of matters of fact can be had only through observation of the world, Hume employs his distinction between ideas and impressions to eliminate unwarranted conclusions that careful observation does not support. His principle, which functions much like Ockham's razor, is that only two types of ideas are admissible in our accounts of the world: (1) those that are direct copies of impressions we have experienced, and (2) those that provide the best explanation of the impressions we have experienced. "Dog" is an example of the first type of idea because we have had many impressions of dogs. "Dinosaur" is an example of the second type of idea because although no human has ever had an impression of a dinosaur, the best explanation of the fossils we have found is that they were the bones of a once-living but now-extinct group of reptiles. An alternative explanation of these fossils is that they were planted by a mischievous fossil-fairy, but because we have no experience of fairies (mischievous, fossil-depositing, or otherwise), "fossil-fairy" is an idea that must be expunged from our accounts of the world (although it might be put to perfectly good use in children's stories).

Hume's insistence that all matters of fact be explained in terms of ideas traceable to impressions does away with much more than the fanciful creatures of childhood imagination. If Hume is right, then God, the self and causality are further casualties of the empiricist principle. The common use of these ideas is, in Hume's view, wholly unwarranted by the facts. We have impressions of particular internal states – such as pain, pleasure, heat and cold – but none of the "self" to whom these states purportedly belong. We have impressions of constantly conjoined phenomena – such as the freezing of water every time the temperature falls below 32 degrees Fahrenheit – but none of the purportedly necessary connection or "cause" that binds them together. We have impressions of the world, but have no credible basis for attributing the creation of this world to a "God", the likes of which we have never encountered.

Kant will challenge Hume's position on each of these three ideas, but it is the attack on causality that leads most directly to scepticism and determinism, and thus inspires the development and defence of the alternative to empiricism with which German Idealism begins.

The attack on causality is especially significant because, as Hume points out, all of our knowledge of matters of fact, other than those of which we are directly aware or retain in our memory, depends upon causal inference. He suggests, for example, that if we were to find a watch on a deserted island we would reasonably infer that other humans had been there before us, for the presence of the watch requires some explanation, and humans are the only beings we have ever known to make and carry watches. The conjunction between watches and human watchowners has been constant, in other words, and it is the constancy of this conjunction that warrants our causal inference and enables us to account for the watches that we occasionally encounter in unusual places.

Hume's insight, however, is that constant conjunction is not equivalent to necessary connection, and thus it is possible that any causal inference, although based upon all available experience, will prove to be false. The watch could have been deposited on the beach by God, or forgotten by a sunbathing alien, or grown on a nearby tree. More plausibly, the watch could have washed up on shore after falling into the ocean from a passing ship. In any of these scenarios, we would be wrong to conclude from the presence of the watch on the beach that humans had already been on the island.

The lesson Hume draws is that our knowledge of matters of fact can never have the same status as our knowledge of relations of ideas. Relations of ideas can be demonstratively proven to be necessarily true, through the use of deductive reason, because their opposites contradict the meaning of the terms in question, and are thus logically impossible. All bachelors are necessarily unmarried, because to get married is, by definition, to forfeit one's bachelorhood. All Euclidean triangles necessarily have interior angles that sum to 180 degrees, because having interior angles that do not sum to 180 degrees is demonstrably incompatible with meeting the conditions that define triangularity in Euclidean geometry. Matters of fact, by contrast, cannot be demonstrated to be necessarily true, because their opposites are not logically impossible. Bachelors may in fact eat too few vegetables, but perhaps unmarried males will someday develop better eating habits. The signs that tell motorists in the USA to yield the right of way are in fact yellow triangles, but a future international commission could resolve to make them purple trapezoids.

Knowledge of matters of fact thus rests not on deductive proof, but rather on inductive generalization: we attend carefully to all of our past experience, identify the most constantly conjoined phenomena, conclude that these stand in relation of cause-and-effect, and predict they will remain conjoined in the future. "Water has always frozen at 32 degrees Fahrenheit" becomes "Water freezes at 32 degrees Fahrenheit". "The sun has always risen every 24 hours" becomes "The sun rises every 24 hours". Further experience may lead us to revise our conclusions ("Water with a sufficiently high salt content freezes at 28 degrees"), but this process of revision is also based on induction.

Inductive reasoning is the foundation of science, and is thoroughly indispensable to our successful navigation of the world. Without relying on induction we could not safely cross the street, much less build computers and send rockets into space. Induction is a tool we literally cannot live without, and a tool that enables us to live very well.

But the problem with inductive reasoning, which Hume recognized and made famous, is that our reliance on it is not rational. Such reasoning takes the following general form: in the past, x has always been the case; therefore, in the future, x will be the case. The question Hume forces us to consider is this: what justifies inferences of this form? The justification is not deductive, for it is not a logical necessity that the future should resemble the past. So the justification must be inductive (since deduction and induction exhaust the types of reasoning): we believe that the future will resemble the past because *in the past* the future has resembled the past. But attempting to justify the practice of inductive inference on the basis of an inductive inference is clearly circular. Such an attempt employs, and thus takes for granted as a hidden premise, the very form of inference that it is supposed to justify: in the past, x has always been the case; therefore, in the future, x will be the case. Despite its reliability and indispensability, then, inductive inference lacks a rational justification.

Hume emphasizes that the inability of reason to justify induction does not mean we should no longer use this form of inference. We have no choice. But he wants us to recognize that our knowledge of matters of fact, all of which rests on causal inferences, all of which are inductive, ultimately rests on habit or custom rather than reason. We are in the habit of expecting the future to resemble the past, and this habit has served us well. We expect it to continue to serve us well. But there is no rational justification for this expectation. Why the future should resemble the past, we cannot say. And thus no matter how regular our experience has been to date, we have no *reason* for expecting the future course of events to resemble it. What we have is a deep-seated faith.

Scepticism regarding the capacity of reason to justify our beliefs about matters of fact is thus the first important consequence of Hume's attack on causality. The second important consequence of this attack is determinism.

It might seem surprising that Hume's analysis of causation as constant conjunction would lead him to deny free will. After all, if free will is understood as the capacity to make decisions and initiate actions that are not necessitated by prior conditions and causal forces, then the recognition that we have no impression of necessary connection binding events together might appear to provide an opening for the operation of freedom.

Hume points out, however, that we have no impression of free will either, and then offers an account of the fact that we are nonetheless prone to ascribe this capacity to ourselves. He suggests that we tend to consider ourselves free because we do not experience ourselves as subject to the strict causal necessitation that we attribute to nature. But if, as Hume has argued, there is no basis for regarding nature as causally necessitated, then there is also no basis for regarding ourselves as qualitatively different from natural entities. The "necessity" we attribute to nature is simply shorthand for the fact that we have observed natural phenomena to be conjoined with each other in highly regular and predictable ways. But human behaviour is also highly regular and predictable, Hume points out, and thus subject to necessity in precisely the same sense. Of course our behaviour is not perfectly predictable, but neither is the weather. Weather patterns and patterns of human behaviour are highly complex, and sometimes surprising, but they are both correlated to discernible factors in observable ways, and the more extensively and carefully we observe these correlations, the better we become at predicting the resulting outcomes of given sets of conditions. If we are not prepared to grant free will to storm systems, then, we should be consistent and acknowledge that we have just as little reason to grant it to ourselves.

Human behaviour is properly understood, according to Hume, in precisely the same way that all animal behaviour is understood. Animals have biological needs, and various desires, and their behaviour is a function of the attempt to satisfy these needs and desires as best they can in the circumstances in which they find themselves. Changes in the inputs (needs, desires and circumstances) tend to produce changes in output (behaviour). The more we know about the correlation between inputs and outputs for a given species, including the human species, the more precisely we will be able to predict the behaviour of animals of that type.

Rationality, on this account of behaviour, is the ability to respond to the environment in ways that maximize the satisfaction of needs and desires. Reason, in other words, guides behaviour by discerning the most appropriate means to bring about given ends. A rational cat will, when hungry, return to the spot where it is accustomed to finding a bowl full of food. A rational person will, when hungry, return to the refrigerator or find a restaurant. But reason, according to Hume, can neither set goals nor motivate us to pursue them. Reason is, in Hume's famous words, "a slave to the passions", and thus what it is rational to do depends entirely upon the passions we do or do not happen to have. If we do not desire food, then it is perfectly rational not to eat (so long as we do not have another desire, such as preserving our health, that depends upon eating for its satisfaction). If it is sufficiently important to me to avoid even the smallest personal injury, then, Hume writes in *A Treatise of Human Nature*, "It is not contrary to reason to prefer the destruction of the whole world to the scratching of my finger" (*THN*: 267). As an animal I will do whatever it is that I desire, and as a rational animal I will attempt to satisfy my desires as successfully as possible, whatever they may be.

Hume thus shows that empiricism leads ineluctably to the conclusion that the human "self" is merely a complex mechanism, producing behavioural outputs in habitual response to the environmental inputs it encounters. Such a self is incapable of rational self-determination, and therefore incapable of fulfilling the modern aspirations to epistemological, moral and political autonomy. Hume is therefore an important intellectual ancestor of postmodern thinkers and movements, and poses a direct and formidable challenge to those who would, like Kant and the French Revolutionaries, assert and defend the truth of human freedom.

The "critique" of reason and German Idealism

Before becoming aware of the power and significance of Hume's empiricism, Immanuel Kant (1724–1804) enjoyed a successful academic career, following Leibniz and Christian Wolff in the tradition of German rationalism. Between the ages of twenty-five and forty-five Kant published an impressive number of works, on the basis of which he was appointed professor of logic and metaphysics at the University of Königsberg in 1770.

During the decade following his appointment, however, Kant published virtually nothing. It was wondered whether his silence indicated the sudden onset of philosophical barrenness, but the truth was even worse: Kant had become aware that all of his work was vulnerable to Hume's devastating attack on dogmatic rationalism, that none of his writings had lasting philosophical value, and that there could be no value in doing more work of the same kind. Kant thus faced a dilemma: either he could accept empiricism, together with the scepticism and determinism that follow from it; or he would have to develop a radically new philosophical alternative, one that could somehow grant the bankruptcy of rationalism while also managing to avoid empiricism and its consequences.

Kant realized that much more than his own professional legacy was at stake. He saw that Hume's scepticism and determinism constituted a challenge to the very possibility and promise of modernity, and therefore responded to the rude awakening from his comfortable dogmatic slumber by trying to answer Hume in a way that would save the prospects of rational cognition, moral agency and political freedom.

Kant transformed his philosophical direction via the insight that Hume's challenge could be answered by means of a very special form of critique. Modernity calls for a re-evaluation of our ordinary beliefs and practices that brings them into accord with the demands of reason, but Hume's denial of the very possibility of this enterprise gives rise to the need for a critical examination of rationality itself. Philosophy must demonstrate that Hume fails to establish that reason is incapable of directing and motivating human behaviour, and thus fails to establish that human beings are not free. This is the project that defines Kant's "critique" of reason, the central aim of which is to provide a defence of freedom and morality, and in so doing to preserve the prospects of Enlightenment and modernity.

The immediate result of Kant's critique of reason was his own new position, known as transcendental idealism. But the revolution initiated by this development set the philosophical agenda for the next fifty years: all of the subsequent German idealists attempted to execute the Kantian project more rigorously and successfully than Kant himself had done, striving to develop a fully self-critical and rational philosophy, in order thereby to determine the meaning and sustain the possibility of a free and rational modern life.

two

Kant: transcendental idealism

Kant presented his response to Hume in three books – the *Critique of Pure Reason* (1781), *Critique of Practical Reason* (1788) and *Critique of the Power of Judgment* (1790) – that have come to be known, respectively, as the first, second and third critique. The enterprise Kant undertakes in these books is often referred to, unsurprisingly, as critical philosophy. The position that results from this undertaking is called transcendental idealism. Kant claims that transcendental idealism successfully rebuts Hume's scepticism without reverting to dogmatic rationalism, and that it is the only philosophical option that remains tenable in the wake of a thorough critique of reason.

According to Kant, a complete and successful critique of reason must answer exactly three questions:

1. What can I know?
2. What should I do?
3. What may I hope?

The first, epistemological, question is the subject of the *Critique of Pure Reason*, the book that broke Kant's decade of silence and introduced his philosophical revolution. In that work, Kant is concerned to survey the extent of our possible knowledge by determining precisely the capacities and limits of theoretical rationality. Like Hume, Kant aims to deflate unwarranted and superstitious beliefs that exceed our powers of justification. At the same time, however, Kant aims to show that

Hume's scepticism regarding theoretical rationality is itself unjustified, by demonstrating that there are indeed matters of fact that can be known to be necessarily true by means of reason alone. In the course of this demonstration, Kant also claims to defeat Hume's determinism, by proving that one of the things we can know is that we *cannot* know whether or not we are free.

The conclusion that agnosticism is the only theoretically justifiable position with respect to free will is one of the most important results of the *Critique of Pure Reason*, which Kant famously describes as "limiting knowledge to make way for faith". By this he means that the first critique demonstrates that we cannot *know* whether certain things are the case, and thus gives us licence to think and act *as if* they were, so long as they are not logically impossible. Free will is, for Kant, the most significant example of something that is theoretically possible but definitively indemonstrable.

The significance of free will lies in its being necessary to our experience of moral obligation, an experience that only makes sense, according to Kant, on the supposition that we are free. If we lacked freedom, Kant reasons, we could not be obliged to do anything, since all of our actions would already be predetermined and a course of action can only be obligatory if one is capable of choosing to pursue it. So it is the experience of moral obligation, rather than any theoretical demonstration, that sustains Kant's belief in free will.

The *Critique of Practical Reason* makes the case for grounding freedom of the will upon moral experience, and then raises the second of the three questions that define the critique of reason: what should I do? Given that I am subject to moral obligation, what are my particular obligations, and why?

Kant presents his moral philosophy in the *Groundwork of the Metaphysics of Morals* (1787), the second critique, and *The Metaphysics of Morals* (1797). In these works he attempts to establish that, *pace* Hume, reason is not merely an instrument for finding the best means to satisfy our desires, but is itself capable of setting goals and motivating us to pursue them. Kant also offers criteria by means of which he claims we can distinguish between those intentions and motivations that are morally permissible and those that are not. He then uses these criteria to specify our rights and duties.

Kant equates living morally with being worthy of happiness, which he notes is quite different from, and very imperfectly correlated with, actually being happy. Those who strive to be moral are not necessarily more satisfied, and indeed are often less so, than those for whom morality is a matter of indifference. Kant claims, however, that we cannot help caring about both morality and happiness. We are free beings, who feel compelled to perform the obligations that our own rationality imposes upon us, and we are also animals, with desires that demand satisfaction. Consequently, according to Kant, we cannot help hoping that our striving to fulfil our moral obligations will be rewarded with a commensurate degree of happiness. Hence the critique of reason yields its third and final question: what may I hope?

In a certain sense, of course, we may hope for anything. I may hope to become a professional baseball player, or to win the lottery. But I have no good reason to believe that either of these hopes will be fulfilled. I am too old and unskilled to embark on a baseball career, and I do not waste my money on the lottery because I know that the odds are so heavily against me. Hoping to be a baseball star, or to win the lottery, is thus to indulge in wishful thinking.

Kant calls the perfect coincidence of being worthy of happiness with actual happiness, or the coincidence of the rational use of our freedom with the satisfaction of our natural desires, the highest good. The question is whether there is a rational basis for hoping that the highest good may come to pass, that freedom and nature may be reconciled, or whether this is merely wishful thinking. In the *Critique of the Power of Judgment*, Kant answers that although we can never know that freedom is operative in the natural world, we nonetheless have good grounds for the judgement that the purpose of nature itself is the development and exercise of our freedom, and thus for the hope that there is a just God who will someday coordinate moral striving with happiness.

Kant claims that his three critiques complete the tasks demanded by critical philosophy. As he writes in the Preface to the *Critique of Practical Reason*, "the concept of freedom . . . constitutes the *keystone* of the whole structure of a system of pure reason" (*CPrP*: 139). The first critique clears the way for faith in human freedom, by arguing that determinism can never be known to be true. The second critique argues that our experience of moral obligation establishes the reality of human freedom. And the third critique contends that we have good reason to hope that the moral use of freedom will ultimately be coordinated with happiness.

Figure 2.1 indicates the location of the central questions of Kant's critical philosophy within his major works.

	Theoretical Epistemology, metaphysics What can I know?	**Practical** Morality, politics What should I do?
Critical reflection	*Critique of Pure Reason* *Prolegomena to Any Future Metaphysics* What is knowledge? What are the conditions of obtaining it? What kinds of object can and can't we know anything about? What can we know, *a priori*, about all possible objects of knowledge?	*Critique of Practical Reason* *Groundwork of the Metaphysics of Morals* What is morality? What are the conditions of being moral?
Metaphysical results	*Metaphysical Foundations of Natural Science* What can we know, *a priori*, about all possible material objects?	*Metaphysics of Morals* What are our moral and political duties?
Empirical applications	*Transition from the Metaphysical Foundations of Natural Science to Physics* (posthumous) How can our *a priori* knowledge guide our empirical research?	*Anthropology from a Practical Point of View* *On Perpetual Peace* Human nature being what it is, how can we fulfil our moral and political duties?

Critique of the Power of Judgment

What may I hope?

How do the answers in theoretical and practical philosophy fit together?

Religion within the Boundaries of Mere Reason

How can the practical postulate of God's existence be rational, if we cannot know that He exists?

Figure 2.1 Kant's critical philosophy

The limits of knowledge and the possibility of freedom

The Copernican revolution in epistemology

In the Preface to the *Critique of Pure Reason*, Kant boldly promises to deliver a Copernican revolution in epistemology, which he claims is the only thing that can save metaphysics from the twin dangers of dogmatism and scepticism. Copernicus revolutionized astronomy by rejecting the hypothesis that the heavenly bodies move around the earth in favour of the hypothesis that the earth moves around the sun. The heliocentric hypothesis was confirmed when it enabled Copernicus to solve a number of outstanding problems that had confounded geocentric astronomers. The epistemological equivalent of the geocentric hypothesis in astronomy, according to Kant, is the assumption that knowledge requires the knowing subject to conform his mental representations to the object that is to be known. If this were the case, then the problem of metaphysical knowledge would be insoluble, and Humean scepticism would be unavoidable. On this hypothesis, all knowledge of the object would have to derive from experience, and Kant grants Hume's point that experience can yield only provisional inductive generalizations, which can never amount to the necessary and universal truths demanded by metaphysics.

Kant's Copernican move is to reject the hypothesis that the subject must conform to the object in favour of the hypothesis that the object must conform to the subject. If this were the case, then metaphysics would be possible. It would be known of all objects that they must have whatever features are required to enable them to be experienced by the subject. These features would thus apply to the objects of experience necessarily and universally, and knowledge of such features would qualify as metaphysics. On this hypothesis, therefore, the possibility of metaphysical knowledge would be saved, but metaphysics would have to be conducted in a radically new fashion. Dogmatic rationalism, which purported to achieve insight regarding the character of actuality but instead revealed only the implicit content of its own terms and definitions, would have to be replaced by a rigorous examination of the knowing subject's own capacities for representation and experience. Metaphysical knowledge of the objects of experience depends upon knowledge of these capacities, because it is to them that such objects must conform.

Kant initiates his Copernican revolution by refining Hume's classification of the types of knowledge. Hume recognizes only two such types, relations of ideas and matters of fact, and argues that because neither type amounts to metaphysical knowledge, metaphysics is impossible. Kant, however, recognizes four distinct types of knowledge, which he classifies on the basis of a pair of related distinctions.

Kant's first distinction is between *a priori* and *a posteriori* knowledge. Knowledge is *a priori*, or pure, if it is not derived from experience. Knowledge that does derive from experience is, by contrast, *a posteriori*, or empirical. Whether bachelors eat enough vegetables is an empirical question, which can be answered only on the basis of experience. One would need to study human nutrition and then embark on a worldwide survey of bachelors to determine their eating habits. Whether bachelors are married, however, is a question that can be answered by any competent speaker of English without any further experience. It would be absurd to embark on a survey of the world's bachelors to enquire about their marital status. "Bachelors are unmarried" is thus *a priori* knowledge, whereas "Bachelors do not eat enough vegetables" is *a posteriori*.

Kant's second distinction is between analytic and synthetic judgements. Judgements are logical forms that connect a subject and a predicate. The most basic judgements have the form *x is y*, where *y* is a property attributed to the type of entity referred to by concept *x*. Kant defines an analytic judgement as one in which mere analysis of the content implicit in the subject term is sufficient to determine that the predicate can be attributed to it. Analytic judgements thus make explicit the predicates that belong to, or are contained in, a given subject. Synthetic judgements, by contrast, connect subjects to predicates that are not implicitly inherent in them. "Bachelors are unmarried" is an analytic judgement, because the subject term "bachelor" means "unmarried male", and thus the predicate term "unmarried" can be arrived at via analysis of the subject term in which it is contained. "Bachelors do not eat enough vegetables" is a synthetic judgement, because "not eating enough vegetables" is not implicit in "unmarried males", although it may happen to be true of them.

Kant's pair of distinctions defines four distinct types of knowledge: analytic *a priori*; analytic *a posteriori*; synthetic *a priori*; and synthetic *a posteriori*. If Hume is right, however, there can be actual instances of only two of these types. Knowledge of relations of ideas must be analytic *a priori*, because such knowledge depends solely upon analysis of the terms in question. And knowledge of matters of fact must be synthetic *a posteriori*, because such knowledge depends upon experience to reveal the connections that happen to obtain in the world.

Analytic *a posteriori* knowledge is patently absurd, because if a truth is analytic then it requires no experience to be known. And synthetic *a priori* knowledge is the old fantasy of rationalist metaphysicians, whose dream of knowing the truth about actuality by means of reason alone had been thoroughly discredited by Hume.

Kant's response to Hume's scepticism regarding the possibility of metaphysics turns on whether or not he can produce synthetic *a priori* knowledge without lapsing back into dogmatic rationalism. Metaphysics must be *a priori* because it seeks necessary and universal truths, whereas *a posteriori* knowledge can provide only contingent generalizations. Experience can tell us how the world is, but not how it must be. And metaphysics must be synthetic because it seeks to inform us about the world, whereas analytic judgements inform us only about the meaning of our concepts.

Kant rests his hopes for synthetic *a priori* knowledge, and thus for metaphysics, upon his Copernican philosophical turn. His strategy is to examine the knowing subject, in order to identify and describe the capacities that enable such subjects to experience a world of objects. If successful, this examination would reveal the conditions that any possible object of experience must meet in order to be experienced at all. Knowledge of such conditions of the possibility of experience would be synthetic, because it would pertain to the actual objects of experience, and it would be *a priori*, because it would apply necessarily and universally to objects without being dependent upon empirical investigations of them. The central task of the *Critique of Pure Reason* is thus to determine the conditions of the possibility of experience, and thereby to restore and complete metaphysics as a rigorous philosophical discipline, capable of withstanding and responding to Humean empiricist scrutiny.

Kant calls the conditions that make experience possible "transcendental" conditions, and the examination of these conditions "transcendental philosophy". Transcendental philosophy attempts to restore the possibility of metaphysics by drawing a novel distinction between appearances, or *phenomena*, and things-in-themselves, or *noumena*.

The most common interpretation of this distinction – which was advanced and made popular by Friedrich Jacobi, almost immediately after the appearance of the first critique, and has had considerable influence ever since – attributes to Kant the view that there are two separate worlds, which are populated by two separate sorts of objects. On this interpretation, Kant faces several difficulties that may seem insurmountable (as they did to Jacobi, whose challenge to Kant, which was instrumental in spurring the development of German Idealism, will be considered in Chapter 3). First, there is the question of how Kant is justified in referring to things-in-themselves at all. Things-in-themselves, by definition, do not appear in our experience, and thus Kant would seem to have no basis for claiming to know that they exist. Second, if the existence of things-in-themselves is granted, the nature of their relationship to the world of appearances then becomes a mystery highly resistant to explanation.

Because the two-world interpretation of transcendental philosophy generates these problems, which many regard as intractable, a promising alternative attributes to Kant the view that there is but a single world, upon which we are capable of adopting two different perspectives. On the one hand, we can conceive of the world as it is experienced by us, in virtue of our capacities for representation. And on the other hand, we can conceive of the world as it is in itself, independently of being represented or experienced by us. On this interpretation, phenomena and noumena do not designate two separate worlds, but rather two different ways of thinking about or characterizing the only world we know.

Transcendental philosophy attempts to make metaphysics possible by strictly limiting its knowledge claims to appearances, or objects as they are experienced by us. If Kant is right, we can know certain things to be necessarily and universally true of all possible objects of experience, or phenomena. Because it is impossible for us to experience objects that fail to meet the conditions determined by our capacities for representation, we can know *a priori* that *all* appearances *must* meet those conditions. But about objects as they are in themselves, we can know nothing whatsoever. Because we can never encounter things as they are independently of being encountered by us, experience can give us no *a posteriori* knowledge of the noumenal character of the world. Nor can we have *a priori* knowledge of things-in-themselves, because the conditions of the possibility of experience that constrain appearances do not apply. All objects of experience must meet these conditions, or else they could not be experienced, but things-in-themselves need not conform to the constraints imposed by our capacities for representation, since they are by definition never represented.

The limitation of synthetic *a priori* knowledge to objects of experience leads Kant to characterize metaphysics as "transcendentally ideal" and "empirically real". The empirical reality of metaphysics indicates that the conditions of the possibility of experience really do, and indeed must, apply to all of the objects that appear to us. The transcendental ideality of metaphysics indicates that the conditions of the possibility of experience apply *only* to appearances, and can never be attributed to things-in-themselves. This is one of the most important conclusions that Kant draws from his Copernican revolution in philosophy: we must remain resolutely agnostic regarding that which transcends our experience, because we are constitutionally incapable of knowing anything whatsoever about it.

The conditions of the possibility of experience

If metaphysics requires the specification of the conditions of the possibility of experience, then philosophy must begin with an account of experience itself. Experience involves, according to Kant, the mental representation of objects, and he identifies two conditions that are necessary to make such representation possible.

The first condition of the mental representation of an object is that the object be encountered by, or taken into, the mind. Kant refers to the capacity to take an object into the mind as intuition. We intuit objects by means of our senses, and thus Kant refers to the human form of intuition as sensibility. He recognizes as a theoretical possibility a being with the capacity for intellectual intuition, for encountering objects directly through the mind without any sensory mediation, but rejects the view, held by many rationalists, that humans have this ability.

The second condition of the mental representation of an object is that the object be recognized as the particular object it is. Kant refers to the capacity to recognize objects as understanding. Understanding receives indeterminate intuitions from sensibility and employs concepts to make judgements regarding the determinate character of the objects of the experience.

Kant famously writes that concepts without intuitions are empty, but intuitions without concepts are blind. We cannot use concepts to understand the world unless we receive data from the senses upon which we can pass judgement, but intuitions by themselves cannot inform us about the world until they have been understood. The experience of objects thus depends upon the interaction of sensibility and understanding.

The project of specifying the conditions of the possibility of experience therefore breaks neatly into two distinct pieces. Kant first investigates the conditions of the possibility of sensibility in the "Transcendental Aesthetic", and then turns to the conditions of the possibility of understanding in the "Transcendental Analytic", which constitutes the first half of the "Transcendental Logic". The aim of both of these investigations is to determine what can be known *a priori* to be true of all objects of experience.

Figure 2.2 provides a map of the *Critique of Pure Reason*. The particular intuitions that are received through sensibility cannot, of course, be known *a priori*. We cannot know what we will encounter until we have encountered it. Kant believes it is possible, however, to know something *a priori* about the form that any possible sensory intuition must take. All sensory intuitions, Kant contends, appear in time, and all sensory intuitions that refer the mind to something outside of itself appear in space. Kant thus refers to space and time as the forms of intuition.

Kant provides two arguments in support of his position on space and time. The first argument, which he calls a "transcendental exposition", assumes that geometry is synthetic *a priori* knowledge, and reasons that this could be possible only if space and time were *a priori* forms of intuition. This is a classic example of what has come to be known as a transcendental argument. Such arguments assume that *x* is a given fact, and then build a case that some condition or set of conditions must obtain to explain the possibility of *x*. Transcendental arguments can fail if the connection between the stipulated conditions and the given fact that they purportedly make possible is not sufficiently well established, or if the purportedly given fact itself is called into question. Kant's transcendental exposition of space and time is often charged with failing in the latter fashion, since many doubt that geometry is in fact synthetic *a priori* knowledge. If geometry is an analytic discipline, deducing conclusions that are implicit in its initial definitions and axioms, then Kant's transcendental exposition of space and time cannot get off the ground.

Kant's second argument, which he calls a "metaphysical exposition", does not depend upon doubtful claims about the status of geometry. It aims to demonstrate that the ideas of space and time cannot be derived from the experience of particular objects, because the experience of any particular object already presupposes them. The idea of space cannot be arrived at via the inductive inference that every object that has appeared distinct from me so far has been spatial, because in order for me to experience even one object as distinct from me it must be located in space. Likewise, the idea of time cannot be arrived at via the inductive inference that all of my representations that have appeared simultaneously or successively in relation to each other have so far

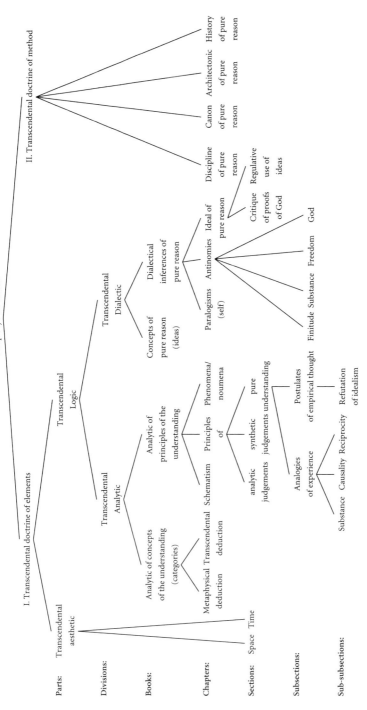

Figure 2.2 Kant's *Critique of Pure Reason*

been temporal, because in order for me to experience even a single set of representations as relatively simultaneous or successive the representations must be located in time. Kant concludes that space and time are *a priori* forms of sensibility, and thus that they are transcendentally ideal and empirically real. All of the objects of our experience must be in space and time, but spatiality and temporality are not properties of things-in-themselves. Indeed, it is only in relation to human sensibility that it makes sense to speak of space and time at all.

Understanding, which Kant equates with thinking, employs concepts to make judgements about sensory intuitions, which is necessary to have experience of determinate objects and events. Sensibility provides us with an ocean of raw data, which Kant calls the manifold of intuition, and concepts are the tools that the mind uses to unify elements of this manifold into discrete perceptions. We respond to sensory stimulation by judging, for example, that "whales are enormous" or "the phone is ringing".

Most of the concepts we employ are derived from experience or, as Hume would have said, from our impressions of the world. If we had never experienced whales or telephones we would not have developed the concepts of "whale" and "phone". The legitimate use of such concepts depends upon an *a posteriori* justification. So long as the world contains whales and phones, our accounts of the world may employ the corresponding concepts. But if there should come a day when whales are extinct or phones have become obsolete, then these concepts will have to be relegated to the writing of history and fiction.

Kant believes, however, that there are also *a priori* concepts, concepts that do not derive from experience but rather contribute to making experience possible. His argument for this claim involves two major steps. The "metaphysical deduction" attempts to demonstrate that a certain set of concepts, which Kant entitles "categories", is necessary to the operation of the understanding, and thus to all thinking whatsoever. The "transcendental deduction" then attempts to demonstrate that these same categories are also necessary conditions of the possibility of the experience of determinate objects. Together these two deductions aim to refute the empiricist principle that all ideas must derive from impressions, by demonstrating that at least some ideas or concepts must be operative in order to make the experience of determinate impressions possible.

The metaphysical deduction asks whether there are any concepts that are presupposed by every act of judgement, and thus by all thinking.

Since there is an indefinite number of possible judgements the question might seem unanswerable, but Kant claims that all possible judgements may be classified into a finite number of types. He enumerates these types in the "Table of Judgments", and then argues that each type presupposes the use of certain concepts, which must therefore be *a priori* and are identified in the "Table of Categories".

Consider the judgements "some people are women" and "some trees are deciduous". These two judgements differ with respect to their content, because they employ different empirical concepts to inform us about very different things. But according to Kant's classification they share the same form, and thus implicitly rely upon the use of the same four categories. The reference to "some" people and trees (as distinct from "one" or "all" of these things) invokes the concept of plurality, the idea that there is more than one of the kind of entity that serves as the subject of the judgement. The verb "are" invokes the concept of reality, the idea that the predicate affirmatively describes the subject. And the categorical assertions that some people are women and some trees are deciduous further invoke the concepts of substance and existence, the idea that there are in fact entities in the world that correspond to the subject term of the judgement, and that possess the property named by the predicate. Thus every judgement of this form, regardless of its particular content, is made possible by the categories of plurality, reality, substance and existence.

Kant's classification allows for precisely 81 distinct types of judgement (because each type is defined by 4 attributes, and there are 3 values that each attribute can take, so there are 3^4 possibilities), which rely on precisely 12 categories (one for each possible value of each attribute, or 3*4). These categories are: unity, plurality, totality, reality, negation, limitation, substance/accident, cause/effect, reciprocal interaction, possibility, existence and necessity. Kant contends that without these concepts, no judging, and thus no understanding or thinking, would be possible. If this is true, then the categories could not derive from experience but must have an *a priori* origin in the mind itself. For this reason Kant also refers to the categories as the pure concepts of the understanding.

The transcendental deduction aims to demonstrate that the categories may legitimately be applied to experience, despite the fact that they do not derive from it. It is therefore upon this notoriously difficult section of the first critique that Kant's reply to empiricism ultimately rests.

The transcendental deduction must show that the categories are not only conditions of the possibility of thinking but also conditions of the possibility of experience. Experience, Kant points out, requires a subject that persists over time and is able to retain and connect its mental contents from one moment to the next. Without such a unified self-consciousness, a subject might receive sensory stimulation but would be incapable of processing these raw data. Each sensory stimulus would be radically isolated from the rest, and whatever awareness the subject might possess could never rise to the experience of determinate objects and events. Such experience thus requires that the raw data of sensation, which Kant calls the manifold of intuition, be synthesized by the mind in various ways. The mind must apprehend the manifold, reproduce it in memory, and recognize it *as* a particular object or event. These syntheses, Kant argues, must employ the categories, the concepts that enable the understanding to unify the material it receives from sensibility. The categories are thus necessary to explain the fact that we have experience of determinate objects and events, and not merely awareness of indistinguishable sensory stimuli.

From the transcendental deduction Kant concludes that Hume is wrong to assert that all ideas must derive from impressions, and so wrong to declare the illegitimacy of every idea whose experiential pedigree cannot be traced. The pure concepts of the understanding do not derive from impressions, but their application in our accounts of experience is perfectly legitimate, because they make experience possible and therefore give us synthetic *a priori* knowledge of its constitution. From the transcendental deduction, in other words, Kant concludes that metaphysics survives the most sceptical empiricist challenge.

Metaphysical knowledge and its limits

The remainder of the *Critique of Pure Reason* is devoted to three tasks: (1) specifying the metaphysical knowledge that the proper application of the categories provides; (2) establishing the proper limits of metaphysical knowledge; and (3) explaining the human propensity to ignore these limits and indulge in unwarranted speculation.

The transcendental deduction is meant to establish the general claim that the categories condition all possible experience, but Kant must still determine the specific features of objects and their interrelations that these conditions make necessary. He must enumerate, that is, the specific synthetic *a priori* judgements sanctioned by the pure concepts of the understanding. Kant calls these judgements the principles of pure understanding, and he identifies precisely twelve of them, or one per category.

The first step in applying the categories is identifying the marks by which they can be recognized in our experience. With respect to empirical concepts this is trivial, because the identifying marks have been abstracted from experience. The concept of "reptile", for example, is partially defined by the mark of "cold-blooded", which has been abstracted from our sensible experience of lizards, turtles, snakes and crocodiles. But the categories are pure concepts, not abstracted from experience, so their defining marks do not correspond to anything sensible. We have never, for example, had the impression of a necessary connection, and thus it is not clear how we could determine and recognize the sensible marks that reveal the operation of causality in our experience.

Kant's solution is to identify a third kind of representation that can mediate between the purely logical concepts of the understanding and the intuitions of sensibility in virtue of having something in common with both of them. What concepts and intuitions have in common is temporality, the form of all representations, and thus these mediating representations, which Kant calls "schemata", are temporal translations of the categories that enable us to recognize the appearances of these pure concepts in our experience.

The category of "substance", for example, is defined as "that which is a subject but never a predicate". But this purely logical definition cannot tell us which sensible appearances qualify as substances, for it does not tell us which sensible characteristics mark something as "that which is a subject but never a predicate". Kant offers as the temporal schema of substance, however, "permanence of the real in time", which enables us to recognize substance as that which abides unchanged in relation to that which is transitory.

The schemata show us how it is possible to apply the categories to sensible experience, but this does not yet provide the synthetic *a priori* knowledge that Kant seeks. Such metaphysical knowledge requires showing how the categories must be found in sensible experience, how the world as it appears to us must conform to the schemata. To this end, Kant produces transcendental arguments intended to prove that each of the twelve schemata serves as a necessary condition of the possibility of a given type of experience. These arguments yield twelve principles, the principles of pure understanding, each of which is a synthetic *a priori* judgement expressing the way that a particular schematized category necessarily structures our experience of the world. The twelve principles are divided into four groups, which Kant calls the "axioms of intuition", "anticipations of perception", "analogies of experience" and "postulates of empirical thought in general".

Table 2.1 presents the relationship between Kant's tables of judgements, categories, schemata and principles.

The most important principle for the purpose of responding to Hume is the second analogy of experience, which contends that we must experience every event as causally determined. The second analogy begins by noting that we experience not only changes in our mental representations, but also alterations of objects, and asks how the latter sort of experience is possible. Kant argues that experiencing the alteration of an object involves more than merely experiencing a change of representations, since the latter occurs even in the experience of static objects that are undergoing no alteration. To experience an alteration, Kant contends, I must regard the order of successive representations as necessary and irreversible, because it is these criteria that distinguish such an experience from the experience of a static object.

To take Kant's example, in perceiving a house I might first take in the roof, then the windows, and finally the door. But I might also survey the house from bottom to top, or left to right, or in any other order I please. In any case my experience is successive, involving a series of representations that replace each other in my mind, but in no case does the mere fact of representational succession suffice to make me experience the house itself as changing. To experience a change in the house itself, such as a window being broken by a ball, I have to regard the order of successive representations as necessary and irreversible.

Whenever I find that it is possible to rearrange the order of experienced representations according to my will – for example, by putting the window back together and returning the ball to the street – then I must regard the experience as the product of my imagination, rather than as the real alteration of an object. To experience real alteration is to experience the order of the representational succession as necessary and irreversible, which requires, Kant claims, regarding the successive representations as following from each other according to a rule, which is to regard them as causally related to each other. We can thus know *a priori*, Kant concludes, that every event must be experienced as having a cause, because otherwise it could not be experienced as an event at all.

The second analogy does not purport to solve the problem of induction, or to demonstrate that we can know *a priori* the causal relationships that obtain between particular phenomena. It does not even purport to demonstrate that our *a posteriori* judgements regarding particular causal relationships will always be accurate. The second analogy does claim, however, to prove the principle of sufficient reason,

Table 2.1 Kant's tables

	JUDGEMENTS	CATEGORIES	SCHEMATA	PRINCIPLES
Quantity				**Axioms of intuition**
	Universal	Totality	All (units)	
	Particular	Plurality	Some (units)	All intuitions are extensive magnitudes
	Singular	Unity	One (unit)	
Quality				**Anticipations of perception**
	Affirmative	Reality	Being	
	Negative	Negation	Non-being	All perceptions have intensive magnitudes
	Infinite	Limitation	Degree of being	
Relation				**Analogies of experience**
	Categorical	Substance/accident	Permanence/impermanence	Substance remains permanent
	Hypothetical	Cause/effect	Rule-governed succession	Events governed by cause–effect
	Disjunctive	Reciprocity	Rule-governed coexistence	Coexisting substances reciprocal
Modality				**Postulates of empirical thought**
	Problematic	Possibility/impossibility	Conceivable existence in time	Agrees with conditions of intuition/conceptualization
	Assertoric	Existence/non-existence	Existence at some time	Agrees with material conditions of experience (sensation)
	Apodictic	Necessity/contingency	Existence at all times	Required by universal conditions of experience

the principle that every event must have a cause, which the rationalists had assumed without justification and Hume had sceptically dismissed. The twelve principles of pure understanding, together with the two forms of pure intuition, exhaust our metaphysical knowledge, according to Kant. We can know *a priori* that all appearances will be spatiotemporal and will conform to the principles that make understanding, and thus experience, possible. But the rest of our knowledge of appearances must be *a posteriori*, derived from particular experiences of particular objects and events. And we can have no knowledge whatsoever of anything that transcends our experience. We can know nothing of the existence of any supposed entities for which our experience provides no evidence, and we can know nothing of things-in-themselves, of things as they are independently of being experienced by us.

Unfortunately, identifying the limits to metaphysical knowledge is not the same thing as abiding by them, and Kant argues that rational creatures are necessarily prone to overstepping the bounds established by their own cognitive capacities. We are prone, that is, to what Kant calls transcendental illusion, a special kind of metaphysical mistake caused by the operation of reason itself.

Reason, which Kant discusses in the "Transcendental Dialectic" (the second half of the "Transcendental Logic"), is the third and final cognitive capacity treated in the first critique. Sensibility is the capacity to receive intuitions, and understanding is the capacity to use concepts to judge those intuitions. Reason, as Kant defines it, is the capacity to make inferences that connect judgements into syllogisms. For example, experience and understanding yield the judgements that "people are mortal" and "the Queen of England is a person". Reason then yields the inference that "the Queen of England is mortal".

The use of reason to draw inferences from our judgements regarding experience is necessary to the unification of our *a posteriori* knowledge into a coherent system of the sort that empirical science aspires to provide. Reason contributes to this task by subordinating particular judgements to increasingly general principles. For example, the judgements that "people are mortal", "fish are mortal" and "birds are mortal" can be subsumed under the more general judgement that "animals are mortal". "Animals are mortal" and "plants are mortal" are instances of the more general truth that "living things are mortal". And "living things are mortal", together with "non-living things decay", is subordinate to the most general judgement of this sequence: "all things pass away".

Kant characterizes this activity of reason as the attempt to find the condition that explains a given judgement or set of judgements.

"People are mortal", for example, because they are subject to the condition that "animals are mortal". "Animals are mortal" because they are subject to the condition that "living things are mortal". And "living things are mortal" because they are subject to the condition that "all things pass away". Reason is not unlike a small child, relentlessly asking "why?" in response to every proffered answer, refusing to cease its questioning in the hope of eventually finding something that is the ultimate condition of everything else and which itself needs no further explanation, something Kant refers to as the unconditioned.

The quest to determine the conditions that explain our experiences is itself unproblematic, and indeed indispensable to the codification of empirical knowledge. At the same time, however, this quest breeds transcendental illusion, according to Kant. Reason is driven by its own activity, he argues, to conceptualize the unconditioned endpoints of its inferential chains, and to speculate about the existence of entities corresponding to these concepts.

Kant calls the concepts generated in this way "ideas", or pure concepts of reason. He identifies precisely three, each of which results from pursuing a distinct form of syllogistic chain to its imagined end. Drawing inferences regarding sequences of causal conditions and their effects, for example, leads to the thought of something that could initiate such a sequence, the thought of an uncaused cause or free being. The other two pure concepts of reason identified by Kant are God and the immortal soul.

The ideas are pure or *a priori* concepts because they do not derive from impressions but rather from the mind's own operation. Unlike the pure concepts of the understanding, however, ideas can tell us nothing about the world. Categories necessarily apply to our experience of the world because they make it possible. Ideas, by contrast, arise from our efforts to unify our empirical knowledge, but are not required to explain the possibility of experience itself. Since they neither derive from experience nor make it possible, the pure concepts of reason have no legitimate application in our accounts of the world.

The illegitimacy of the ideas of reason does not make it any easier to stop thinking about them, however. We are led to them again and again by the normal activities of our own rationality, and this makes it all too easy to fall into speaking and arguing about the soul, freedom and God. One of the central claims of critical philosophy, however, is that such arguments cannot possibly yield any knowledge, since the concepts in question transcend our experience and play no role in making it possible. Thoughts and conversations involving the ideas of reason, according to Kant, lead not to knowledge but to two species of transcendental illusion that he calls "paralogisms" and "antinomies".

The paralogisms result from the mistaken inference that the subject of experience must itself be a substance. Having made this mistake, it is only natural to attempt to characterize the purportedly substantial self, which leads quickly to claims regarding the identity, indivisibility and immortality of the soul. Venerable and fascinating as the discussions surrounding these issues may be, Kant's point is that the entire "discipline" to which they traditionally belong, that of rational psychology, rests on a gross confusion of empirical consciousness with the idea of the soul. The subsequent proclamations about "the soul" and its properties are therefore neither true nor false, but utterly meaningless.

The antinomies are two-sided illusions in which the regressive sequences of rational inference lead to vacillation between mutually contradictory positions on the ideas of reason. Contemplating causal chains, for example, leads to consideration of the possibility that such chains terminate in an uncaused cause, as well as the possibility that such chains are infinite. Contemplating contingent beings, which happen to exist because other beings have brought them about, leads to consideration of the possibility that there is a necessarily existing being, as well as the possibility that all beings are contingent. In similar fashion, reason generates antinomies regarding whether or not the universe is finite, and whether or not the universe is ultimately composed of simple parts that cannot be further subdivided.

For each of the four antinomies, Kant constructs a pair of arguments that claim to show that each of the opposed positions leads necessarily to the other. In the third antinomy, for example, the assumption that there is freedom in the world generates a contradiction and therefore proves that there can be only uninterrupted causal chains. Conversely, however, the assumption that there are only uninterrupted causal chains also generates a contradiction and therefore proves that there must be freedom. If both arguments are sound, as Kant insists they are, then reason would seem to be left spinning helplessly between the two alternatives with no basis for deciding between them.

The antinomies can be resolved, Kant urges, but only by strictly distinguishing between appearances and things-in-themselves. We know from the second analogy, for example, that we must experience every event as having a cause, which is to say that we will never experience freedom. This means that the antithesis of the third antinomy, which asserts that there is no freedom, must be true of appearances. It is permissible, however, to think of the thesis, which asserts that there is freedom, as being true of things-in-themselves. This would resolve the antinomy because the thesis and antithesis would not in fact contradict each other, since one would pertain to the world as it appears and the other to the world as it is in itself. Although this resolution does not constitute a proof that there truly is freedom in the world, because it remains impossible to know anything whatsoever about that which transcends our experience, it does serve as an important reminder that it is possible to think of freedom as being compatible with the causal necessity that governs all of our experience.

It is to these various transcendental illusions that Kant refers in the famous opening sentence of the Preface to the *Critique of Pure Reason*, where he writes: "Human reason has the peculiar fate in one species of its cognitions that it is burdened with questions which it cannot dismiss, since they are given to it as problems by the nature of reason itself, but which it also cannot answer, since they transcend every capacity of human reason" (*CPR*: 99). The task of the first critique is not to pretend to answer these questions, but rather to establish the limits of human knowledge and thereby demonstrate that they are unanswerable.

On the basis of his assessment of our cognitive capacities, Kant concludes that it is demonstratively certain that no one could ever know whether or not there is immortality, or freedom or God. This may sound disappointing, but Kant regards it as a great victory, for it means that Hume's determinism is dogmatic and unjustified. If Kant is right, the possibility of freedom remains alive.

The obligations of freedom and the autonomy of reason

Practical reason

Imagine two copulating spiders. The male impregnates the female, at which point she finds that he is no longer useful to her. And she is hungry. So she dismembers her partner and eats him. This is fascinating animal behaviour, the stuff of documentary films and high-school science courses that inspire awe at the wonders of nature. The female spider is the star of the show.

Now imagine two copulating humans. The male, having satisfied himself, finds that the female is no longer useful to him. And he is hungry. So he dismembers his partner and eats her. This is not fascinating animal behaviour. This is a horrific crime, for which the male is responsible and deserves to be punished. The only show in which he stars is his own trial.

Kant insists that we can justify the distinction we draw between these two cases only if we attribute freedom to ourselves. If determinism were true, we could still register our repulsion and horror when one person killed another, but it would make no more sense to hold the killer morally responsible than it would to blame the spider for killing her mate. On the deterministic hypothesis, one of these cases would certainly upset us more than the other, but there would be no basis for drawing a sharp, qualitative distinction between them. Both cases would be instances of animals performing the deeds that the prevailing conditions and forces compel them to perform. And thus in neither case would it make sense to blame the animal for its deed, since an animal cannot be blamed for doing something that it is strictly forced to do. The rain cannot be blamed for making us wet, the sun cannot be blamed for burning our skin, and if determinism is true, then people cannot be blamed for doing unpleasant things either. If determinism is true, then people are simply complicated animals, and like all animals we are akin to weather systems, producing a variety of effects, some of which we find more pleasant than others, but none of which are ultimately our responsibility. Holding ourselves responsible for our actions, and passing moral judgement on our behaviour, thus depend upon rejecting determinism and attributing freedom to human beings.

The *Critique of Pure Reason* does not prove that we are free, but it does allow us to think of ourselves as free, since its examination of the limits of knowledge issues in the conclusion that determinism cannot be known to be true. The *Critique of Practical Reason* begins with a reminder of this result, and then undertakes an examination of the role of rationality in human action. Its primary aim is to show that the human will is capable of being determined by pure reason, that reason alone can be "practical" in the sense that it can set ends and motivate us to pursue them. Kant equates such rational determination of the will with freedom, and thus with the capacity for moral agency, because it amounts to being self-determining, rather than being determined by external conditions and forces for which we are not responsible. After arguing that pure reason can be practical, the second critique then attempts to specify the criteria that determine our duties, and to assess the appropriate relationship between religion and morality.

Kant defines the will as "a faculty either of producing objects corresponding to representations or of determining itself to effect such objects (whether the physical power is sufficient or not), that is, of determining its causality" (*CPrR*: 148). For example, if I am hungry and have a pizza in mind, I am capable of willing if I am able to resolve to produce an actual pizza. There is a variety of ways in which I might accomplish this goal – make a pizza myself, drive in search of a pizza, order a pizza to be delivered – and just as many ways that I might fail. But to have a will is simply to be able to adopt the pursuit of a goal, to be able to guide one's action by means of intentional principles.

Kant takes it as given that we are capable of willing. The central question, however, is whether our willing can be determined by purely rational considerations, or whether the goals we adopt are always conditioned by empirical factors. Examples of such empirical conditioning abound: if we are cold, we adopt the goal of getting warm; if we are hungry, we adopt the goal of finding food; if we are tired, we adopt the goal of getting some rest. Each of these goals is a reasonable response to the stipulated conditions. But responding to given conditions in a reasonable way does not qualify as rational willing in Kant's sense. Purely rational willing involves determining ourselves to adopt and pursue goals that are entirely unconditioned by empirical factors, goals that are not merely reasonable if certain conditions obtain, but which stem from the nature of reason itself, and thus must be adopted by any and all agents who claim to be rational.

A goal incumbent upon all rational agents to adopt would be an objectively required intentional principle, which Kant calls a law. Whether purely rational willing is possible thus depends upon whether any subjective principles or "maxims" that people use to guide their behaviour qualify as laws that derive their obligatory force from reason alone.

Most maxims clearly do not have this status. Agents normally guide their actions according to principles chosen in virtue of their expected success in satisfying the needs and desires of the individual in the circumstances in which he finds himself. These principles do not rise to the status of objective laws because needs, desires and circumstances vary. The principles that maximize the satisfaction of one individual might serve others poorly or not at all.

Kant concludes, therefore, that no maxim defined by the desire for a particular object or outcome could qualify as a law binding upon all rational agents. We all seek happiness, but the variation in the particular things that make us happy means that the validity of maxims aimed at satisfying desires extends only to those who contingently happen to have the desires in question. Such maxims represent what Kant calls "hypothetical imperatives", intentional principles one must adopt only *if* they serve as means to the ends one happens to have. Laws of reason, by contrast, would apply necessarily and universally to all rational agents. Such principles would be absolutely or "categorically" binding, and it would therefore be incumbent upon all of us to adopt them as ends in themselves, regardless of whether they served to further or to frustrate the other ends any of us happened to have.

It is through our awareness of such absolute obligations, Kant contends, that we become aware of the ability of reason to be practical, and thus of our freedom. We are all aware, Kant claims, of the absolute necessity of abiding by certain principles, and of our ability to die for these principles rather than forsake them. It is this awareness of our ability to sacrifice everything for certain principles that reveals to us their absolutely binding character, the precedence they take over every natural desire and social convention.

Kant does not claim that every human actually would sacrifice happiness in order to fulfil his obligations, but he claims that every rational agent is aware that he ought to do so. Kant refers to this immediate consciousness of absolute obligation as the "fact of reason", and he thinks consciousness of freedom follows from it. Kant famously declares that "ought implies can", which means that an agent can only be obliged to do something that he is capable of doing. I cannot be obliged to leap over my house, because it is beyond my abilities. So if I am absolutely obliged to abide by certain principles, which Kant insists is an immediate and undeniable certainty, then I must be capable of living up to such absolute obligations. But living up to absolute obligations is possible only if one is capable of recognizing them and giving them precedence over all of the conditional ends one happens to have. In other words, one can be subject to absolute obligation only if one is a rational agent and reason is practical, able to set ends and motivate us to pursue them. This practicality of reason, as revealed by the experience of absolute obligation, makes us aware of the freedom that Kant believes theoretical reason is incapable of demonstrating.

Morality

Creatures capable of freely responding to the absolute obligations of reason are moral agents, qualitatively distinct from spiders and all other non-rational animals. Such animals can behave only as their instincts and desires compel them to, but moral agents can set aside or defer the satisfaction of their desires in favour of fulfilling their responsibilities and performing their duties.

Kant thinks that most of the time our duties are apparent to us. We know what must be done, even if we often fail to do it. We do not need philosophy, therefore, to specify our duties, but it does play an important role in articulating the criteria that lie behind the moral intuitions that Kant assumes to be universal.

The two fundamental constituents of moral action, Kant argues, are the intentions and motives that determine the will of the agent. Famously, he holds that the consequences of action are irrelevant to an agent's moral worth. We cannot be held responsible for the outcomes of our deeds because they do not lie entirely within our control. The best of intentions can lead to disastrous results, for which we should not be blamed, just as evil intentions can accidentally produce positive consequences, for which no praise is deserved. Moral worth depends exclusively upon those features of our action for which we are fully responsible, and these are our maxims – the intentional principles by which we guide our actions – and our motives – the reasons that we have for adopting those principles.

The content of an intentional principle cannot make it absolutely obligatory, since the particular things that satisfy individual agents are empirically conditioned and variable, so if maxims are to qualify as moral laws it must be in virtue of having a distinctive form. And Kant declares it to be self-evident that the distinctive form of an objective law can only be "universality" (*CPrR*: 161). This captures the intuition that if a principle is absolutely obligatory, then it must be universal in scope, equally binding upon all rational agents.

Kant defines the universality, and thus the morality, of intentional principles in the following formulation of the categorical imperative: "I ought never to act except in such a way that I could also will that my maxim should become a universal law" (*G*: 57). A maxim is immoral, in other words, if I cannot act upon it while also willing that it should become a determining principle for the action of all agents. The immorality of acting upon a principle that I could not will all others to adopt would lie in making an unjustifiable exception for my own behaviour.

This "universalizability" test for the morality of intentional principles can be failed in two distinct ways. The most serious sort of failure is a logical contradiction between my willing a particular intentional principle and my willing all others to will the same principle. Such a principle would be self-defeating, in the sense that if everyone acted upon it then no one would be able to accomplish his intention. The second and lesser failure of the test involves a principle that could be adopted by all without logical contradiction, but which nonetheless no one could will to become a universal law.

Kant regards maxims that cannot be universalized without defeating themselves as absolutely immoral, and believes that we have a "perfect duty" never to act upon them. Kant offers telling the truth as an example of a perfect duty, because if lying were universalized then no one would ever expect anyone to be truthful, and lies would cease to be effective. Telling a lie to accomplish my aims thus constitutes making an exception for my own behaviour, which is the touchstone of immorality. Kant therefore considers lying to be immoral in absolutely every circumstance.

The converse of a perfect duty is a right: all rational agents have an absolute right to expect and demand that all other rational agents perform their perfect duties. The most fundamental right is that of having one's freedom respected by other free beings, since freedom is the ultimate condition of the possibility of morality, duties and rights. The regulative political ideal is therefore "a constitution providing for the greatest human freedom according to laws that permit the freedom of each to exist together with that of others" (*CPR*: 397).

Maxims that are not strictly self-defeating but which no one could will to become a universal law are also immoral, although the duty not to act upon them is only "imperfect". This means that I may not make such maxims into a general rule for my behaviour, but the prohibition is not absolute. For example, Kant believes that no one could will to live in a world in which people did not develop their talents, and thus regards it as a duty to develop one's own. It is not, however, incumbent upon me to develop my talents at every single moment. It is acceptable to engage in activities that do not contribute to the actualization of my potential, so long as I do not indulge in such recreation to an extent that stunts the flourishing of my capacities.

We do not have a right to demand that others fulfil their imperfect duties, but those who do so are to be regarded as virtuous, according to Kant. It is virtuous to develop one's talents, although no one can demand this of me as their right. Likewise, the virtuous person will assist other people, although no one can claim a right to such help.

The universalizability test thus sorts intentional principles into those that are morally permissible and those that are not. Maxims that pass the test are acceptable to act upon at the discretion of the agent. Morality is completely indifferent, for example, to whether I choose to wear blue or green on Tuesdays, because whatever principle of colour choice I might construct could be universalized without contradiction. Maxims that fail the test are immoral, and it is therefore prohibited to act upon them and morally required to act on their opposites. I may not, for example, tell lies or completely neglect the development of my talents. And I must, conversely, tell the truth and strive to actualize my potential.

Intending to perform one's duties is the first necessary condition of moral action, but Kant emphasizes that it is not sufficient. Moral worth depends, Kant argues, not only on trying to do the right thing, but also on trying to do it for the right reason. Striving to act in accordance with duty is always a good thing, but it is morally praiseworthy only if I am fully responsible for the adoption of the maxim in question, and am not led to it by external forces beyond my control. Kant refers to an externally determined will as "heteronomous", which he contrasts with a self-determining or "autonomous" will. Moral worth depends upon autonomously choosing intentional principles that accord with the rational law, and then striving to act upon them.

Kant recognizes two possible sources of motivation for choosing intentional principles that accord with duty: inclination and respect for the moral law. I may be inclined to help others, for example, because I expect to be repaid with reciprocal assistance, or because I enjoy being highly regarded by my neighbours. In this case, according to Kant, no matter how valuable my help may be, it is undeserving of moral praise. To do good deeds on the basis of inclination is to act like an animal that is well behaved in the hope of receiving a kind word or a piece of meat. Such animals do not deserve moral praise any more than killer spiders deserve moral condemnation, because they are not responsible for the inclinations that determine their behaviour. Of course we prefer the friendly dog to the dog that bites, but moral judgements do not apply to creatures that have no choice but to act upon their most powerful inclinations. Such judgements therefore apply to humans only because, *pace* Hume, we are capable of ignoring all of our inclinations, even those that pull us towards doing our duty, in order to perform our obligations out of pure respect for the moral law.

Because the moral law has its source in our own rationality, to be motivated by respect for it is to act autonomously, which is to be self-determining and free. It is in doing our moral duty for its own sake, then, that we actualize the freedom of which Kant believes we are capable, and in which he locates our dignity as rational animals.

Religion

Rational animals are, in Kant's view, especially interesting and conflicted creatures. Animals that lack rationality are motivated solely by the satisfaction of their desires; they seek happiness, and are neither concerned with nor capable of moral action. A purely rational creature, by contrast, would act upon the commands of reason automatically; lacking desires, such a creature would have no conception of happiness. Rational animals, however, are motivated by both desires and reason. As rational creatures, we are acutely aware of our obligations, and of the moral worth that comes only from striving to perform them. But as animals we are also acutely concerned with happiness.

The highest good for a rational animal would thus be the coincidence of happiness and morality, the ultimate satisfaction of happiness that is well deserved. Unfortunately, it is all too obvious that happiness and morality are only contingently related. Striving to obey the moral law can be met with misfortune and misery, and it is possible, conversely, to satisfy one's desires while displaying utter disregard for obligation.

Kant worries that this undeniable disconnection between our two deepest interests may undermine our moral resolve. We ought to strive to fulfil our obligations whether they lead to happiness or not, but as animals we simply cannot help being concerned with the satisfaction of our desires. If obeying the moral law does not contribute to happiness, and in certain circumstances may even diminish it, then our animal nature may overwhelm our good intentions and lead us to neglect our duties.

Because moral resolve is our most fundamental obligation, Kant concludes that we must suppose to be true whatever is required to sustain it. We must believe, therefore, that moral striving and happiness will eventually coincide. Since there is no evidence of their correlation in a normal human lifetime, we must suppose both that the individual person persists after death, and that there is a power capable of recognizing and rewarding the moral worth of each individual. We must, that is, live *as if* there were a God and immortal souls, despite the fact that there can be no theoretical justification for these suppositions.

Practical reason thus demands and generates, according to Kant, "rational faith". It calls for and supports belief in two of the ideas of pure reason – God and the soul – for which there is neither empirical evidence nor good argument. Theoretical reason must be agnostic with respect to these ideas, since it can demonstrate the impossibility of ever proving whether anything actually corresponds to them. But practical reason cannot remain agnostic because, if Kant is right, we must act, and we recognize an absolute obligation to act morally, and we cannot sustain a lifelong commitment to fulfil this obligation unless we believe in God and our own immortality. Kant thus refers to God and the immortal soul as necessary postulates of practical reason.

Belief in the practical postulates qualifies as "faith" because we do not, and cannot, have knowledge of God or the soul. There is no question of waiting for evidence, or developing better arguments. The first critique has shown that it is strictly impossible to know anything about entities that transcend our experience. But this faith is "rational" because it is non-arbitrary and universally demanded by reason itself. We are not licensed to believe whatever we please, but we are required to believe whatever must be supposed in order to enable us to respond to the fact of moral obligation. The rationality of these beliefs also stems from the fact that they are not imposed by any external authority, but rather emerge from our own reflection upon our own practical experience.

It is important to be aware of the roles that these religious postulates do and do not play in Kant's moral theory. God cannot be the source of the moral law, because this would make the duties it specifies arbitrary and external impositions, rather than the product of autonomous reason; for Kant, as for Plato, God must be conceived as loving what is intrinsically good, rather than as defining what is good through the bestowal of love. God also cannot provide the incentive to perform any particular obligation, because doing our duties out of fear or the expectation of reward would deprive our actions of moral worth, which can lie only in respect for the law itself. Kant even claims that a wise and benevolent God would make us incapable of knowing of His existence, since such knowledge would make it impossible for us to ignore our fear of punishment and do our duty for its own sake; God would, in other words, care more about morality than anything else, and would therefore make it possible for us to be moral by concealing His own existence. The postulation of God's existence can thus sustain our resolve to be moral, to use our freedom to fulfil the obligations of reason without regard for our inclinations, but it can neither tell us what those obligations are nor motivate the performance of any particular action.

The place of freedom in the natural world

The *Critique of Pure Reason* argues that all natural phenomena must be experienced as subject to causal necessitation, but that it is nonetheless possible to think of ourselves as free. The *Critique of Practical Reason* argues that we must attribute freedom to ourselves in order to account for our experience of moral obligation, despite the fact that we can never observe the operation of our freedom in the natural world. Thus, even if the two works successfully respond to Hume by offering accounts of the possibility of rational cognition and action, they do so only at significant cost, as Kant himself recognizes:

> There is an incalculable gulf fixed between the domain of the concept of nature, as the sensible, and the domain of the concept of freedom, as the supersensible, so that from the former to the latter (thus by means of the theoretical use of reason) no transition is possible, just as if there were so many different worlds, the first of which can have no influence on the second: yet the latter *should* have an influence on the former, namely the concept of freedom should make the end that is imposed by its laws real in the sensible world; and nature must consequently also be able to be conceived in such a way that the lawfulness of its form is at least in agreement with the possibility of the ends that are to be realized in it in accordance with the laws of freedom. (*CPJ*: 63)

The *Critique of the Power of Judgment* endeavours to explain how it is legitimate to judge that the natural universe and the operation of freedom are indeed harmonized, and so to bridge the gulf between our theoretical and practical experience, our scientific and moral perspectives on the world. The problem is that all natural phenomena, including human behaviour, appear to be explicable purely in terms of mechanistic or efficient causality: scientific accounts of the world present sequences of events in which the successive moments bring each other about but do not aim in any particular direction or serve any particular purpose. Such accounts resolutely eschew all teleology, rejecting the attribution of what Aristotle called final causes, or purposes, to the natural world. But the absence of purposes or intentions is incompatible with conceiving of ourselves as moral agents, and instead reduces us to complicated machines, the operation of which is governed by the same physical forces that control all other natural phenomena. The second critique insists that because we have an obligation to intervene freely in the natural world we must be capable of doing so, but the first critique rules out the possibility of there ever being direct evidence of such intervention. The third critique is thus intended to complete Kant's system by arguing that there is indirect evidence of the efficacy of freedom, of the impact of invisible purposes on the visible natural world.

The third critique, like the first two, supports its central claim by means of a transcendental argument that moves from a given fact to the necessary conditions of its possibility. In this case, the given fact is that we make a certain distinctive type of judgement, which Kant calls "reflective", and the conclusion is that reflective judgements are possible only if we regard nature as a system that contains purposive beings (not merely efficient causes) and itself serves the purpose of providing the conditions within which free, purposive beings can perform the moral actions of which they are capable.

Kant defines "reflective" judgements in contrast to the "determinative" judgements that provide the basis for the metaphysical deduction of the categories in the first critique. Determinative judgements, as their name suggests, determine the objects that they judge. They do this by applying a universal concept to the particular object in question, and so identifying the object as an instance of the type of being that the concept names. Making such a judgement requires that one already possess the concept to be applied, in order to be able to recognize that the features of the object correspond to it. With knowledge of the properties that define the concept "tree", for example, I may stroll through the park and make quite a few successful determinative judgements: "These plants are trees", "Those plants are trees", "And those are trees as well". If I stumble upon an unfamiliar plant, however, one with features that do not match any of my available concepts, I will not be able to determine what it is. Instead, I will have to begin by carefully observing and describing the object, and then search for a concept to which its features correspond. It is this process of moving from a particular object toward an appropriate universal concept that characterizes reflective judgement.

Kant distinguishes between two species of reflective judgement – the aesthetic and the teleological – each of which, he claims, implicitly relies upon the attribution of a specific sort of purposiveness to nature. Aesthetic judgements presuppose that nature is "subjectively purposive", or suited to being judged by us and to giving us a distinctive pleasure when we experience its beauty. Teleological judgements presuppose that nature is "objectively purposive", or contains purposive beings and itself aims at enabling the free, purposive beings within it to fulfil their moral calling.

Aesthetic judgements of natural beauty emerge, Kant argues, from our efforts to comprehend our experience by developing universal concepts, principles and laws that describe and predict the behaviour of particular phenomena. This is the task attributed to reason in the first critique, and the third critique makes explicit that it is accomplished by means of reflective judgement, which moves from particulars in search of the universals that explain them. Kant claims that this operation of reflective judgement, which is essential to rationality, depends upon the implicit attribution of subjective purposiveness to nature. The quest to find and formulate universal laws that govern particular objects and events presupposes that nature comprises a regular system, one suited to being judged by us. Although the conditions that make our experience possible guarantee that nature will exhibit causality, they do not guarantee it will exhibit systematic unity, that the particular phenomena will be ordered according to universal laws, and so we take pleasure in finding the regularity that reason leads us to expect. This pleasure that we take in the regularity of nature characterizes the aesthetic experience of beauty.

Kant highlights the essential features of aesthetic experience by distinguishing it from two other ways in which we respond to nature. When we encounter regularity in nature three responses are possible. We may understand the phenomenon by applying a concept to it, in which case we make a determinative judgement ("Those distant shapes are mountains") and have a cognitive experience. Or we may take pleasure in the material of the phenomenon, in which case we make a judgement of agreeableness ("The air is refreshingly cool today") and have a sensory experience. But we may also simply appreciate the form of the phenomenon, in which case we make a judgement of beauty ("The horizon is gorgeous") and have an aesthetic experience.

In order to enjoy aesthetic experience, Kant contends, we must abstract from our interests in cognition and sensory satisfaction. Only if we are truly disinterested in what an object is, and in how it might satisfy our desires, is it possible for us to appreciate its formal qualities for their own sake. If I am flying an aeroplane, for example, and I want to know whether the approaching mass is a mountain or a cloud, the importance of the cognitive judgement to my impending sensory experience will prevent me from enjoying whatever beauty the formation might possess. Sitting safely on the ground, however, I may be able to abstract from my desires and cognitive interests and so enable myself to perceive the purely formal qualities in which beauty resides.

The significance of aesthetic experience for attributing subjective purposiveness to nature lies in the specific ways in which it is similar to and different from cognitive and sensory experience. Judgements of beauty are, according to Kant, universally binding upon rational agents, all of whom have the same mental capacities for recognizing and responding to the regularity of natural forms. In this respect aesthetic experience is like cognitive experience (if something is a mountain, it is a mountain for everyone), but unlike sensory experience (the mountain air may refresh me, while it may give you frostbite). But aesthetic experience is like sensory experience, and unlike cognitive experience, in providing us with pleasure. Beauty is thus unique in giving pleasure to all rational agents. Nature appears beautiful precisely when it appears as if its forms had been arranged for the purpose of pleasing us by stimulating the play of our mental capacities.

In addition to beauty, Kant also recognizes one other form of aesthetic experience, that of sublimity. Although Kant's treatment of the sublime in the third critique has been quite influential, it is far less important to the completion of his own critical philosophy than his treatment of beauty. Whereas beauty involves the experience of natural forms that seem to suggest that nature was intended for our appreciation, and thus hint at a reconciliation of nature and freedom, sublimity involves the experience of formless natural phenomena that exceed our capacity to comprehend. Some phenomena trigger the experience of sublimity in virtue of being infinitely vast, like the night sky, and others are incomprehensibly powerful, like a tsunami.

The significance of the sublime lies in the fact that it demonstrates our ability to respond to infinitude, although it exceeds the capacity of our senses to take it in. This evokes, according to Kant, our ability to respond to the moral law, despite the fact that its appeal is entirely non-sensory. Nature's ability to overwhelm our senses thus reminds us of our mind's superiority to nature, of our capacity to abstract from all natural intentions and motivations in order to respond to the higher calling of morality.

The experience of sublimity is therefore less important than the experience of beauty for the project of reconciling freedom and mechanistic causality because, although it teaches us something about ourselves, it teaches us nothing about nature itself. Kant writes that beauty

> expands not our cognition of natural objects, but our concept of nature, namely as a mere mechanism, into the concept of nature as art: which invites profound investigations into the possibility of such a form. But in that which we are accustomed to call sublime in nature there is so little that leads to particular objective principles and forms of nature corresponding to these that it is mostly rather in its chaos or in

its wildest and most unruly disorder and devastation, if only it allows a glimpse of magnitude and might, that it excites the ideas of the sublime. From this we see that the concept of the sublime in nature is far from being as important and rich in consequences as that of its beauty, and that in general it indicates nothing purposive in nature itself, but only in the possible *use* of its intuitions to make palpable in ourselves a purposiveness that is entirely independent of nature.　　　　　　　　　　　　　　　　　　　　　　　(*CPJ*: 130)

Because beauty "does not actually expand our cognition of natural objects", Kant refers to the purposiveness that it points us toward in nature as "subjective". Natural beauty sanctions the judgement that nature appears purposive, in the sense that it appears to serve the purpose of pleasing our ability to appreciate formal regularity (as works of art do), and so leads us to undertake "profound investigations" of how nature could both be mechanistic and appear as if purposively ordered for our benefit. But natural beauty does not sanction the attribution of purposes to particular beings within nature, or to nature itself as a whole. The attribution of such "objective purposiveness" to nature cannot be justified by aesthetic experience.

The second part of the third critique, which is devoted to teleological rather than aesthetic judgement, aims to demonstrate that we must judge (although we cannot know) nature to be objectively purposive, and must judge (although we cannot know) ourselves to be the final purpose of nature. Kant argues, first, that we are driven to the reflective judgement that nature is objectively purposive by our experience of organisms, the existence of which, he contends, cannot be explained by mechanistic processes alone. He then offers a long and complex argument for the claim that we can judge nature to be objectively purposive only if we regard it as having been designed by an intelligent being with the intention of creating free and rational animals. Kant believes we must judge, in other words, that God has arranged the natural mechanisms investigated by science in such a way that they are inherently oriented toward the emergence of creatures with the capacity for morality. Regarding the world as governed by divine providence bridges the gap between nature and freedom, and thereby completes Kant's transcendental philosophy, by conceiving of nature's own purpose as the creation of the conditions in which human beings can exercise their freedom for moral ends.

Summary of key points

- Kant's epistemological revolution attempts to establish metaphysical knowledge by determining the necessary conditions of the possibility of experience.
- Kant limits knowledge to appearances, and denies that we can know anything at all about things-in-themselves.
- The limitation of knowledge to appearances refutes dogmatic assertions of determinism. Kant argues that our experience of moral obligation makes sense only if we are truly free.
- Morality, according to Kant, requires us to ignore our inclinations and perform our duties out of pure respect for the rational law that is their source.
- Kant contends that we, as rational animals, necessarily hope that moral worth and happiness will coincide. He contends that this hope can be sustained only by postulating the existence of God and the immortality of the soul.
- Kant argues that our experience of organic forms in nature leads us to judge that an intelligent being created the world for the purpose of enabling rational animals to use their freedom for moral ends.

three

Sceptical challenges and the development of transcendental idealism

German intellectual life in the wake of Kant's philosophical revolution was astonishingly rich and varied. The late eighteenth and early nineteenth centuries gave rise to Hamann and Herder; Goethe, Schiller and Hölderlin; the early Romantics, including Novalis and the Schlegels; and Schopenhauer. All of these authors made lasting contributions to philosophy and literature. The focus of this book, however, is the thinkers whose explicit aim was to complete the project of critical philosophy, and whose work towards that end contributed most significantly to the development of the movement now known as German Idealism. The key figures in this story are Fichte, Schelling and Hegel, who are the subjects of the next three chapters. This chapter offers an account of some of the initial responses to Kant that influenced the trajectory of these later idealists. The individuals discussed in this chapter – Jacobi, Reinhold and Schulze – have been selected for the direct role they played in the emergence of Fichte, and the specific texts discussed have been chosen for both their importance and their availability in English. The early Romantics are treated in the Conclusion, because although their work helped to propel the transition from Fichte to Schelling and Hegel, their primary tendency was to undermine, rather than attempt to fulfil, the philosophical aspirations of German Idealism.

Kant's *Critique of Pure Reason* did not fall "stillborn from the press", as Hume had described the reception of his own *Treatise of Human Nature* some forty-five years earlier, but it did fall subject to pervasive misunderstanding that served to rejuvenate scepticism regarding the

cognitive capacities of reason. Kant was initially interpreted as a subjective idealist in the mould of George Berkeley, who had moved Locke's
empiricism in the direction of Hume's scepticism by arguing that
the ideas with which we are directly acquainted provide no basis for
believing in mind-independent material substance. Berkeley denied
the existence of matter and held that the universe comprises nothing
but ideas, finite minds like our own, and the infinite mind of God. Kant
vigorously denied the association of his position with the metaphysics
of subjective idealism, but recognized that at least some of the confusion was due to the complexity of his thought and the infelicity of his
prose, and therefore attempted to express himself more clearly.

In 1783, a scant two years after the appearance of the first critique,
Kant published the *Prolegomena to Any Future Metaphysics That Will
Be Able to Come Forward as Science*. This short but remarkable book
summarizes the results of the first critique, with the stated intention
"to convince all of those who find it worthwhile to occupy themselves
with metaphysics that it is unavoidably necessary to suspend their
work for the present, to consider all that has happened until now as if
it had not happened, and before all else to pose the question: 'whether
such a thing as metaphysics is even possible at all' " (*P*: 53).

The *Prolegomena* proved insufficient, however, to enable readers to
distinguish transcendental idealism from Berkeley's idealist metaphysics,
and so in the second edition of the *Critique of Pure Reason*, published
in 1787, Kant added a new section that addressed this issue directly.
The "Refutation of Idealism" does not, Kant insists, add anything of
substance that cannot already be found in the first edition, but simply
makes explicit the implications of the position he had already tried to
articulate. The "Refutation" begins with a three-sentence dismissal of
Berkeley's "dogmatic" idealism, on the grounds that the positive denial
of material substance is decisively undermined by the argument in the
"Transcendental Aesthetic" that the character of things-in-themselves
is completely unknowable. The main target of the "Refutation" is thus
not Berkeley but Descartes, whose "problematic idealism" Kant considers much more respectable and worthy of response: "Problematic
idealism, which . . . professes only our incapacity for proving an existence
outside us from our own by means of immediate experience, is rational
and appropriate for a thorough philosophical manner of thought"
(*CPR*: 326). Kant hopes to defeat problematic idealism in the "Refutation"
by means of a proof "that even our *inner experience*, undoubted by
Descartes, is possible only under the presupposition of outer experience" (*ibid.*). Transcendental idealism thus claims, in direct contrast to

subjective idealism, that the fact of experience can be explained only if we suppose the existence of an external world of material substance.

Whether Kant can in fact defeat scepticism regarding the external world, and so avoid lapsing into a form of subjective idealism, remains a matter of contemporary dispute, and it was regarded by the first readers of the *Critique of Pure Reason* as the single most pressing issue raised by the work. With the publication of the *Groundwork* (1785) and the second critique (1788), Kant's practical philosophy also drew attention, but since it was understood, rightly, to depend upon the work done in the first critique, the focus remained on the theoretical philosophy, and especially on questions regarding the justification of the basic premises of transcendental idealism.

The most influential early response was offered by Friedrich Heinrich Jacobi (1743–1819), in a short piece entitled "On Transcendental Idealism", which he appended as a supplement to his second major work, *David Hume on Faith, or Idealism and Realism, a Dialogue* (1787).

Jacobi's sceptical challenge to Kant

Jacobi's response to Kant was influential largely because of the reputation he had established in 1785 with his first major work, *Concerning the Doctrine of Spinoza in Letters to Herr Moses Mendelssohn*. Jacobi provoked the famous Mendelssohn (1729–86) into corresponding with him by claiming that the highly regarded Gotthold Ephraim Lessing (1729–81) had confessed on his deathbed to being a Spinozist, and so to being a pantheist. Mendelssohn leapt energetically to the defence of his deceased friend, and Jacobi then published his own half of the correspondence, which addressed not only the narrow question of Lessing's personal beliefs, but also the more general issue of whether rationalism and theism are compatible. Jacobi claimed that to be a rationalist is necessarily to be a pantheist, which he equated with being an atheist who continues to use (and abuse) the word "God". To be a theist, Jacobi concluded, one must make a leap of faith.

By 1787 Jacobi was well aware of, but completely unpersuaded by, Kant's attempt to refute subjective idealism. "On Transcendental Idealism" was published a few months before the second edition of the *Critique of Pure Reason*, but in 1815 Jacobi added a note in which he emphasized Kant's own insistence that the second edition affected only the form of presentation, but not the substantive position, of the critical philosophy. Jacobi took this to indicate that "On Transcendental

Idealism" retained all of its argumentative force, and that Kant's purported "Refutation of Idealism" was a dismal failure.

Phenomena and noumena revisited

Jacobi's main claim is that despite Kant's talk of outer experience and an external world, the transcendental idealist uses the term "object" to refer to mental representations and is never able to establish the existence of mind-independent entities. "So," Jacobi laments, "what we realists call actual objects or things independent of our representations are for the transcendental idealist only internal beings *which exhibit nothing at all of a thing that may perhaps be there outside us, or to which the appearance may refer. Rather, these internal beings are merely subjective determinations of the mind, entirely void of anything truly objective*" ("OTI": 334). In other words, Kant is a subjective idealist like Berkeley, but lacks the courage to admit it. Kant's talk of "objects" is merely, in Jacobi's estimation, self-deceptive verbiage that prevents him from acknowledging that his own position implies the impossibility of encountering or knowing anything that is independent of the mind.

Jacobi grants that Kant distinguishes between objects of experience, or phenomena, and objects as they are independently of being experienced, or noumena. But this distinction hardly solves the problem, in Jacobi's view, for it makes the mind-independent object unknowable:

> If we abstract from the human form, these laws of our intuition and thought are without any meaning or validity, and do not yield the slightest information about the laws of nature in itself. Neither the principle of sufficient reason, nor even the proposition that nothing can come from nothing, apply to things in themselves. In brief, our entire cognition contains nothing, nothing whatsoever, that could have any *truly* objective meaning at all.   ("OTI": 337)

Moreover, the relation between noumena and the phenomena we experience is thoroughly opaque. Attempting to be generous, Jacobi writes, "even if it can be *conceded* under Kant's view, that a transcendental somewhat *might* correspond to these merely subjective beings, which are only determinations of *our own being*, as their *cause*, where this cause is, and what kind of connection it has with its effect, remains hidden in the deepest obscurity" (*ibid.*: 336).

Jacobi concludes that Kant's critical philosophy is caught in the contradiction of relying upon a presupposition that is ultimately incompatible with the transcendental idealism resulting from it. In order to account for cognition Kant assumes that the subject must receive access to objects via intuition, which in human beings takes the form of sensibility. But this presupposes that objects "make *impressions* on the senses and that in this way they bring about representations . . . For . . . the word 'sensibility' is without any meaning, unless we understand by it a distinct real intermediary between one real thing and another" (*ibid.*). "It is not possible", claims Jacobi, "to see how even the Kantian philosophy could find entry into itself without this presupposition and manage some statement of its hypothesis," but at the same time, "it is plainly impossible to stay within the system with that presupposition" (*ibid.*). The presupposition violates the system by speaking of a causal relation between noumena and phenomena, despite the fact that transcendental idealism itself insists that the category of causality applies only to objects of our experience and that nothing whatsoever can be known of objects in themselves.

Jacobi's final verdict is that Kant's critical philosophy cannot be saved from scepticism and subjective idealism "unless you give an alien meaning to every word . . . For according to the common use of language, we must mean by 'object' a thing that *would be present outside us in a transcendental sense*. And how could we come by any such thing in Kantian philosophy?" (*ibid.*: 338). Jacobi's answer to his own rhetorical question, of course, is that we cannot. If Kant is right, then the "objects" we know are mind-dependent representations, which are not truly objects at all in the ordinary sense of the word. Regarding mind-independent objects Kant proclaims "*absolute and unqualified ignorance*" (*ibid.*), and is thus a nihilist (a term first made popular by Jacobi), one who knows nothing, or knows a mere appearance that is itself nothing. Jacobi concludes his essay by proclaiming that "the transcendental idealist must have the courage, therefore, to assert the strongest idealism that was ever professed" (*ibid.*).

Faith and reason revisited

The fact that "On Transcendental Idealism" was appended as a short supplement to a much longer work reveals that Jacobi regarded his attack on Kant's particular position as peripheral to his more general assault on all attempts to know the truth by means of rational explanation. Indeed, in his earlier book, *Concerning the Doctrine of Spinoza*,

Jacobi had already argued that every effort to explain our experience necessarily results in determinism and atheism, and thus that belief in free will and God depend upon making a leap of faith.

Jacobi's argument begins with the premise that to explain a phenomenon is to identify its efficient cause. The project of explaining all phenomena thus implicitly assumes the principle of sufficient reason, which states that there must be an efficient cause of everything that comes to be or transpires. But to assume that all phenomena are explicable in terms of efficient causes is to assume the truth of determinism, which leads immediately to what Jacobi calls "fatalism", the view that human actions, like all other events, result necessarily from the currently prevailing conditions and forces. Free will is incompatible with this view, as is a personal God who providentially guides the course of the world: "If there are only efficient, but no final, causes, then the only function that the faculty of thought has in the whole of nature is that of observer; its proper business is to accompany the mechanism of the efficient causes . . . The inventor of the clock did not ultimately invent it; he only witnessed its coming to be out of blindly self-developing forces" (*CDS*: 189). The logical conclusion of the project of explanation is thus the pantheistic determinism of Spinoza, which Jacobi regards as atheism by another name.

Jacobi finds it impossible to believe in fatalism, and consequently considers the project of rational explanation self-refuting by means of a *reductio ad absurdum*: "I have no concept more intimate than that of the final cause; no conviction more vital than that *I do what I think*, and not, *that I should think what I do*. Truly therefore, I must assume a source of thought and action that remains completely inexplicable to me" (*ibid.*: 193). He simply refuses to give up the belief in free will, in other words, and therefore must reject whatever is incompatible with it, including the principle of sufficient reason and the quest for explanation. Jacobi portrays himself as one "who does not want to explain what is incomprehensible, but only wants to know the boundary where it begins and just recognize that it is there", and claims that it is through this recognition of the point where explanation founders on the inexplicable that one "gains the greatest room within himself for genuine human truth" (*ibid.*: 194). This "genuine human truth," which Jacobi takes to include free will and the personal God of Christianity, is "what cannot be explained: the unanalyzable, the immediate, the simple" (*ibid.*).

Jacobi acknowledges that he has never been able to find "grounds that are sound enough to counter Spinoza's arguments against the personality and understanding of a first cause, against free will and final causes" (*ibid.*: 214–15). But he cheerily declares: "I extricate myself from the problem through a *salto mortale*" (*ibid.*: 189) or leap of faith. He proceeds, in other words, from unprovable convictions of which he is immediately certain, and is quite unembarrassed to do so, since he believes that the most rational philosophical arguments, including those of Spinoza, must ultimately rest on presuppositions for which they cannot account: "If every *assent to truth* not derived from rational grounds is faith, then conviction based on rational ground must itself derive from faith, and must receive its force from faith alone" (*ibid.*: 230).

Having made the leap to the standpoint of faith, Jacobi then declares, without argument, his unshakeable beliefs in the existence of material bodies, in freedom, and in God. The first two of these Jacobi claims to be "a revelation of nature that not only commands, but impels, each and every man *to believe*" (*ibid.*: 231). He holds, in other words, that no one can seriously doubt that he has a body or that his will is free, despite the fact that philosophers can produce clever arguments on behalf of metaphysical idealism and determinism. Jacobi grants that faith in God is not compelled by nature in this way, and instead attributes it to a practical decision to adopt the Christian way of life: "Try to grow in a virtue perfectly, that is, to exercise it *purely* and *incessantly*. Either you desist in the attempt, or you'll become aware of God in yourself, just as you are aware of yourself" (*ibid.*: 243). Since Christian faith emerges from Christian practice, the initial decision to adopt the latter must be made without understanding the reasons for it. Jacobi therefore counsels "complete submission to a superior authority; strict, holy, obedience" (*ibid.*: 244) and warns that "the less can man discern the command's inner good before obeying it, the less capable is his reason to accept it, the more does he need authority and faith" (*ibid.*: 245–6).

In response to those who fail to see the truth of Jacobi's position, his only recourse is to declare their vision lacking: "I do not in any way intend to advance [these propositions] as theses or to defend them against every possible attack . . . Just as it is impossible to make objects somehow visible to a blind man through art, as long as the man is blind; so too it is impossible for a seeing man not to see them, when there is light" (*ibid.*: 236). Jacobi does not feel compassion for these poor souls who cannot see the truth, because he holds them responsible for their own blindness, and for the unpleasantness he experiences when forced to look upon them. In the opening passages of *David Hume on Faith* he declares that "what I hate is the malaise, the disgust that follows upon having to summon contempt from the bottom of one's soul – having to spit in the presence of *men* because they have impudently done violence to their own feeling of what is right and true and have yielded, unscrupulously, to the lie" (*DHF*: 262).

Jacobi is well aware that with his unabashed embrace of a faith for which there can be no argument, and his denigration of those who do not share it, he runs the risk of being dismissed as the worst sort of fanatic. Indeed, in his first book Jacobi portrayed Lessing as raising this very complaint against him: "The boundary that you want to establish [between the explicable and the inexplicable] does not allow of determination. And moreover, you give free play to phantsies, nonsense, obscurantism" (*CDS*: 194). And in his second book Jacobi attempts to defend his reliance on faith by linking his position to that of David Hume, whom no one would accuse of fanaticism.

Jacobi asserts in the Preface that he holds all knowledge to come from sensation, and that he understands reason to be the capacity of drawing inferences regarding relations of propositions. Such inferences yield apodictic certainty regarding the necessity of the propositional relations in question, which claims regarding the existence and properties of objects can never enjoy. "So", Jacobi confesses, "an idealist, basing himself on this distinction, can compel me to concede that my conviction about the existence of real things outside me is only a matter of *faith*. But then, as a realist I am forced to say that all knowledge derives exclusively from faith, for *things* must be *given* to me before I am in a position to enquire about relations" (*DHF*: 256). The entire book, Jacobi then announces, constitutes a development of this single point, intended to demonstrate that all knowledge depends upon an antecedent faith in the senses, and that such faith is not blind, irrational or embarrassing, but an inevitable consequence of the finitude of the human condition.

To drive this point home, Jacobi then proceeds to quote extensively from the *Enquiry Concerning Human Understanding*, in which Hume argues that "all the difference between *fiction* and *belief* lies in some sentiment or feeling, which is annexed to the latter, not to the former, and which depends not on our will", which is to say that "belief is nothing but a more vivid, lively, forcible, firm, steady conception of an object, than what the imagination alone is ever able to attain" (*DHF*: 270–1). Jacobi triumphantly exults that the great authority Hume shares his thesis that "faith is the element of all cognition and action", and his view that "without faith, we cannot cross the threshold, sit at table, or go to bed" (*ibid*.: 272).

Jacobi's readings of both Hume and Kant are partial and tendentious. His interpretation of Kant's distinction between phenomena and noumena assumes that the two are different sorts of object, between which there must be a mysterious causal relation. Jacobi does not recognize the possibility that for Kant the phenomenal and the noumenal designate two distinct perspectives on one and the same object, in which case "appearances" are every bit as real as "things-in-themselves", and are by definition the only sort of object we could ever encounter or come to know. Jacobi's interpretation of Hume fails to make any distinction between habitual reliance on induction and superstitious faith in entities and capacities for which there is no evidence. Jacobi does not recognize, or at least does not acknowledge, that for Hume inductive generalization from particular experiences is necessary to the human condition, whereas superstition that transcends all experience is dangerous and strenuously to be avoided.

But for Jacobi the subtleties of interpretation were really beside the point. Kant and Hume served as representative foils for the two positions that Jacobi cared to distinguish: one that attempts to know the truth about nature, human beings and God without reliance on faith, and results in idealism, determinism and atheism; and one that acknowledges that only faith can secure the truth of realism, freedom and theism. Hume and Kant might not be exactly as Jacobi portrayed them, but such interpretive quibbles could hardly affect the necessary logic of the only available positions concerning faith and reason.

The imperfection of Jacobi's interpretations also mattered little to his contemporaries, who were for the most part so perplexed by Kant's works that they were unable to recognize the points at which Jacobi's attack on transcendental idealism might be parried. The most important attempt to defend Kant from Jacobi's charges came from Karl Leonhard Reinhold (1757–1823), whose work would transform transcendental idealism in ways that led, first, to renewed sceptical attacks, and then to the efforts of Fichte, Schelling and Hegel to secure and complete the critical philosophy.

Reinhold's transformative defence of Kant

Reinhold made his reputation as an expositor of Kant, at a time when exposition of the critical philosophy was sorely needed. Beginning in 1786, he produced a series of *Letters Concerning the Kantian Philosophy*, which were collected and published in two volumes in

1790 and 1792. These efforts to popularize transcendental idealism were welcomed by the public, and initially by Kant himself, who thought that Reinhold was the first to have understood the *Critique of Pure Reason* properly. Very quickly, however, Reinhold came to believe that Kant's critical philosophy lacked the foundation it needed to withstand sceptical attacks on its positive claims. Reinhold continued to conceive of himself as a Kantian, but set himself the task of supplying a proper foundation for transcendental idealism. He took the first steps toward fulfilling this task in *The Foundation of Philosophical Knowledge*, published in 1791, which attempts to identify the limitations in Kant's own work, to establish criteria for overcoming them, and to propose a foundational principle for philosophy that meets the established test.

Reinhold characterizes the question that motivates him in the following way: "Suppose that the *Critique of Pure Reason* already is authentic science: where are then the principles which, together with the one which is the highest, would make up its foundation?" (*FPK*: 87). He then assesses the contribution he hopes to make: "To my knowledge, no defender of Kant's philosophy has conceded, or even expressed as a mere conjecture, the view that there might be, and actually are, objections to the *Critique* that cannot be answered from the *Critique*; or that its *foundation* might need to be argued for and justified independently of anything that is already constructed on it" (*ibid.*: 93). Although Kant would have disputed that his philosophy needs a foundation of the sort that Reinhold sought to provide, and future philosophers would judge that the foundation provided by Reinhold was insufficient to do the needed work, Reinhold's attempt to defend the Kantian project transformed critical philosophy in ways that made possible the subsequent achievements of Fichte, Schelling and Hegel.

The foundationalist response to scepticism

Reinhold seeks to defeat scepticism by establishing an unassailable principle with which philosophy can begin, and from which careful deduction can ensure truthful results. He rules out the law of non-contradiction as a candidate, for reasons already recognized by the empiricists, Kant and Jacobi: deductive reasoning can preserve truth by ensuring that the conclusions drawn from true premises are derived by means of valid inferences, but it cannot guarantee the truth of the initial premises themselves. In Reinhold's words:

The use of the principle of contradiction presupposes in every case . . . the *correctness of what has already been thought* without in any way establishing it . . . For its correct application, the principle of contradiction presupposes a ground different from it; hence it is not at all the *fundamental principle* of philosophy. The ground that it presupposes concerns nothing less than the *reality* of the propositions to which it is applied.

(*FPK*: 54–5)

Hume takes this limitation on the law of non-contradiction, which he describes as its being restricted in scope to establishing relations of ideas, to be the death knell of rationalism, since it implies that knowledge of matters of fact can come only from experience. He then argues for the impossibility of using experience to ground necessary and universal truth, and concludes that metaphysics must give way to empirical science.

Reinhold considers Kant's innovative response to Hume to be decisive, however. He writes that, in response to Hume, "Kant discovered a new *foundation of philosophical knowledge*", derived "from the *possibility of experience* which is found *determined* in the mind *prior to all experience*" (*FPK*: 61). Kant then succeeded, in Reinhold's view, in distinguishing the *a priori* aspects of experience contributed by the mind from those given *a posteriori*, and in so doing defeated empiricism and the scepticism to which it leads. Kant also managed to do this, in Reinhold's estimation, without lapsing back into the indefensible rationalist assumption that our minds are furnished with a stock of innate ideas that inform us about the world. Reinhold judges, in other words, that Kant actually accomplished everything he set out to achieve.

The somewhat surprising problem identified by Reinhold, however, is that Kant was not quite ambitious enough:

With Hume, Locke, and Leibniz, philosophical reason had imposed certain requirements upon itself which Kant met by demonstrating that the foundation of philosophical knowledge lies in the *possibility of experience*. Yet, however successful he was in this, it still cannot be denied that his [newly] uncovered foundation fails to ground the *whole* of philosophical knowledge; on the contrary it can *only* ground ONE PART of it. (*FPK*: 63–4)

Reinhold regards metaphysics as the part of philosophy successfully grounded by Kant, and he recognizes that this grounding is achieved by means of Kant's Copernican revolution: "The *Critique* showed that if metaphysics is to be the science of knowable, real objects, it has to be a metaphysics of *sensible nature*, i.e., the science of the necessary and universal characteristics of appearances, the sum-concept of which constitutes the *sensible world* or the *domain of experience*" (*ibid*.: 65). Reinhold also grasps that Kant's revolution effects a radical reconception of what it is to be an "object", which was never imagined by either the rationalists or the empiricists, and never understood by Jacobi: "This result secures a *concept* of 'object proper' and of 'knowable object' of a kind that neither Locke nor Leibniz had in mind when defending their theses, nor Hume when challenging the foundation of real science. By 'knowable object' they understood, each and all of them, not just an object distinct from its mere representation, but the *thing-in-itself*" (*ibid*.).

Despite its revolutionary reconception and grounding of metaphysics, however, Kant's achievement remains partial, in Reinhold's eyes, because the first principle of transcendental philosophy itself remains ungrounded. Reinhold identifies this foundation as the proposition that Kant himself calls "the highest principle of all synthetic judgements", namely, "every object stands under the necessary conditions of synthetic unity of the manifold of intuition in a possible experience" (*ibid*.: 66). The problem, as Reinhold sees it, is that this proposition, "like any other first principle . . . *is not*, and *cannot* be, *demonstrated* in the science it grounds, or through it" (*ibid*.). The entirety of Kant's transcendental idealism hangs on this proposition, but the proposition as stated is neither specific enough nor adequately justified. It remains to be specified what is meant by "experience", and how the mind makes it possible, but Reinhold regards the answers to these questions as presupposed, rather than demonstrated, by the first critique. He concludes that "the fate of Kant's newly founded metaphysics depends, therefore, on this explication of how experience is made possible in the mind, i.e., of how the faculty of cognition is originally constituted" (*ibid*.: 67).

The completion of critical philosophy thus demands, Reinhold insists, that the science of metaphysics be supplemented and preceded by a science of the faculty of cognition. Reinhold recognizes the same three cognitive capacities identified by Kant: sensibility, understanding and reason. Each of these is a mode of receiving or manipulating mental representations, so Reinhold considers them three species of the most general cognitive capacity, that of representation. The foundation of philosophy must therefore be a science of the faculty of representation, which will ground not only the subsequent theoretical sciences but also practical philosophy, since all willing and action involve the capacity to represent a desired outcome.

Reinhold names the foundational science of representation the "Philosophy of the Elements", and declares that "the object of this science is all that can be known *a priori* concerning the representations of sensibility, understanding and reason – and nothing else" (*ibid.*: 68). The name Reinhold gives to his foundational science is immediately reminiscent of the "Doctrine of Elements" in Kant's first critique, which includes both the "Transcendental Aesthetic" (the account of sensibility) and the "Transcendental Logic" (the account of understanding and reason). Reinhold is quick to distinguish the two, however, pointing out that Kant's goal in the "Doctrine of Elements" was to prepare the way for a scientific metaphysics, whereas the goal of the "Philosophy of the Elements" is to secure the account of representation that Kant presupposes.

Reinhold's central complaint is that Kant takes for granted certain basic concepts – including thought, intuition, sensation, concept and judgement – without offering anything like a rigorous exposition of their meaning. Kant either assumes that his own use of these terms is unproblematic, or adopts without question the prevailing use in the standard logic texts of his day. Reinhold's point is not necessarily that Kant's account of these elements of cognition gets something in particular wrong, but rather that it lacks the sort of justification that could provide an adequate foundation for a truly scientific philosophy. Reinhold sums up his charges against Kant in the following way:

> The *foundation* of the *Critique of Pure Reason* is neither *universal* enough (i.e., all-encompassing) nor *firm* enough to carry the *whole philosophical edifice* of philosophy. Not *universal* enough: for the critique of *theoretical* reason grounds only *metaphysics* . . . Not *firm* enough: for however *true* all that the *Critique* presupposes as *established* regarding its own groundwork may be, (or all that on which it actually erects its edifice) it is equally true that none of it HAS BEEN ESTABLISHED *as true*.
>
> (*FPK*: 92)

Reinhold aims to rectify the situation in his "Philosophy of the Elements" by achieving a true comprehension of the specific aspects of cognition by means of an analysis of their root in the general faculty of representation. Reinhold claims that he will "reduce systematically to *one* what [Kant] . . . abstracts *rhapsodically* from *many*", and thereby "establish what is assumed as established in the *Critique of Pure Reason*" (*ibid*.: 93). Here Reinhold charges Kant with making the very same mistake that Kant himself famously accuses Aristotle of making. In his metaphysical deduction of the categories Kant takes pride in having rigorously derived the basic concepts of thought from the nature of judgement itself, while denigrating Aristotle's *Categories* as having "arisen rhapsodically from a haphazard search for pure concepts", in which Aristotle "had no principle" but merely "rounded them up as he stumbled on them" (*CPR*: 213). Reinhold's language makes it clear that he finds Kant's account of the elements of cognition equally haphazard and unprincipled. The "Philosophy of the Elements" is thus to improve upon the *Critique of Pure Reason* by providing a foundational first principle of the science of representation that can ground the account of the cognitive capacities that in turn ground metaphysics and practical philosophy.

The principle of consciousness as the foundation of philosophy

Before introducing the only principle that he believes is capable of providing an adequate foundation for philosophy, Reinhold briefly considers the main criterion that such a foundational principle must meet. Because the principle must justify everything within philosophy, it cannot itself be philosophically justified: "What has to stand at the *head* of the *Philosophy of the Elements* – and hence of all philosophical explanations and proofs – cannot itself be established through a proof drawn from any part of philosophy whatever, nor for that matter can any philosophy, past or future prove it" (*FPK*: 70). Any attempt to argue for the foundational principle of philosophy, that is, would be manifestly circular, and thus invalid. The principle must, therefore, be self-evident, a fact whose truth is immediately apparent: "the criterion of the *foundation* of the Philosophy of the Elements is the immediate evidence of its *content* discoverable by mere reflection, independently of any reasoning – the unanalyzable nature of the concepts in which it is originally exhibited, or the *de facto* nature of its characteristics" (*ibid*.: 84).

Reinhold refers to the foundation of his philosophy of the elements as the "principle of consciousness", which he claims to meet the criterion just established: "It is not through any inference of reason that we know *that in consciousness representation is distinguished through the subject from both object and subject and is referred to both,* but through simple *reflection* upon the actual fact of consciousness" (*ibid.*: 70). Philosophy begins, in other words, when the subject attends to what is implicit in the incorrigible fact of his own consciousness. This attentive reflection makes explicit that consciousness involves being aware of an object by means of a representation. Consciousness is thus constituted by a subject, an object of its awareness (which may be a spatiotemporal thing in the world, such as a rock, or may be one of its own internal states, such as hunger), and a representation of that object, each of which must be present and distinguished from the others. The philosophical science of cognition, according to Reinhold, can take its departure only from this self-evident truth.

Immediately after introducing the principle of consciousness, Reinhold emphasizes that it is not a definition. He does this in anticipation of being charged with relapsing into rationalism, which begins by defining terms and axiomatic principles from which further propositions are then deduced. The problem, of which Reinhold is well aware, is that although the rationalist method can inform us about the relations of ideas contained in its definitions, it cannot guarantee that its defined starting points correspond to the matters of fact that obtain in the world. Reinhold's lengthy insistence that his foundational principle is not a definition is thus intended to prove that his philosophy meets the empiricist stipulation that knowledge of the world must originate with the experience of matters of fact.

Reinhold argues that because "the concept of *representation* . . . is *immediately* drawn from consciousness . . . it is entirely *simple* and incapable of analysis", from which it follows that "the principle of consciousness, far from being a *definition,* qualifies rather as the *first principle* of all philosophy precisely because it presents a concept that does not allow definition" (*FPK:* 70). He claims that "the concept of representation can only be drawn from the CONSCIOUSNESS of an *actual fact*" (*ibid.*), and complains that "anyone who accuses me of *building upon mere definitions . . .* is misinterpreting the entire foundation on which my system rests" (*ibid.*: 71).

Reinhold recognizes that by basing his philosophy upon a purportedly immediate fact he avoids the charge of rationalism only to risk the charge of arbitrariness. Without mentioning Jacobi by name, he takes pains to distinguish his position from one "driven by [the] whims and prejudices" of fantasy or imagination (*ibid.*: 72). Reinhold's account of how it is possible to draw this distinction results in the identification of a number of additional criteria that the foundational principle of philosophy must meet. These criteria were important not only for Reinhold's own project, but also for the development of Fichte, Schelling and Hegel, all of whom adopted aspects of Reinhold's test for the grounding of philosophy, while agreeing that his own principle fails to pass it.

Reinhold's first criterion for a non-arbitrary foundational principle is that it be "*self*-determined in the sense that any possible explanation of the concepts that it exhibits is only possible through it; for its part, on the other hand, it does not allow of any explanation, and it needs none" (*FPK*: 72). A principle in need of explanation cannot be foundational, since its own meaning and justification rest upon additional explanatory principles more basic than itself. The same is true of any principle that incorporates concepts dependent upon anything external to the principle for their explanation. A truly foundational principle must therefore be self-evident or self-explanatory, and it must determine or specify the meaning of all of the concepts that it employs. Such a principle, which depends upon nothing but itself for its meaning or justification, is self-determining.

From the fact that the ground of philosophy must be self-determining, Reinhold immediately deduces a second characteristic of the foundational principle: "The self-determinacy of the principle confers upon it its rank of the ABSOLUTELY FIRST among all possible principles, and upon the foundation expressed by it, the property of being ULTIMATE" (*FPK*: 85). A self-determining principle, in other words, is also an unconditioned principle, since its meaning and truth are not conditional upon the meaning and truth of any other propositions. The first principle of philosophy must therefore be an unconditional principle, which is precisely how Reinhold regards his own starting point: "I call the definition of representation the '*absolutely* fundamental explanation' of the Philosophy of the Elements because it includes no characteristic that would either allow of explanation or need any" (*ibid.*: 80).

To characterize the first principle as unconditional is also to characterize it as rational, given Reinhold's Kantian understanding of the activity of reason as the investigation of chains of conditions in pursuit of their ultimate, unconditioned terminus. The unconditional is rational, in this sense, both because it is self-explanatory and because it enables comprehension of all of the propositions that it conditions, and thus completes the process of explanation. With the discovery of the unconditional principle reason is finally satisfied, because it no longer makes sense to ask "why?".

From the unconditionality of the first principle Reinhold next deduces a third characteristic of the foundation of philosophy, its ability to secure the certainty of the results that are derived from it, which he regards as indispensable to achieving scientific status:

> Probability, which the Philosophy of the Elements simply cannot tolerate if it is ever to realize philosophy as science, gives place to apodictic certainty in the science of the faculty of representation. In virtue of the principle of consciousness, the one absolutely fundamental explanation is determined through and through; and in it the original concept of representation is exhaustively drawn out in all its characteristics, none of which is further analyzable. (FPK: 80–81)

Reinhold does not claim or demand that the entirety of philosophy be derived from the first principle alone, but does insist that because the first principle is implicated in all further philosophical results, getting it wrong would compromise everything else: "the accuracy of the highest characteristic does not alone determine that of the subordinate ones; but its inaccuracy makes their accuracy impossible" (ibid.: 77).

Finally, Reinhold concludes that a truly scientific philosophy, one based upon a self-determining, unconditional principle that issues in apodictically certain results, must be a systematic philosophy. Such a philosophy would be characterized by its "scientific form, the thoroughgoing interconnection of its material, the unity under one principle of the manifold that makes up its content – in a word, its systematic character" (ibid.: 84). The formal criterion of this scientific philosophy "is its rigorous systematization – the thoroughgoing determinacy, based on principles, of its theorems and corollaries, and the subordination of all its principles under a single one" (ibid.: 84–5). The Philosophy of Elements, it goes without saying, was intended by Reinhold to be the one truly scientific and systematic philosophy, and thereby to fulfil the promise implicit in Kant's transcendental idealism.

Conclusion

The great idealists who followed Reinhold – Fichte, Schelling and Hegel – agreed with him that any philosophy deserving of the name must be scientific, and that a truly scientific philosophy must be systematic. Philosophy must be scientific in order to ward off the sceptic without lapsing into dogmatism. Only by demonstrating the necessity of its truth claims can philosophy defeat scepticism without falling prey to arbitrariness and prejudice. And only by being systematic can philosophy demonstrate that its truth claims are indeed necessary, in virtue of following strictly from an unconditional starting point.

The central disputes among the idealists, as we shall see, revolved around how to select a starting point that can actually meet the criteria of unconditionality and self-determinacy, and how to proceed from that starting point in a way that can actually meet the criterion of systematicity. They also argued over how much philosophy can systematically determine, and over how the necessary truths of philosophy relate to the contingent truths of other disciplines and ordinary experience. Despite these disagreements, however, the post-Kantian idealists were united by the search for a truly scientific philosophical system, and the conviction that only such a system can answer the challenge posed by the sceptic and thereby realize the aspirations of philosophy.

Reinhold's closing prediction in *The Foundation of Philosophical Knowledge* would therefore look prescient, and sooner than he thought:

> Twenty years hence it will no longer be so difficult to comprehend that without *universally binding first principles*, neither *logic* proper nor *metaphysics* (the metaphysics of sensible and super-sensible objects), neither *moral* nor *natural* law, nor any other particular part of philosophy hitherto dubbed 'science' can attain the rank, the stability and the advantage of authentic *sciences*.   (*FPK*: 96)

First, however, scepticism was to raise its head again, this time in the form of an essay by Gottlob Ernst Schulze (1761–1833), which attacked Reinhold's *Foundation* directly, and more generally called into question the potential of critical philosophy. It was Schulze's provocation that would give the immediate impulse to Fichte's attempt to defend transcendental idealism, which led eventually to the development of Fichte's own distinctive position.

Schulze's sceptical challenge to Reinhold

Schulze's essay appeared in 1792, just one year after Reinhold's *Foundation*, with a remarkable title that made its ambitions clear: *Aenesidemus, or, Concerning the Foundations of the Philosophy of the Elements Issued by Professor Reinhold in Jena together with a Defence of Skepticism against the Pretensions of the Critique of Reason.* The piece takes the form of a constructed conversation between two characters named after actual men who lived in ancient Greece: Aenesidemus, a sceptic, and Hermias, a devotee of Plato and Aristotle. Aenesidemus, who represents Schulze's position (although the essay was published anonymously), mounts attacks on both Reinhold and Kant, and argues that neither has successfully defeated Humean scepticism.

Aenesidemus portrays the thesis of critical philosophy as being that "a large portion of the determinations and characteristics with which the representations of certain objects occur in us are to be grounded in the essence of our *faculty of representation*" (*A*: 106). He then states his intention to give a proper estimation of the true value of critical philosophy, and says that in order to do so "we must give special consideration to the grounds and principles from which, and in accordance to which, it establishes that there is in our knowledge something determined *a priori* by the mind, and that this something constitutes the form of the material given to our knowledge *a posteriori*" (*ibid.*). Aenesidemus then emphasizes that "in this examination . . . we must also pay special attention to the demands of Humean skepticism . . . It is of great consequence . . . in adjudicating the value of the whole of critical philosophy to press the question whether the *Critique of Reason* has done justice done to the demands made by Hume" (*ibid.*).

Although this initial portrayal of the critical philosophy does not distinguish between Kant and Reinhold, Aenesidemus acknowledges that there are apparent differences between the two, and he proceeds to examine them separately. The conclusion of his examinations, however, will be that the differences between Kant and Reinhold are merely apparent, and that both fall prey to the same self-contradictions and sceptical objections. Fichte took Schulze's scepticism quite seriously, and one of his first important publications would be a review of *Aenesidemus*, in which he took up the challenge of defending critical philosophy.

Reinhold insists that the foundation of philosophy must be a fact rather than a definition, and that his own science of representation rests upon the simple fact of consciousness. Aenesidemus, however, immediately challenges the purported factuality of Reinhold's foundational principle. He grants that we are conscious, but denies that reflection upon consciousness can reveal anything about the actual constitution of our minds or the process of representation.

Aenesidemus prefaces this criticism with the introduction of several of the basic claims made by Reinhold in his "Philosophy of the Elements". Aenesidemus is most interested in the claim that from the consciousness of representations we can infer the existence of a faculty of representation, and the claim that this faculty of representation plays a causal role in the constitution of those representations. Aenesidemus quotes from Reinhold's *Theory of the Faculty of Representation* (1789):

> Representation is the only thing about whose actuality all philosophers agree. Indeed, if there is anything at all about which there is agreement in the philosophical world, it is representation. No idealist, no solipsist, no dogmatic skeptic, can deny its being. *Whoever grants a representation, however, must also grant a faculty of representation, i.e., that without which no representation can be thought.*   (*A*: 107–8)

Aenesidemus pounces upon this argument, which he charges with confusing the necessity of *thinking* that x is the case with the necessity of it *being true* that x is the case. He writes that "the proof really consists in the following argument: Any two things that cannot be *thought* apart from one another can also not *be* apart from one another; the being and actuality of representations cannot be *thought* apart from the being and actuality of a faculty of representation; hence a faculty of representation must also exist objectively" (*ibid.*: 108).

Aenesidemus finds this slippage particularly ironic and unforgivable, coming from a critical philosopher, since transcendental idealism is built upon the distinction between the conditions of the possibility of experience and the conditions of the possibility of being, and is normally so fastidious about denying our ability to have any insight whatsoever into the latter. To forget this distinction, as Reinhold appears to have done, is to forsake the critical stance and lapse back into discredited rationalism: "If this syllogism were right, and were it to prove anything at all, then Spinozism would be invulnerable to attack, as well as the Leibnizian system and idealism – in fact, the whole of dogmatism in all its diverse and contradictory claims about the thing-in-itself " (*ibid.*). In other words, "all that Kant has asserted and believes to have demonstrated, about the inability of the understanding and of reason to discover by thought the nature of things-in-themselves – all this would be false and wrong-headed; we would instead possess a principle by which we can discover the nature of things as they are outside our representations" (*ibid.*). Aenesidemus concludes that Reinhold is guilty of the most blatant self-contradiction: "The Philosophy of the Elements, by deriving actual representations from a faculty which it takes to be something objectively actual, and by defining it as the cause of the representations, contradicts its own principles as well as the results of the *Critique of Reason*" (*ibid.*: 109).

Aenesidemus does not deny that we have representations, nor even that we have representations of ourselves as having a faculty of representation that possesses the distinct capacities sensibility, understanding and reason. What he rejects is the inference from the presence of these representations to the conclusion that we in fact have such a faculty that plays a causal role in giving form to the representations themselves. This attribution of causality to the supposed faculty of representation amounts, Aenesidemus believes, to applying the category of cause-and-effect to things-in-themselves, which the critical philosophy expressly prohibits. This mistake strikes Aenesidemus as so obvious that he is perplexed as to how Reinhold could have made it: "It is . . . simply incomprehensible whence the Philosophy of Elements obtains the right, in laying down its foundations, to apply the categories of *cause* and *actuality* to a super-sensible object, viz., to a particular faculty of representations which is neither intuitable nor given to any experience" (*ibid.*: 110).

To make matters worse, Aenesidemus contends, the explanatory inference from representations to a faculty of representation is not only invalid but also useless. For "to appeal to some particular cause or faculty behind an alteration, or some other matter of fact, in order to explain it, as is commonly done, amounts to no more than a repetition of the phenomenon or actual fact whose properties we wanted to explain, with the addition of the word *power* or *faculty*" (*ibid.*: 111). Trying to explain the presence and alteration of representations by reference to our having a faculty of representation is, according to Aenesidemus, as vacuous as trying to explain the fact that water droplets stick to objects by referring to the objects having a "faculty of attracting water". In neither case have we said anything meaningful about the mechanism behind the phenomenon, and thus Aenesidemus concludes that "answers of the sort are nothing else but admissions of human ignorance regarding the ground of the given facts, or of the changes in sensible objects" (*ibid.*).

Aenesidemus' own view is that philosophy has yet to discover a sufficient basis for deciding the questions raised by the undeniable experience of representations:

Whether or not [faculties of representation] have actual being outside our representations of them; whether or not the thought of something that ought to make intuitions, concepts and ideas possible in us in the first place is totally void of objective value; and where the representation of this something might originate – these are, according to skepticism, totally *undecided issues*. (*Ibid.*: 109)

He is careful not to declare the issues undecidable, but insists that they cannot be decided until philosophy succeeds in establishing a principle that sanctions inferences from representations to things-in-themselves, and so allows us to determine the truth about actual things from the representations with which we are immediately acquainted. Aenesidemus claims to be open to the possibility of such a principle being established, but he emphatically rejects Reinhold's "principle of consciousness" as a candidate for securing the foundation of critical philosophy.

Aenesidemus next turns his attention to Kant, and argues that the original exposition of the critical philosophy is subject to precisely the same objections already raised against Reinhold. Schulze uses as a title for this section of the work the question that guides Aenesidemus' investigation: "Has the Critique of Reason Really Refuted Hume's Skepticism?"

Aenesidemus begins with a clear statement of the deciding issue that will determine how the question is to be answered. It all depends, he writes, on "whether David Hume could have found Mr. Kant's proof that the necessary synthetic judgements must originate in the mind, in the inner source of representations, and that they are the form of experiential cognition, significant and compelling" (*A*: 112). Aenesidemus concludes, of course, that Hume would find Kant's proof far short of compelling, and for the same reasons that Aenesidemus has already adduced to condemn Reinhold's purported science of representation.

Schulze's ultimate judgement is that the positive claims of critical philosophy, whether advanced by Kant or Reinhold, are as arbitrary as the "facts" that Jacobi claims to know on faith. They may be true, or they may be false, but in any case they are not adequately justified, and they surely do not deserve to be called scientific. The proper response to all the claims is the suspension of judgement, the *epoche* that the ancient sceptics advocated not only for its intellectual honesty but also for the peace of mind that they claimed only it could bring. For Schulze, as for Jacobi, Hume remains unrefuted, and if the pretensions of reason can ever be made good, it will take a new and heroic effort.

Conclusion

Ten years after the *Critique of Pure Reason* first appeared, the debates that it inaugurated remained unsettled and, to those involved, as pressing as ever. No consensus had been achieved on the fundamental questions concerning the possibility, source and scope of synthetic *a priori* knowledge. All the major German intellectuals granted, as Hume had not, the existence of such knowledge, but that was the extent of their agreement. Schulze contended that the source of necessary synthetic judgements was a complete mystery, and that all of Kant's claims regarding the structure and operation of the mind were shamelessly dogmatic. Jacobi joined Schulze in rejecting the idea that reason alone could determine the scope of synthetic *a priori* knowledge, and insisted that philosophy has no choice but to begin with the deliverances of faith. Reinhold defended the project of critical philosophy, but conceded that it needed a better foundation than Kant himself had been able to provide. Reinhold's attempt to base philosophy upon a theory of representation founded upon the so-called principle of consciousness, however, was thoroughly unpersuasive.

These debates in epistemology and metaphysics remained pressing not only in virtue of their intrinsic philosophical interest, but also because they were seen, by all involved, to have great practical consequences. At stake in the disputes over rationality and freedom were moral and political questions regarding how humans should live. The French Revolution of 1789 had been driven by the call to reject traditional authority in favour of a free life guided by reason, and the German intellectuals felt a powerful need to determine what such a life would involve, whether it was possible and desirable for human beings, and how their own circumstances could and should be transformed.

Defenders of the Kantian project saw critical philosophy as the only hope for determining the conditions of a free and rational life. The logical alternatives, represented in the flesh by Schulze and Jacobi, were a scepticism that could provide no basis for challenging prevailing customs and authorities, and a religious dogmatism that espoused unquestioning submission to the dictates of Christianity. Resistance to these dispiriting choices demanded the development of a philosophy that could defeat scepticism and determinism, and establish the conditions of the actualization of freedom, thereby providing the standard against which all modern social, political and religious institutions and practices must be measured.

It was this task that Fichte inherited and sought to accomplish. He aimed to defeat the scepticism of Schulze and Hume by putting philosophy on the sort of foundation that Reinhold had called for but been unable to provide. Fichte's primary goal, in other words, was to make philosophy truly scientific, by identifying an unassailable first principle, and then deriving all subsequent knowledge claims from it in strictly systematic fashion. With this derivation he hoped to refute Jacobi's claim that philosophical explanation is necessarily deterministic, by establishing the truth of human freedom and specifying the moral and political conditions of its actualization.

Summary of key points

- Jacobi charges that Kant's limitation of knowledge to appearances makes him a subjective idealist, incapable of justifying our belief in a mind-independent reality.
- Jacobi claims that only a leap of faith can secure belief in the external world, freedom and God.
- Reinhold attempts to defend Kant by establishing the "principle of consciousness" as an unassailable foundation upon which transcendental idealism can be made scientific and systematic.
- Schulze objects that Reinhold's principle falsely assumes that the way the mind appears to work must be the way that the mind actually works.
- Schulze regards the claims that Reinhold and Kant make about the operation of the mind as violating transcendental idealism's own insistence that we can know nothing about things-in-themselves.

four

Fichte: towards a scientific and systematic idealism

Johann Gottlieb Fichte (1762–1814) burst onto the German philosophical scene in 1792 (the same year in which *Aenesidemus* appeared) with the publication of *An Attempt at a Critique of All Revelation*. The essay, which develops Kantian themes in the philosophy of religion, was first printed anonymously, and the public initially assumed that it had been written by Kant himself, who had in fact approved the piece in advance and helped to get it published, harbouring hopes that the young Fichte would prove to be a worthy champion of transcendental idealism. When Fichte's authorship became known he was immediately accorded an elevated status in the intellectual community. In 1793 he published two political essays ("Reclamation of the Freedom of Thought from the Princes of Europe, Who Have Oppressed It Until Now" and "Contribution to the Rectification of the Public's Judgment of the French Revolution") that further established his commitment to freedom and his willingness to espouse controversial views, even at the risk of angering powerful authorities.

In 1794, at the age of thirty-two, Fichte was named to replace Reinhold in the prestigious chair of philosophy at the University of Jena, and at the same time he also assumed Reinhold's mantle as the most prominent defender of the critical philosophy. His first important contribution to the ongoing methodological debates was a review of *Aenesidemus*, which appeared in February. This was followed several months later by Fichte's first presentation of his own approach to philosophy, and especially to the foundational issues raised by Jacobi, Reinhold and Schulze. This work, "Concerning the Concept of *The Science of Knowledge*", was written as a prospectus for the students at the University of Jena, intended to introduce them to the new professor of philosophy. The foundation of Fichte's own philosophical system was to be called *The Science of Knowledge*, and in this prospectus Fichte endeavoured to explain the tasks that systematic philosophy must accomplish, and the methods by which it could accomplish them.

During the academic year 1794–95 Fichte gave the lectures that formed the basis for the first published version of *The Science of Knowledge*. He then turned his attention to practical philosophy, attempting to treat political and moral issues "scientifically" by grounding his account of them in the foundational principles of *The Science of Knowledge*. This effort resulted in the publication of the two other works that completed Fichte's system: *Foundations of Natural Right* (1797) and *The System of Ethics* (1798).

In 1798 Fichte also published an essay in the philosophy of religion, "On the Basis of Our Belief in a Divine Governance of the World", that led him to be charged with atheism and initiated a controversy that prematurely ended his career in Jena. The controversy was inflamed in 1799 when *The Science of Knowledge* was denounced by Jacobi as "nihilistic" and by Kant as overstepping the bounds of a truly critical philosophy. The university responded by firing Fichte, who moved to Berlin, where he continued to rework *The Science of Knowledge*, and to write a variety of pieces intended to introduce his system to the intellectual public, all in the hope of striking upon a form of presentation that would win his philosophy the universal acclaim he was sure it deserved. Fichte's frustration at his inability to achieve this recognition was perhaps most evident in the remarkable title of an essay published in 1801: "A Crystal Clear Report to the General Public Concerning the Actual Essence of the Newest Philosophy: *An Attempt to Force the Reader to Understand*". His reputation continued to wane, however, and in the first decade of the nineteenth century Fichte was surpassed by Schelling and Hegel, who became the new standard-bearers of German Idealism.

Response to Schulze's scepticism: "Review of *Aenesidemus*"

Fichte's philosophical development was strongly influenced by Schulze's sceptical attacks on Kant and Reinhold. In his "Review of *Aenesidemus*", Fichte undertook a critical assessment of Schulze's scepticism, granting its philosophical value while rejecting its claim to have undermined transcendental idealism.

The very first sentence of Fichte's review concedes to Schulze that "it cannot be denied that philosophical reason owes every noticeable advance it has ever made to the observations of skepticism upon the precariousness of the position where it has for the moment come to rest" ("R": 137). The resting point of the moment, of course, was the principle of consciousness, which Reinhold had offered as the foundation of his account of representation, which he claimed to be the *sine qua non* of a fully justified critical philosophy. In his review Fichte explains that although he hopes and expects that the principle of consciousness will indeed prove to be true, the objections raised by Aenesidemus have persuaded him that the principle remains in need of an adequate justification, and therefore that Reinhold's philosophical position is indeed precarious. Fichte thus declares that Schulze's essay has convinced him of the necessity of discovering an even more fundamental starting point for philosophy, from which the truth of the principle of consciousness can be deduced *a priori*.

At the same time that he lauds scepticism for spurring philosophy to shore up its foundations, Fichte criticizes Schulze for misunderstanding Kant and the nature of knowledge more generally. Schulze's scepticism, according to Fichte, stems from the misguided assumption that the object of knowledge is the thing-in-itself. On this assumption, knowledge would indeed be impossible, but to continue to desire access to things-in-themselves is to demonstrate a complete failure to appreciate Kant's basic point: any object of which we are aware must already have been processed by the cognitive apparatus that enables our awareness, and thus can be known only as it appears in the light of such processing. The proper conclusion to draw is not that knowledge is impossible, but rather that things-in-themselves cannot be known; the only possible objects of knowledge are appearances, the phenomena that result from the interaction of our cognitive faculties with the world. The genuine philosophical problem, Fichte insists, is not to explain how we can know things-in-themselves (because we cannot), but rather to explain how we can have synthetic *a priori* knowledge of appearances.

Schulze had granted that we do in fact have such knowledge, but argued in *Aenesidemus* that Kant's explanation of its possibility need not be true, even if it is the only one we are able to imagine. Perhaps Kant is right that the mind contributes necessary forms to the objects of knowledge, but perhaps the necessity that characterizes some of our judgements has an alternative source that we have yet to grasp. So long as this is the case, Schulze had concluded, the proper stance is a sceptical restraint that refuses to make assertions that exceed our capacities of justification.

Fichte is also critical of this line of reasoning, however, contending that it fails to appreciate the difference between empirical and *a priori* explanations. Empirical explanations are always provisional hypotheses resulting from inductive inference upon all of the available evidence, and as such they remain open to revision or replacement in the face of newly acquired information or counterexamples. *A priori* explanations, by contrast, confer deductive necessity upon their conclusions, so long as they employ indisputably valid inferences to draw out the implications of indisputably true premises. The transcendental explanation of the possibility of necessary synthetic judgements can be definitively established, therefore, if it can be shown to result from a sound *a priori* deduction. Such a deduction would provide critical philosophy with a foundation impervious to Schulze's sceptical worry about the possibility of alternative explanations that we have simply failed to imagine.

Fichte's reflections upon *Aenesidemus* thus lead him to the conclusion that his philosophical calling is to develop a foundation for transcendental idealism that rests entirely upon indisputable premises and valid *a priori* reasoning. Fichte takes this to be his own task because he agrees with Schulze that Reinhold utterly failed to accomplish it, but he does offer high praise to Reinhold for having recognized what must be done to complete and perfect the Kantian revolution: "After Kant, Reinhold gained for himself the immortal merit of drawing the attention of philosophical reason to the fact that the whole of philosophy must be traced back to one single principle, and that one cannot discover the system of the permanent modes of operation of the human spirit prior to the discovery of its keystone" ("R": 150).

Fichte's review of *Aenesidemus* also contains provocative hints about the foundation for philosophy that he intends to develop. The indisputable premise or principle from which Fichte will begin is the fact of self-consciousness, which he credits Descartes with recognizing as the only appropriate philosophical starting point. Fichte then plans to proceed in transcendental fashion, reflecting upon the conditions that are necessary to explain the possibility of the fact of self-consciousness. He credits Kant with recognizing, most explicitly in the "Refutation of Idealism", that one of these conditions of selfhood is the intuition of a world that is experienced as distinct from and external to the self. Fichte's own philosophical programme would amount to the deduction of all of the features of the world, the self and their interaction that are necessary to account for self-consciousness.

Fichte's first attempt to establish the foundation of his philosophical programme appeared two years after the "Review of *Aenesidemus*", in *The Science of Knowledge* of 1794–95. Before undertaking this foundational enterprise, however, Fichte first endeavoured to specify the method by which it must proceed, and the criteria by which its success must be evaluated. He published this preparatory work under the title "Concerning the Concept of *The Science of Knowledge*", the prospectus of his philosophy with which he introduced himself to the students at Jena.

Systematic idealism: "Concerning the Concept of *The Science of Knowledge*"

In the Preface to the first edition of his prospectus Fichte again acknowledges Kant, Reinhold and Schulze as his most important predecessors. The opening sentence reports that "reading the modern skeptics, in particular *Aenesidemus* . . . has convinced the author of this treatise [that] . . . philosophy has not yet been raised to the level of a clearly evident science" ("CC": 94). Fichte goes on to add that he is "just as sincerely convinced that nothing, following Kant's spirit of genius, could contribute more to philosophy than Reinhold's systematic spirit" (*ibid.*: 96). Fichte clearly conceives of himself as applying Reinhold's systematic spirit in the service of Kant's original genius for the purpose of vanquishing Schulze's scepticism.

In the Preface to the second edition of the prospectus, which appeared in 1798, Fichte distinguishes between the role of this preliminary essay, and that of *The Science of Knowledge* itself (which by this time had been written and published). *The Science of Knowledge* is a study in metaphysics, which Fichte is careful to note "does not have to be a theory of the so-called things in themselves, but may be a genetic deduction of what we find in our consciousness" ("CO": 97). "Concerning the Concept" is "critique", which Fichte defines as an investigation "into the possibility, the real meaning, and the rules governing" the science of metaphysics (*ibid.*). "Concerning the Concept" thus aims to prepare the way for *The Science of Knowledge* by defining its tasks, explaining its methodology, and establishing the criteria for its successful completion.

"Concerning the Concept" is divided into three parts, the first of which attempts to define "Science of Knowledge" more precisely. Fichte begins by noting that it is universally agreed that philosophy is a science. There is broad disagreement, however, about the objects and methods of this science, because the meaning of "science" has been left unspecified.

Fichte joins Reinhold in defining "science" as a body of propositional knowledge that has systematic form, and in defining systematic form as the unification of all the propositions through a single first principle. If the propositions are to qualify as knowledge, Fichte reasons, the first principle must itself be certain, and its certainty must be conveyed to all the subsequent propositions in virtue of their systematic connection. Systematicity is thus not an end in itself, but a means to the certainty that science demands. The systematicity required, however, is of a very strong sort, for the propositions must not only be interrelated (which is all that a weak notion of "system" might entail) but also connected in such a fashion that if the first principle is certain, then so is every other proposition.

Fichte notes that these first reflections on the meaning of "science" immediately raise two essential questions: "How can the certainty of the first principle be established? And what is the warrant for that specific kind of inference by which we infer the certainty of other propositions from the certainty of the first principle?" ("CC": 105). These questions must be answered, Fichte insists, if we are to be able to determine whether our knowledge has a sound foundation (and thus whether we in fact have knowledge at all).

Fichte begins to address the first question by pointing out, again in agreement with Reinhold, that a first principle cannot be proven, for the result of a proof is dependent upon the premises from which the proof proceeds and therefore by definition not a *first* principle. The certainty possessed by the first principle must therefore be immediate, rather than mediated by any process of deduction.

The question that now emerges, however, is whether there are in fact any principles that enjoy immediate certainty. Fichte candidly admits that the answer is not obvious. It is possible that there are no such principles, in which case there is none that could serve as the foundation of philosophical science, in which case none of our knowledge is certain. And it is possible that there are several such principles, in which case the knowledge that rests on each of them is certain, but our knowledge as a whole cannot be unified into a single science. And, finally, it is possible that there is exactly one immediately certain principle that can serve as the foundation of all of our knowledge.

The only way to determine which of these possibilities obtains, Fichte argues, is to make the effort to identify and examine candidate propositions:

Everything depends on the experiment. Should we discover a proposition possessing all of the internal conditions necessary for the first principle of all human knowledge, we will then inquire whether it also possesses the external ones, namely whether we can trace back to it everything that we know or believe that we know. If we succeed in this, then we will have shown – by actually constructing it – that such a science is possible and that there is a system of human knowledge which it portrays. If we fail to construct such a science, then either there is no such system at all or else we have just not discovered it and must leave this discovery to our more fortunate successors. ("CC": 113)

The Science of Knowledge will constitute Fichte's attempt to reconstruct all human knowledge on the basis of a single, immediately certain first principle.

Having defined "Science of Knowledge" more precisely in the first part of "Concerning the Concept", Fichte turns in the second part to questions concerning the method by which the science of knowledge must proceed, and the relation of this foundational science to the other sciences.

One of the first methodological questions Fichte addresses is that of how it is possible to know that "The Science of Knowledge" is complete. Fichte has already argued that philosophical science must begin with an immediately certain first principle, and that all subsequent propositions of the science must be deduced *a priori* from this principle in order to guarantee the certainty of the results. But, he now wonders, how can we know that this process of deduction has run its course, that all possible knowledge has been extracted from the first principle? We might find it impossible to deduce any further consequences from the principle but, Fichte points out, this could indicate a limit to our abilities rather than the completion of the system. The only way to rule out the possibility of additional propositions being added to the system, Fichte concludes, is if the deduction arrives back at its original starting point, thus guaranteeing that any subsequent inferences will simply retrace steps already taken rather than demonstrate anything new. Scientific philosophy must, that is, form a closed and circular system, setting out from a single foundational principle and ultimately returning to it by means of careful deductive steps that ensure the completeness and certainty of the resulting body of propositions.

Having discussed how philosophy must begin and end, Fichte next gives an account of the objects of philosophy – that which philosophy claims to know – and of the method by which philosophy can come to know them. Fichte takes the first object of philosophy, as already indicated in his review of *Aenesidemus*, to be the self-conscious subject, the existence of which he takes to be an immediate and incorrigible certainty. The further objects of philosophy are then determined, Fichte argues, by the attempt to explain the necessary conditions of the possibility of self-consciousness. Because he shares Kant's view that only the mind can furnish such transcendental conditions, Fichte specifies these objects of philosophy as the acts of the mind that are necessary to its becoming aware of itself.

The reconstruction of the mental acts necessary to selfhood is what Fichte meant earlier when he described the metaphysical task undertaken in *The Science of Knowledge* as the "genetic deduction of what we find in our consciousness". As a matter of fact, we find that we are aware of ourselves, of an external world, and of various forms of interaction between ourselves and the world. The task of philosophy, as Fichte conceives it, is to explain how it is that each of these elements of which we are aware (each of which can be construed as a mental act – the mental act of becoming aware of the element in question) is not simply a contingent matter of fact, but rather a necessary condition of our being self-conscious.

The objects of philosophy are thus the acts of the mind without which there would be no "mindedness" at all. Philosophy does not aim to describe the order in which we happen, as a matter of empirical fact, to become aware of these mental operations. Rather, it aims to give a systematic account of the mind that deduces in a purely *a priori* fashion all of the mental acts that are necessary conditions of the possibility of the immediate fact of self-consciousness. If this deduction is successful, then the mental acts that it reconstructs should correspond to those that we are in fact conscious of performing, even though the order of performance, awareness and philosophical reconstruction need not be the same.

Fichte notes that the method by which philosophy reconstructs the necessary acts of the mind is itself one more mental act, that of reflection. Philosophy involves the mind turning upon itself and becoming explicitly aware of the modes of its own action, which will have been in operation for some time before their philosophical reappropriation. Fichte further notes that such reflection involves abstracting these modes from the concrete forms in which they naturally occur, considering each in isolation from the others, in the order in which they appear in the *a priori* reconstruction of self-consciousness.

At this point Fichte takes the opportunity to distinguish himself from Reinhold by pointing out that although the philosophical act of reflection is a form of representation (it represents the mental acts upon which philosophy reflects), not all of the mental acts that it reflects upon are necessarily acts of representation. In other words, although representation is the basic act of philosophy, it may not be the basic act of the mind itself, as Reinhold assumed. Philosophy therefore cannot take representation as a given, much less as a foundational principle, but rather must deduce the necessity of representation from the more basic fact of self-consciousness.

While declaring his own method to be more systematic and truly foundational than Reinhold's, Fichte also forthrightly draws attention to the fact that it is inevitably circular. Philosophy operates by means of reflection and deduction, and therefore must presuppose rules for the proper performance of these mental acts that can only be sanctioned on the basis of the deductions that these presuppositions enable. Fichte sees no way to escape this circle of justification, and concludes that it is impossible to exclude the possibility that systematic philosophy, no matter how completely and necessarily unified it may seem, rests upon a false deduction. He confesses that "one may never claim infallibility", but rather than seeing this as a reason to reject the project of systematic philosophy, he places the burden back upon those who would criticize it: "if someone doubts the tenability of our system, we may demand *that he point out to us the error in our reasoning*" ("CC": 130). If such an error can indeed be identified, then the system will require revision, but the mere fact that the possibility of error cannot be ruled out should not deter us from making our best efforts to secure the foundation of knowledge.

Fichte offers several strategies for increasing our confidence that our philosophical reflections are sound, including repeating them, and running through them in reverse order, but ultimately offers no consolation for the fact that our reasonings are never indefeasible, and our philosophical conclusions are at best "probable". The objects of our defeasible philosophical reasonings and probable conclusions, however, are the necessary conditions of the possibility of self-consciousness, and their necessity is not impugned by our fallibility.

Fichte acknowledges that defining the objects of philosophy in terms of their necessity to self-consciousness requires the philosopher to discriminate between those acts of the mind that are necessary to its operation and those that are contingent or accidental. But again he is happy to grant that there is no infallible rule for making this discrimination. We have no choice but to make the experiment of systematic philosophy to the best of our ability, and to remain open to revising our deductions and conclusions whenever we become aware of having made mistakes.

This distinction between the necessary and the contingent actions of the mind plays an important role in Fichte's account of the relation between philosophy and the other sciences. Philosophy, which begins from the immediately certain principle of self-consciousness, must serve as the foundation for all of the other sciences, for otherwise their conclusions would lack the certainty that Fichte regards as the criterion of scientific knowledge. As the foundation of the other sciences, philosophy must provide the principles from which they begin, but if these sciences are to be distinguished from philosophy proper, then something extra-philosophical must be added to their initial principles. Fichte suggests that because all the principles of philosophy are necessary operations of the mind, the objects of the other sciences must be mental operations that are contingent or free.

Fichte offers several examples to illustrate this point. He considers it part of the task of philosophy to deduce the necessity of the experience of a natural world to our own self-awareness, but regards the particular laws that describe the behaviour of objects in the world as contingent with respect to our selfhood (since this could emerge in a variety of possible worlds, but not if there were no natural world at all), and so assigns the examination of these laws to the natural sciences rather than to philosophy. Likewise, Fichte expects philosophy to deduce the necessity of space to our experience of the world (which Kant had already tried to do, but without success in Fichte's opinion), but regards the construction and manipulation of particular spatial figures that are not necessary conditions of self-consciousness as the province of geometry.

It is the fact that philosophy is concerned solely with the necessary operations of the mind that enables it to form a closed system, in contrast to the other sciences, which are open-ended or "infinite", since additional experiments or constructions are always possible. The natural scientist can always gather more data, and the geometer can always imagine another figure, but the task of philosophy comes to an end when all of the necessary conditions of self-consciousness have been deduced. Of course, our fallibility means that any account of these conditions must always remain open to revision and improvement, but the scope of philosophical investigation is fixed by, and limited to, the nature of the mind's necessary operations.

Fichte takes special care to distinguish philosophy from logic, since both claim to be universal sciences, in contrast to the particular sciences that depend upon them. The key difference, in Fichte's view, is that logic is a purely formal discipline, whereas philosophy also provides content, or substantive knowledge of the mind and the world. Logic, as Fichte understands it, proceeds by means of abstracting the form of propositions from their content, and thus cannot be a foundational discipline, since it is parasitic upon other disciplines, including philosophy, to provide it with the propositions from which it abstracts the formal qualities. Fichte thus concludes, uncontroversially, that metaphysics cannot be deduced from formal logic alone. He goes on, however, to declare that the validity of logical laws cannot be assumed by the metaphysician, but rather must be derived from the certain principles of "The Science of Knowledge". This highly controversial subordination of formal logic to metaphysics receives a more thorough explication in the opening section of *The Science of Knowledge*, which is discussed below.

The third and final part of "Concerning the Concept", entitled "Hypothetical Division of *The Science of Knowledge*", is quite brief, but provides valuable insight into the overall structure of the philosophical system that Fichte is on the verge of developing. Here Fichte notes that the first principle of philosophy is the self-conscious subject, or the "I", and asks the reader to suppose what he will later claim to have demonstrated, namely, that the I can be self-conscious only in virtue of distinguishing itself from the world, or the "not-I", which is therefore the second principle of philosophy. He then points out that there are only two ways in which the I and the not-I can be further determined. Either the not-I can determine the I (the world can affect the subject), or the I can determine the not-I (the subject can affect the world). In the second of these modes of determination the I functions as a "will", a conscious subject striving to realize its ends in the world. In the first mode of determination the I functions as an "intellect", a conscious subject registering the impacts of the world upon it. Fichte's philosophical system will begin with a deduction of the basic principles that are fundamental to all self-consciousness, and will then branch into theoretical philosophy, which treats the necessary conditions of intellectual activity, and practical philosophy, which treats the necessary conditions of willing.

The Science of Knowledge

Introducing The Science of Knowledge

The Science of Knowledge is preceded by not one but two introductions, a fact that reflects Fichte's frustration that his philosophical system failed to win immediate and universal acceptance from his contemporaries. Fichte opens the second introduction by declaring that the original introduction is "perfectly adequate for the unprejudiced reader" and that the current effort is aimed at "those who already have a philosophical system" (*SK*: 29) preventing them from giving Fichte's work the reception it deserves. Significant portions of the second introduction are thus explicitly polemical, directed in response to specific misunderstandings that Fichte feels compelled to rectify, but these polemics also serve to complement the first introduction (which is much shorter), so that the text is best approached by reading the two together.

Fichte introduces *The Science of Knowledge* by declaring that philosophy must "furnish the ground of all experience" (*SK*: 6), and then offering a brief analysis of the concept of experience itself. He begins by stating that experience involves a relation between a thing that is experienced and a subject that experiences. He then reasons that attempts to explain the fact of experience can proceed in only two possible ways, because the only available explanatory grounds are the thing and the subject. "Idealism", as Fichte uses the term, is defined by the attempt to trace experience back to the conscious subject, whereas "dogmatism" (which might be referred to more helpfully as "materialism") seeks the ultimate explanation of experience in the thing-in-itself.

Fichte then announces, somewhat surprisingly, that neither idealism nor dogmatism is capable of refuting the other, because they proceed from contrary first principles for which no justification can be offered. The idealist postulates the existence of a free and independent self, which the dogmatist regards as an illusion due to its incompatibility with his mechanistic presuppositions. And the dogmatist postulates the existence of things-in-themselves, which are regarded by the idealist as mere figments of thought that have no independent reality.

Having denied that reasons can be given for choosing either idealism or dogmatism over its opposite, Fichte proposes that the factors driving the decision must be inclination and interest. He then adds, however, that dogmatism is unable to explain the basic fact that must be explained, that of "representation", and is therefore untenable. The fact of "representation" is equivalent to that of consciousness, to the fact that there are beings that have experience of themselves and of other beings. Dogmatism cannot explain this fact because there is no possible transition from its fundamental explanatory ground – the thoroughly material thing-in-itself – to that which must be explained – the immaterial phenomenon of consciousness. Fichte reasons that all dogmatism is necessarily materialism, all materialism is necessarily mechanism, and no mechanism can account for consciousness. Dogmatism is thus left with no choice but to deny the fact of consciousness, which the idealist regards as a *reductio ad absurdum* of the dogmatist position, and which also contradicts the dogmatist's own behaviour and treatment of others. Fichte consequently concludes that idealism is the only possible philosophy.

Fichte's denial that dogmatism is a possible philosophy does not amount to a retraction of his claim that the idealist will not be able to persuade the committed dogmatist of the untenability of his position. Fichte does not claim that dogmatism is impossible to hold, but rather highlights the implications of holding its commitments. These implications include, in Fichte's view, an inability to explain experience that ultimately forces the denial of experience, and so forces a schism between the way one acts (like a conscious being) and the way one talks (as if there were no such thing as conscious beings).

Thus Fichte grants that "dogmatism" can be held, and is in fact held, even by those who recognize its radical implications, and he harbours no hope of converting to idealism those who are willing to deny the existence of consciousness. He does insist, however, that dogmatism cannot qualify as a tenable *philosophy*, since he understands philosophy as the project of accounting for the possibility of experience, which is a project the consistent dogmatist has no interest in undertaking (since he holds that there is in fact no experience to explain).

Fichte's own task is to provide an idealist account of experience, which involves explaining how the mind can be the source of the conditions that make possible its awareness of itself and the external world. Fichte credits Kant with having recognized this as the definitive philosophical task, but faults Kant for having provided inadequate deductions of the forms of intuition and the categories of understanding. Fichte's aim, however, is not simply to improve upon the details of Kant's deductions, but rather to undertake the entire task from scratch, offering an *a priori* account of how all the essential features of our experience are necessary to explain the existence of self-consciousness, which he takes to be an immediately certain fact, and which he claims is the only assumption that his philosophy makes.

Fichte's idealist programme, in other words, is to explain how the constitutive elements of our conscious experience (the "determinations of consciousness" in Fichte's language) are generated by the activity of the mind itself. This is the "genetic deduction of what we find in our consciousness" promised in "Concerning the Concept of *The Science of Knowledge*", which serves as Fichte's answer to Kant's metaphysical deduction of the categories. Fichte's deduction will proceed by reflecting upon the mental acts that are necessary to self-consciousness, and deriving from them the definitive aspects of our conscious experience, the most obvious of which include an external world full of material objects, the existence and behaviour of which appear to be largely independent of the activity of our minds. Fichte explains that idealism will account for this apparent independence of the world by attributing it to the necessary character of the mental acts that are its true source. Because our minds must, in virtue of their nature, act in certain ways, we experience the presentations that result from these actions as necessary or inevitable, and it is this necessity, rather than mind-independence, that accounts for the objectivity of the world. Fichte therefore rejects the need for a transcendental deduction of the categories, since he regards the world of objects as being constituted by, and therefore necessarily conforming to, the conditions that make experience possible.

In introducing *The Science of Knowledge* Fichte offers remarks on the method by which he intends to carry out his idealist programme that elaborate on the earlier discussion in "Concerning the Concept", and which ultimately provide important insights regarding the relationship between his philosophical project and that of Kant. Fichte writes that idealism

> *shows that what is first set up as fundamental principle and directly demonstrated in consciousness, is impossible unless something else occurs along with it, and that this something else is impossible unless a third something also takes place, and so on until the conditions of what was first exhibited are completely exhausted, and this latter is, with respect to its possibility, fully intelligible . . .* If the hypothesis of idealism is correct and the reasoning in the deduction is valid, the system of all necessary presentations or the entirety of experience . . . must emerge as the final result, as the totality of the conditions of the original premise.
>
> (*SK*: 25–6)

The idealist philosopher seeks to provide, that is, an *a priori* reconstruction of what is given in experience *a posteriori*.

The elements that emerge in this reconstruction will be, as already indicated in "Concerning the Concept", the mental acts that are necessary conditions of the possibility of self-consciousness. In deducing these acts the philosopher "merely makes clear to himself what he actually thinks, and always has thought, when he thinks of *himself*; that he thinks of himself is, however, an immediate fact of consciousness for him" (*SK*: 36).

Although self-consciousness is experienced as an immediate fact by the philosopher (and by everyone else), Fichte contends that this experience must be preceded by an original act of self-constitution, without which there would be no conscious subject at all. Fichte writes that "it is only through this act, and first by means of it, by an act upon itself, which specific act is preceded by no other whatever, that the self *originally* comes to exist for itself" (*ibid*.: 34).

Fichte famously characterizes the original act of self-constitution, whereby an existing being develops reflexive awareness, and thereby becomes a "self", as one of "intellectual intuition". He appears to adopt Kant's assumption (without explicitly saying so) that there are only two sorts of mental act through which subjects relate themselves to the objects of which they are aware: conception and intuition. He further assumes that conceiving of an object is dependent upon first intuiting it, for only after encountering an object through intuition is it possible to develop a conception of it. The original act that brings the self into being thus cannot be one of self-conception, but must rather be one of intuition. This intuition cannot be sensory, however, because the self is not an object that can be encountered through the senses; it is impossible to see, hear, smell, touch, or taste the self. The only remaining possibility is that the self comes into being through an original act of intellectual intuition, through a constitutive moment in which it becomes immediately and directly aware of its own mental activity.

Fichte is well aware of Kant's famous denial that humans have a capacity for intellectual intuition, and he characteristically takes pains to argue that his own position is not only consistent with that of his great predecessor, but actually expresses what Kant really intended to say. Kant broke with the rationalist tradition, and aligned himself with the empiricists, in rejecting the claim that we are capable of knowing objects directly with our minds. All human access to objects, Kant insisted, is mediated through the senses, and without the intuitions they provide our concepts are "empty" or incapable of informing us about the world. Fichte quickly notes that he too rejects the possibility of knowing things-in-themselves with our minds, and emphasizes that the capacity for "intellectual intuition" that he ascribes to us has nothing to do with this, and in fact names a capacity that Kant himself recognizes under a different name: "The intellectual intuition alluded to in *The Science of Knowledge* refers, not to existence at all, but rather to action, and simply finds no mention in Kant (unless, perhaps, under the title of *pure apperception*)" (*SK*: 46).

Fichte goes on to explain that he uses "intellectual intuition" to name the idea at the very heart of Kant's transcendental idealism: the condition of both sensory intuition and conceptual thinking is the unity of the conscious subject, and the establishment of this unified subject requires an act of pure spontaneity that cannot be experienced, but without which experience is impossible to explain. Fichte then cites several passages from the *Critique of Pure Reason* in defence of his interpretation. First, he notes Kant's declaration that "the supreme principle of the possibility of all intuition, in its relation to understanding, is that all the manifold of intuition should be subject to conditions of the original synthetic unity of apperception" (*SK*: 48). Then, Fichte points to Kant's recognition that the condition of the unity of apperception is that "it should be *possible* for my presentations to be accompanied by the 'I think'" (*ibid*.). And finally, Fichte triumphantly seizes upon Kant's claim that "this representation ('I think') is an act of *spontaneity*, that is, it cannot be regarded as belonging to sensibility" (*ibid*.: 49). Since this spontaneous act that makes possible selfhood and experience is precisely what Fichte means by "intellectual intuition", he concludes that his apparent difference from Kant is merely semantic and not at all the betrayal of the critical philosophy of which he has been accused.

Having expended significant effort to defend the Kantian credentials of his fundamental principle, Fichte immediately anticipates and dismisses another objection. Although Kant and Fichte both begin from the spontaneity of self-consciousness, it will be argued, the two philosophers assign quite different roles to self-consciousness in the constitution of experience. "According to Kant", Fichte's critics are sure to point out, "all consciousness is merely conditioned by self-consciousness, that is, its content can be founded upon something outside self-consciousness", but "according to *The Science of Knowledge*, all consciousness is determined by self-consciousness, that is, everything that occurs in consciousness is found, given and introduced by the conditions of self-consciousness; and there simply is no ground whatever for it outside of self-consciousness" (*SK*: 50).

Fichte insists once again, however, that this apparently significant deviation from Kant is in truth no deviation at all. He concedes that his own position is that the contents of consciousness must be thoroughly determined by the self-conscious subject, independently of any and all external givens. But he then tries to make the case that this is in fact Kant's position too. Citing Jacobi's essay "On Transcendental Idealism" as an authority, Fichte claims that "Kant knows nothing of any somewhat distinct from the self " (*SK*: 54). Of course Kant makes reference to things-in-themselves, but only as "something which we merely append *in thought* to appearances" (*ibid.*: 55). Since things-in-themselves are merely an invention of our own thinking, Fichte reasons, the only remaining candidate to be the real ground of the appearances that comprise experience is self-consciousness itself, and this must therefore have been Kant's own view. Fichte concludes that "our knowledge all proceeds from *an affection*; but not affection *by an object*. This is *Kant's* view, and also that of *The Science of Knowledge*" (*ibid.*: 60). Making sense of this notion that knowledge proceeds from the mind's self-affection is one of the major tasks of *The Science of Knowledge*, and Fichte's difficulty in making a persuasive case for the plausibility of the idea ultimately proved to be one of the major obstacles to the acceptance of his philosophy.

Fichte summarizes the position that he proposes to defend in the following way: "Intellectual intuition is the only firm standpoint for all philosophy. From thence we can explain everything that occurs in consciousness; and moreover, only from thence. Without self-consciousness there is no consciousness whatever; but self-consciousness is possible only in the manner indicated: I am simply active" (*SK*: 41). Fichte will also defend the claim, however, that self-consciousness necessarily involves the consciousness of an existence external to it, and thus that "intellectual intuition is . . . constantly conjoined with an intuition of *sense*. I cannot find myself in an action without discovering an object on which I act, in the form of a conceptualized sensory intuition" (*ibid.*: 38).

The Science of Knowledge thus seeks to establish *a priori* that all the determinations of consciousness are necessary to, and grounded in, the existence of self-consciousness itself. The most basic of these determinations, which is definitive of consciousness, is the opposition between the subject and the objects of its awareness, so Fichte's deduction must show that without the experience of an external world there can be no self-consciousness, no experience of subjectivity. A major portion of *The Science of Knowledge* is then concerned with accounting for the relations that obtain between the self-conscious subject and the external world.

Fundamental principles of the entire science of knowledge

The first part of *The Science of Knowledge* proper introduces and attempts to justify the three principles upon which Fichte claims all of our knowledge rests. He refers to these three principles, respectively, as the principle of identity, the principle of opposition, and the principle of grounding.

The first principle, as we already know from the "Review of *Aenesidemus*", "Concerning the Concept", and the two introductions to *The Science of Knowledge*, cannot be argued for without losing its status as the *first* principle. Fichte therefore begins by asserting and examining a proposition, the certainty of which everyone will grant without argument: A = A. Fichte then converts this statement of logical identity into conditional form: if A exists, then A exists. Since this proposition is equivalent to the original, he reasons, everyone must grant its certainty, and thus the necessity of the connection that binds the antecedent and the consequent. But what, Fichte asks, could be responsible for this connection that constitutes the form of judgement in question? The only possibility, he answers, is the self that performs the judgement. Designating the connection as "X", Fichte writes that "X is at least *in* the self, and posited *by* the self, for it is the self which judges in the above proposition, and indeed judges according to X, as a law" (*SK*: 95).

Fichte's basic point is that without judgement there can be no experience at all, and that without the self there can be no judgement. Consequently, the most simple and certain experience depends upon the existence of the self. "Hence", Fichte concludes, "it is a ground of explanation of all the facts of empirical consciousness, that prior to all postulation in the self, the self itself is posited" (*ibid.*: 96).

The self is thus the first principle of experience and knowledge, and the act whereby it comes into existence is the intellectual intuition discussed by Fichte in the second introduction. Here he describes this intellectual intuition as a "self-positing": "The *self posits itself*, and by virtue of this self-assertion it *exists*; and conversely, the self *exists* and *posits* its own existence by virtue of merely existing. It is at once the agent and the product of action; the active and what the activity brings about" (*ibid.*: 97).

"Posit" is one of Fichte's favourite verbs (indeed, the editors of the English edition of *The Science of Knowledge* remark that at times it seems to be the only verb he knows), and is notoriously difficult to translate. The German *setzen* is etymologically related to the English "set", and means roughly to "set forth", "put forward" or "establish". The German word for "law" is *das Gesetz*, that which has been set forth or established. As Fichte uses it, consciousness "posits" the objects of its awareness. The idea he is trying to communicate is that becoming consciously aware of an object requires an activity on the part of the subject, a focusing that sets or establishes the object as the centre of attention.

The subject may "posit", or take as the object of its attention, either an ordinary thing, such an apple, or its own self. When an ordinary thing is posited, the subject simply becomes aware of a previously existing object. But in the case of self-positing the act of becoming aware of the object actually brings the object into existence, because the self is a very peculiar sort of entity, the existence of which is defined by reflexive awareness. In Fichte's language: "*That whose being or essence consists simply in the fact that it posits itself as existing, is the self as absolute subject*" (*SK*: 98).

Fichte's view is thus that it is true of the self, but not of any other object, that to be is to be posited. If and only if the self is posited, or is the object of its own awareness, does the self exist. Fichte elaborates by asking rhetorically, "*What* was I, then, before I came to self-consciousness? The natural reply is: *I* did not exist at all; for I was not a self. The self exists only insofar as it is conscious of itself " (*ibid.*). The positing of the self is thus constitutive of its reality, and Fichte takes the establishment of the self as the first principle of philosophy to be equivalent to the deduction of "reality" as the first and most basic category (*ibid.*: 100).

There is an obvious paradox that threatens Fichte's account (and with it his entire philosophical system): if the self does not exist, then it cannot bring about its own existence; but if the self exists, then it need not bring about its own existence. Fichte's strategy for diffusing this objection is to distinguish between the self as an action and the self as an entity. The "absolute subject" is nothing but pure activity, and it is only as a result of this activity that the self emerges as an entity: "The self presents itself to itself, to that extent imposes on itself the form of a representation, and is now for the first time a *something*, namely an object; in this form consciousness acquires a substrate, which *exists*" (*SK*: 98).

The first principle of knowledge in Fichte's system is thus the pure activity that brings into being a conscious self capable of making the intuitions and judgements by means of which experience is constituted. In case this sounds strange or mysterious, Fichte calmly tells us that it is really nothing new: "That our proposition is the absolutely basic principle of all knowledge, was pointed out by *Kant*, in his deduction of the categories . . . *Descartes*, before him, put forward a similar proposition: *cogito, ergo sum* – which . . . he may very well have regarded . . . as an immediate datum of consciousness" (*ibid*.: 100). Complicated reasoning and forbidding terminology aside, Fichte seems to be saying, the point is quite simple: the existence of the self consists in, and is confirmed by, the immediate awareness of its own thinking, and this thinking self is the necessary condition of the possibility of experience and knowledge.

Fichte ends his discussion of the first fundamental principle of knowledge with a brief reflection on the procedure he has followed, which also sheds light on his understanding of the relation between logic and metaphysics: "We started from the proposition A = A; not as if the proposition 'I am' could be deduced therefrom, but because we had to start from something given with *certainty* in empirical consciousness. But it actually appeared in our discussion that it is not the 'I am' that is based on 'A = A' but rather that the latter is based on the former" (*SK*: 99). In order to ensure the certainty of knowledge, in other words, methodological priority must be granted to those facts that are immediately and incorrigibly given in consciousness, and the proposition representing logical identity is the best example of such a fact. But transcendental philosophy investigates the conditions that are necessary to account for the possibility of these given facts, and these investigations reveal that ontological priority must be granted to the self, without which there could be no judgements, including judgements of identity. Rephrasing the point in more explicitly Kantian language, Fichte writes that "the form of this proposition [A = A], so far as it is a purely logical proposition, is really comprehended under the highest of forms, the condition of *having form* at all, namely, the unity of consciousness" (*ibid*.: 102).

Fichte follows the same procedure in his explication of the second fundamental principle of knowledge, the principle of opposition. The immediate and certain fact from which Fichte begins is the proposition: not-A ≠ A. The condition of making this negative judgement is that the judging subject make a distinction between an object, A, and that which is other than the object, not-A. Fichte helpfully refers to the activity of opposing a posited object to that which is distinct from it as "counterpositing". He then reasons that because the only entity that has yet to be posited (in the first principle) is the subject itself, the initial act of counterpositing must involve drawing the distinction between the self and that which is distinct from it, or the not-self. Fichte concludes that "as surely as the absolute certainty of the proposition not-A is not equal to A is unconditionally admitted among the facts of empirical consciousness, *so surely is a not-self opposed absolutely to the self* . . . And with this we have also discovered the second basic principle of all human knowledge" (*SK*: 104). The discovery of this principle is also equivalent, he tells us, to the deduction of the category of "negation" (*ibid.*: 105).

The third and final fundamental principle of knowledge is deduced in a different fashion. Rather than beginning with another logical proposition, Fichte reflects upon the first two principles, finds an apparent contradiction between them, and then derives the third principle as that which is required to enable their reconciliation (which is necessary, since both have been established as absolutely certain). The reconciliation of an apparent contradiction between established principles by means of the addition of a new principle then becomes Fichte's general method for the *a priori* expansion of his system of philosophical knowledge.

The original contradiction emerges, according to Fichte, when consciousness posits the actuality of the not-self (as it does in the second principle), and thereby displaces the self as the sole object of consciousness (which it had been in the first principle). Consequently, if consciousness can only "posit" the actuality of one object, then the first and second principles are incompatible. The obvious solution is to recognize that consciousness must be capable of positing the self and the not-self simultaneously, and thereby attributing actuality to each, which entails recognizing that each is limited or determined by the other. "Determination" is thus the category that is deduced in the course of establishing the third principle.

Fichte describes the result of this reconciliation as the synthesis of the self and the not-self. They are synthesized, or brought together, in the sense that they are recognized to have something in common, which in this case is simply the fact that they are both actual. This synthesis depends, Fichte points out, on the prior positing of the two theses in question, without which there would be nothing to synthesize. It also depends on the antithesis or opposition of the two theses, without which there would be no need for their reconciliation. The third fundamental principle of knowledge thus emerges from the statement of two theses, the identification of their mutual antithesis, and the derivation of their synthesis.

Fichte claims that all subsequent knowledge will have to be generated by applying this same basic method (thesis–antithesis–synthesis) to this original union of self and not-self: "All other syntheses, if they are to be valid, must be rooted in this one . . . We have therefore to seek out opposing characteristics that remain, and to unite them through a new ground of conjunction . . . And this we must continue so far as we can, until we arrive at opposites which can no longer be altogether combined" (*SK*: 112–13).

A proper appreciation of German Idealism requires noting and emphasizing that this method was invented and practised by Fichte, rather than by Hegel, to whom it is often falsely attributed (a long tradition of misunderstanding popularized by Marx). Hegel's remarks on method and his own philosophical practice, both of which we will consider in Chapter 5, are sharply at odds with Fichte's programme of transcendental synthesis.

Foundation of theoretical knowledge

Fichte begins his account of theoretical knowledge with a succinct summary of the position from which it must begin and the method by which it must proceed:

> We have established only three logical principles; that of *identity*, which is the foundation of all the others; and then the two which are reciprocally based upon it, the principle of *opposition* and the *grounding* principle . . . In the first synthetic act, the fundamental synthesis (of self and not-self), we have likewise established a content for all possible future syntheses . . . But if anything is to be derived from it, there must be still other concepts contained in those it unites, which have not yet been established; and our task is to discover them . . . All synthetic concepts arise through a unification of opposites. We ought therefore to begin by seeking out such opposed characteristics in the concepts already postulated (the self and the not-self) . . . and this is done by reflection.
>
> (*SK*: 120)

The self and the not-self are so far determined only as two opposed and mutually limiting actualities. Fichte's practical philosophy will be concerned with the ways that the self ought to limit or determine the not-self, the ways that the subject ought to strive to impose its will upon the world. His theoretical philosophy is concerned with the ways that the self is limited or determined by the not-self, the ways that the world imposes itself upon the knowing subject.

In positing itself, *qua* knowing subject, as determined by the not-self, the self must posit the world as causally efficacious, or active. Conversely, the self must posit itself as passive, as receptive to the world that confronts it. Although this is consistent with our ordinary understanding of how empirical knowledge is acquired, and therefore likely to strike us as unproblematic, Fichte points out that the passivity of the self is incompatible with its being purely active and self-determining, which is the first principle from which his idealism proceeds. In order to reconcile this contradiction, the self must be posited as being actively responsible for its own passivity. Fichte famously claims that the activity of the subject must be "checked" in a way that makes possible the subsequent experience of being determined by an external world. The precise mechanism by which this check occurs, Fichte confesses, lies beyond the ability of philosophy to determine, but it must transpire with the "concurrence" of the self's own activity, so that the subsequent limitation is ultimately a self-limitation. Fichte attributes the subject's amenability to being checked to the power of the imagination, which he thus regards as "the basis for the possibility of our consciousness, our life, our existence for ourselves, that is, our existence as selves" (*SK*: 202). In conclusion he dramatically declares that "our doctrine here is therefore that all reality – *for us* being understood, as it cannot be otherwise understood in a system of transcendental philosophy – is brought forth solely by the imagination" (*ibid.*).

This rather remarkable doctrine provides the transition to Fichte's practical philosophy, because it indicates that our capacity for knowing the world depends on our capacity for actively constituting the world that we know. The practical self thus has ontological priority over the theoretical self, in the sense that it generates the not-self that is the object of intellectual activity. The theoretical self, however, has philosophical priority over the practical self, in the sense that we only come to know the truth about our practical capacities through the reflective work of philosophy.

Foundation of practical knowledge

Fichte's practical philosophy considers the self as an absolutely active being, capable of determining itself and the world in accordance with its will. In order to determine the not-self, the self must be capable of causally affecting it. But, Fichte suggests, this generates another contradiction: if the not-self is under the control of the self, then it cannot be regarded as a *not*-self, as something truly distinct from and other than the subject; but if the not-self resists the control of the self, then the self cannot be regarded as absolutely independent and self-determining. The contradiction, in other words, is that to be self-determining the subject must be "infinite", unlimited by anything external to itself, but to be a self at all the subject must be "finite", limited by an external world from which it distinguishes itself.

Fichte's solution to this contradiction is to regard the self as infinite in one sense, and finite in another. The self must be infinite in the sense that its *striving* to make the not-self conform to the dictates of its will is unlimited, but finite in the sense that this conformity always remains incomplete. The self must therefore have an absolute drive to transform the world, but this drive must always be partially frustrated, leaving the subject longing to accomplish more.

Fichte regards the central concern of practical philosophy proper as the determination of the particular transformations of the world that rational agents ought to strive to accomplish. Fichte treats these issues in the *Foundations of Natural Right* and *The System of Ethics*, his major works of political and moral philosophy, both of which appeared within three years of the publication of *The Science of Knowledge*.

Foundations of Natural Right and The System of Ethics

Fichte's practical philosophy is best known for its endorsement of a number of unsavoury provisions designed to establish and preserve political order. Fichte argues, for example, that individuals may not assemble without the awareness and consent of the authorities, and that every citizen must carry an identification card (preferably with a pictorial likeness of the bearer) at all times to assist the authorities in keeping track of everyone's whereabouts. Although these particular doctrines are certainly regrettable, and not to be ignored, it is unfortunate that they have tended to inhibit and obscure the more general reception of Fichte's political and moral philosophy, which on the whole is appealing and original, and which develops several themes that had a significant influence on the work of Hegel and Marx.

The primary appeal of Fichte's practical philosophy is its central concern with freedom. Like Kant before him, Fichte aimed to liberate people from their irrational subordination to unjustified political and religious authorities, in favour of a life determined by their own reason. Fichte intended the primary contribution of his own philosophy to this project to be the deduction of the conditions of rational self-determination. But Fichte also believed, as he argues in "Some Lectures Concerning the Scholar's Vocation" and other pieces written for popular consumption, that intellectuals have a responsibility to communicate their knowledge to the wider public, and thereby to accelerate the worldly realization of freedom.

The originality of Fichte's practical philosophy is both methodological and substantive. In keeping with his insistence that philosophy must be strictly systematic, Fichte attempts to derive all his political and moral prescriptions without presupposing anything other than the principles he takes to have been established in *The Science of Knowledge*. The result of this methodological innovation is a conception of freedom importantly different from that of Kant. Whereas Kant had conceived of self-determination or autonomy in terms of the capacity of an individual agent to be an uncaused cause, Fichte reconceives freedom as a fundamentally communal ideal, such that the liberation of rational agents is seen to depend upon their establishing the right sorts of relationships with each other.

Fichte's insight essentially amounts to a transcendental deduction of the Aristotelian notion that humans are political animals, and it is hard to overstate the importance of this philosophical development. One consequence is the reversal of the priority that Kant had given to morality over politics. For Kant, freedom is a metaphysical capacity that must be postulated to account for our experience of moral obligation. Our overriding concern, in Kant's view, must always be using our freedom to attempt to live up to the demands of the moral law. Consequently, the goal of politics (as well as of education and religion) can only be to serve morality by creating conditions that are conducive to the proper use of our freedom (war, ignorance and atheism are to be struggled against because they increase the tendency of people to act immorally). For Fichte, however, freedom is not a metaphysical given but rather a condition that can only be enjoyed in communities that develop certain essential characteristics, the establishment of which is therefore regarded as an end in itself, and not merely as a means to the sustenance of individual morality.

A second important aspect of Fichte's communal conception of freedom is his realization that the necessary conditions of self-determination are not only political but also economic. Fichte emphasizes that without an appropriate level of resources and opportunities people are not free in a meaningful sense, and thus puts economic issues at the centre of discussions concerning social justice. This idea, together with the more general point that the freedom of each rational agent depends upon the freedom of all rational agents, would later be appropriated by Hegel and Marx, who would make them defining elements of German social and political theory.

Foundations of Natural Right

The introduction to the *Foundations of Natural Right* describes the object and task of political philosophy, as Fichte conceives it. Political philosophy is concerned with those actions that follow from the concept of rational agency, which Fichte understands to be those actions that are necessary conditions of the possibility of self-consciousness. This follows from his assumption that beings can be rational only if they are self-conscious, and therefore must do whatever their self-consciousness requires in order to realize their potential for rationality. Political philosophy must determine as precisely as possible the particular requirements of rational agency, which Fichte regards as equivalent to deducing the rights possessed by all free beings.

The body of the *Foundations of Natural Right* comprises three main divisions: the first division deduces the concept of right from the principles of *The Science of Knowledge*; the second division deduces the conditions that are minimally necessary for the concept of right to be applicable to the world; and the third division develops a detailed account of the application of the concept of right to social and political institutions.

The deductions that Fichte develops in the first and second divisions of the *Foundations of Natural Right* proceed by means of a series of "theorems", the first of which states that "*a finite rational being cannot posit itself without ascribing a free efficacy to itself*" (*FNR*: 18). This is simply a restatement of one of the primary conclusions of *The Science of Knowledge*, in which Fichte also argued that this ascription of freedom to oneself also requires positing the existence of an external world, upon which causal efficacy can be exercised. The second theorem of the *Foundations of Natural Right* builds upon the first theorem, and exceeds what was established in *The Science of Knowledge*, by proclaiming that "the finite rational being cannot ascribe to itself a free efficacy in the sensible world without also ascribing such efficacy to others, and thus without also presupposing the existence of other finite rational beings outside of itself " (*FNR*: 29).

It is simple enough to say what the remarkable second theorem means, although more difficult to reconstruct Fichte's argument for it. The import of the proclamation is that "*if there are to be human beings at all, there must be more than one*" (*ibid.*: 37). This does not amount to a denial of the possibility of an apocalyptic future in which a single surviving member of the species *Homo sapiens* walks alone upon a charred and polluted earth. Fichte's point is rather that an animal of the species *Homo sapiens* can become self-conscious of its freedom, and thereby a human being, only in the presence of other animals to which it also ascribes freedom and humanity. The life of the animal begins *in utero*, and could perhaps be sustained after birth in the company of a sufficiently clever pack of chimpanzees, but the development of the animal into a person, Fichte claims, happens only if and when it is raised in a community of free beings that gradually elicit its awareness of its own freedom.

Fichte's transcendental argument for the essentially communal nature of human beings turns (as it must if he is to satisfy the require-ments of systematic philosophy by presupposing nothing but the principles already established in *The Science of Knowledge*) on a further specification of the conditions of the possibility of self-consciousness. In *The Science of Knowledge* Fichte argues that the emergence of self-consciousness requires the subject to "posit" itself, and acknowledges that this requirement generates a paradox unless a distinction is made between the self as pure activity, and the self as an object of awareness brought about by the action. Fichte's argument for the second theorem of the *Foundations of Natural Right* seems to be that the purely active self must be solicited to posit itself as an object of awareness, and that this solicitation or "summons" can only come from another free being, which demands and inspires the other being to actualize its potential for freedom. Fichte writes that this "summons to engage in free self-activity is what we call upbringing" (*FNR*: 38), and thus places educa-tion at the heart of his account of the means by which animals with the capacity for rational agency can develop into persons. Anticipating Marx's famous description of humanity as a "species-being", Fichte concludes that "the concept of the human being is not the concept of an individual – for an individual human being is unthinkable – but rather the concept of a species" (*ibid.*).

The third theorem, which concludes the first division's deduction of the concept of right, states that "*the finite rational being cannot assume the existence of other finite rational beings outside it without positing itself as standing with those beings in a particular relation, called a relation of right*" (*ibid.*: 39). Here Fichte is elaborating on the conditions under which rational animals can issue and respond to the solicitations without which they cannot actualize their freedom. The main condition of such solicitations, he argues, is that both parties *recognize* the other's rationality: if the person capable of issuing the summons does not recognize the rationality of the animal with which it is confronted, then he will not issue a summons at all (one does not demand of a squirrel, for example, that it become a person); conversely, if the animal receiving the summons does not recognize the rationality of the being confronting him, then he will either reject its summons or not recognize it as a summons at all (one does not interpret the playful behaviour of a pack of squirrels, for example, as a call to join them in a community of self-determining persons). A successful summons to the exercise of self-conscious freedom, therefore, depends upon the parties' mutual recognition of their rationality, and this, Fichte believes, depends upon their according each other the respect that rational beings deserve: "*I can expect a particular rational being to recognize me as a rational being only if I myself treat him as one*" (*FNR*: 42).

Fichte's conclusion is that the emergence of freedom depends not merely on the existence of a plurality of rational animals (which is the condition established by the second theorem), but also on those animals forming a community that establishes and secures a "relation of right" between them. Such a relation requires each prospective member of the community to limit the exercise of his own freedom in recognition that every member deserves and must enjoy the right to be free.

The implications of Fichte's third theorem are profound. Most importantly, it follows that there can be no truly human persons in the absence of just communities that foster the development and recognition of each individual's capacity for rationality. This insight, which makes social and political relations a prior condition of the possibility of moral agency, is directly at odds with Kant's practical philosophy, and was later prominently adopted by Hegel and Marx.

A second implication of the theorem, to which Fichte draws attention, is that there can be no such thing as "animal rights". This is not to say that animals other than *Homo sapiens* cannot have rights, but rather that the having of rights can only be conferred in virtue of a being's rationality, rather than its animality. Perhaps dolphins or chimpanzees or extraterrestrial organisms do in fact have the capacity for personhood, in which case we could (and should) form communities with them that secure their rights, but this rightful relation would be granted in recognition of their status as rational agents rather than merely living things.

Having completed his deduction of the concept of right as a necessary condition of the possibility of self-conscious subjectivity, Fichte next turns to the conditions of applying the concept of right in the world. His account of these conditions introduces two additional theorems to the *Foundations of Natural Right*.

The fourth theorem proposes that "*the rational being cannot posit itself as an individual that has efficacy without ascribing to itself, and thereby determining, a material body*" (*FNR*: 53). Self-consciousness, Fichte has previously argued, depends upon the subject positing both itself as a causal agent, and the external world as a field upon which the subject can exercise its causality. The external world, as the not-self, is posited as a realm of material substance, in distinction from the immaterial consciousness that is definitive of selfhood. In order to act in and upon this world, therefore, the self must be capable of controlling a material body, by means of which it can transfer its conscious intentions to the objects around it.

The fifth theorem then adds that "*the person cannot ascribe a body to himself without positing it as standing under the influence of a person outside him, and without thereby further determining it*" (*FNR*: 58). This follows from the combination of the second theorem, which states that the person cannot become self-conscious at all without the solicitation of another self-conscious being, and the fourth theorem, which claims that the actions of self-conscious beings must be accomplished by means of their bodies. Any self-conscious being must therefore regard his own body as having been influenced by the other self-conscious being who summoned him to develop and exercise his capacity of rational agency.

Fichte goes on to argue that it is the sight of human bodies like our own that encourages us to ascribe rationality to other beings. Our presumption, in other words, is that animals sharing our shape also share our capacity for free agency, which Fichte takes to mean that "the human shape is necessarily sacred to the human being" (*FNR*: 79). Of course, it is conceivable that some animals with human form might not be rational agents, and also that a species of animals with a completely different sort of body might be capable of rationality and freedom. But our predisposition, Fichte believes, is to recognize all and only those animals that have human bodies as rational creatures.

The final division of the *Foundations of Natural Right* is by far the longest of the three, and it treats in some detail the specific rights that Fichte believes can be deduced as necessary conditions of establishing the sort of community in which persons can develop. Before this division, all that has been said about such communities is that each member must limit his own freedom out of recognition and respect for the freedom of the other members. But this very general stipulation, Fichte recognizes, must be made much more specific if it is to be the foundation of an applicable political theory.

Fichte first discusses those rights that he regards as directly entailed by the freedom of persons, which he refers to as "original rights". The most basic of these is the right to be a causal agent, and not merely a thing determined by external causes. From this right Fichte derives the right to the inviolability of one's body, and also the right to property, both of which he considers necessary to enable people to be effective agents in the world. Without a body, one could not act at all, and without at least some property the ability to act is insufficient to guarantee a meaningful degree of freedom, since the possession of material objects is a prerequisite for accomplishing almost any intention one might have. Finally, Fichte also argues for the "right of coercion", which allows members of the community to exercise control over any individuals who fail to respect the rights of others and thereby forfeit their own freedom.

Fichte next justifies the existence of the political state on the grounds that it is necessary to secure the original rights of persons. Although people may in fact respect each other in the absence of a political authority, this respect is precarious, contingent upon the mutual trust of the individuals involved. To establish the inviolability of the body and the possession of property as *rights*, therefore, this contingency must be overcome and replaced by a guarantee that individuals will not violate each other. Such a guarantee is only meaningful if it is backed up by a credible threat to coerce those who do commit violations, so it must be provided by an authority that has been designated to exercise the right of coercion on behalf of the community.

Political authority is only legitimate, however, if it does in fact secure the freedom of the members of the community, and Fichte emphasizes that submission to a political authority is rational only on this condition. Individuals therefore have the right, he reasons, to examine and consider the laws that any prospective political authority intends to impose, and to grant ultimate power only to those laws, rather than to any particular person whose will might be fickle or arbitrary.

If a group of persons do agree to establish a legitimate political authority, the result is a contract to create a commonwealth or state. Fichte distinguishes his version of social contract theory from others, however, by complaining that "the only way in which anyone until now has conceived of the whole of the state has been by thinking of an ideal aggregate of individuals; and so true insight into the nature of this relation has been obstructed" (*FNR*: 180). Fichte's own view is that "the most appropriate image for illustrating this concept is that of an organic product of nature" (*ibid.*). The most salient difference between an aggregate and an organism is that in the latter, but not the former, membership in the whole is actually constitutive of the essential character of the parts. A marble that is removed from an aggregate of marbles is still a marble; but a foot that is removed from a human being is a rotting piece of flesh. Fichte characterizes the state as an organism because he has argued that individuals can be persons only as members of just political communities; outside of such communities individuals may continue to live as animals, but not as rational agents. This idea, which actually dates to Aristotle, is another central aspect of Fichte's practical philosophy that is later prominently endorsed by Hegel, although he will reject the larger social contract theory within which Fichte embeds it.

The only features of the state that can be philosophically deduced, in Fichte's view, are those that are necessary to establish and secure the rights of rational agents. Fichte uses the term "constitution" to refer to the set of necessary features that any political authority must have in order to qualify as a state. All other aspects of particular states that lie outside the constitution must be decided upon empirically, and are beyond the ability of philosophy to determine.

Fichte regards the core of the constitution as the legislative, judicial and executive authorities that enable the state to define and defend the rights of its citizens. He also argues, however, that the state must offer a constitutional guarantee that all citizens who are willing and able to work can make a living from their labour, since this, like the right to own property, is a precondition of meaningful freedom. Whenever the state cannot make good on this guarantee, it must offer assistance to those citizens who have done everything in their power to support themselves. Fichte memorably concludes that "there ought to be no poor people in a rational state . . . [and] no idlers" (*FNR*: 186–7). This insistence that economic issues are central to political justice is yet another aspect of Fichte's political philosophy adopted by Hegel and Marx.

The System of Ethics

Moral theory is often assumed to precede political theory, because morality treats individual agents whereas politics treats collections of those agents. According to this common assumption, there could be moral agency without political community, but no political community without moral agents, and thus theorizing about political entities is regarded as parasitic upon a prior understanding of the human individual. Fichte turns this way of thinking on its head, however, by arguing that there are no truly human individuals outside of political communities that enable the emergence of rationality and secure the actuality of freedom. His political philosophy therefore precedes his moral philosophy; only after he has determined the necessary conditions of free agency in the *Foundations of Natural Right* does Fichte turn in *The System of Ethics* to the question of what individuals are obliged to do with the freedom that their communities afford them.

The System of Ethics has the same basic structure as the *Foundations of Natural Right*. The first part of the book deduces the concept at issue, which in this case is "ethics", and the general conditions of its applicability to the world. The second part of the book then applies the concept as concretely as possible.

Fichte identifies ethical actions as those that follow from the necessary laws of rationality. The necessary laws of rationality he understands to be those laws that the subject must give itself in order to be autonomous, rather than ruled by inclinations for which it is ultimately not responsible. An ethical subject is therefore one that uses its capacity for action (its free will) in order to become self-determining, independent of all external determination, and thus free in the fullest sense. Because the freedom that ethical action actualizes is the definitive characteristic of rational agents, Fichte attributes to all such agents an impulse to act ethically for its own sake, without regard for any ulterior motives.

Fichte understands his moral philosophy to be entirely consistent with that of Kant, although he considers himself to have improved upon his predecessor by deducing the specific laws of ethical life as necessary conditions of the possibility of rational agency. Doing so, Fichte crows, makes comprehensible the so-called categorical imperative. The latter no longer appears to be some sort of hidden property (*qualitas occulta*), which is what it previously appeared to be, though of course no positive pretext for such an interpretation was provided by the originator of the critique of reason. Thanks to this derivation, that dark region of sundry, irrational enthusiasm, which has opened itself in connection with the categorical imperative (e.g., the notion that the moral law is inspired by the deity) is securely annihilated.   (*SE*: 52)

Fichte's criticism of Kant is not entirely transparent (which is not surprising, since he wants to avoid the appearance of criticizing Kant at all), but it appears to be twofold: first, Kant takes consciousness of moral obligation to be a brute (and therefore mysterious or occult) fact, rather than deriving it as a necessary condition of self-conscious experience itself; and second, by treating moral obligation as a brute fact, Kant leaves the way open for "irrational enthusiasm" to spell out our specific duties in any variety of ways. Fichte regards his own deduction as solving this problem by determining precisely which actions are necessary to self-consciousness and therefore obligatory for all rational beings.

Fichte states his own version of the categorical imperative at the conclusion of the first part of *The System of Ethics*: "*Always act in accordance with your best conviction concerning your duty*, or, *Act according to your conscience*" (*SE*: 148). He then turns immediately to the "application" of this principle, devoting the second part of the book to the specification of those acts that the conscience of a rational agent ought to register as duties.

Fichte claims that there must be an absolute criterion by means of which we can test the correctness of our convictions regarding our duties, because otherwise morality would be impossible. This he regards, apparently on the basis of a Kantian belief that "ought implies can", as a *reductio ad absurdum*. We *ought* to be moral and thus, Fichte reasons, it must be possible for us to be moral, and therefore it must be possible for us to determine whether our convictions regarding our duties are accurate.

The only criterion Fichte is able to offer for a healthy conscience, however, is the accompaniment of our convictions by a feeling of truth and certainty. This feeling, he insists, can be distinguished from other feelings in virtue of the immediacy of the certitude it brings, as well as the peace and satisfaction it provides.

If we attend carefully to these feelings, Fichte further claims, it will be impossible for conscience ever to err, and impossible for us ever to be mistaken about whether conscience has passed judgement. Consequently, morality is indeed possible, and all any rational agent must do is heed the convictions of his conscience. One implication Fichte draws is that morality can never involve acting upon the authority of others, since to do so is to lack certainty regarding one's own judgements, and so to act unconscientiously.

Although he believes that the conscience of every rational agent serves as a built-in morality detector, Fichte also thinks it must be possible for philosophy to provide an *a priori* derivation of the duties that conscience will confirm. Such a derivation can only begin from the fact that the ultimate purpose of ethical life is the absolute independence and self-sufficiency of rational agents. The ethical agent, therefore, "*wills that reason and reason alone should have dominion in the sensible world.* All physical force ought to be subordinated to reason" (*SE*: 262).

From this general prescription, Fichte derives a number of specific duties. The first is that every self-conscious being should make himself into a tool of the moral law, using all his capacities to further the actualization of rationality. Every such being also has a duty, therefore, to help establish the conditions in which he can be an effective tool. This means cultivating his own body so that it can serve his pursuit of the ends of reason, while resisting the temptation to use it as a means to the enjoyment of merely sensuous pleasures. It also means caring for other individuals who are potential tools of morality, by respecting the property that they need to accomplish their aims, by showing them benevolence when the state fails to provide the livelihood or assistance they need in order to maintain themselves, and by setting a good example. Finally, every rational agent also has the duty, Fichte concludes, to bring the entire sensuous world under control, taking possession of all natural objects as property that can be employed as additional tools in the arsenal of reason.

Fichte refers to a group of rational agents who serve each other in their mutual service of morality as an ethical commonwealth or "church". One feature of such rational churches is that they must not limit the free thinking and communication of their members, since such freedom is necessary to attain the certainty of conviction and clarity of conscience that ethical life requires. The ethical commonwealth will therefore accept no prescribed direction for its thoughts and actions, but will insist upon its right to determine for itself the obligations to which its members are called.

Conclusion

In 1798, the year in which *The System of Ethics* appeared, Fichte also published an essay entitled "On the Basis of Our Belief in a Divine Governance of the World". This essay made explicit, as careful readers of *The System of Ethics* would also realize, that Fichte espoused the subordination of religion to morality. The place of a "church", in his view, was neither to restrict thinking in favour of the assertion of dogma, nor to issue commandments on the basis of revelation rather than reason. The only true church was the ethical commonwealth described in Fichte's moral philosophy, a community of rational agents committed to determining the obligations of reason for themselves, and to performing those obligations freely and for their own sake.

Fichte was quickly accused of atheism, and his attempt to defend himself was made more difficult when Kant denounced *The Science of Knowledge* as having betrayed the critical philosophy. Jacobi added fuel to the fire by describing Fichte's system as a form of "nihilism", and in 1799 Fichte was dismissed from Jena. He retreated to Berlin, where he wrote a number of popular essays, and undertook several substantial revisions of *The Science of Knowledge*, but his stature in German philosophy was never the same again.

Summary of key points

- Fichte adopts Reinhold's foundationalist strategy for making transcendental idealism scientific, systematic and able to withstand sceptical challenges, but rejects "the principle of consciousness" as a starting point for philosophy.
- Fichte begins with the fact of self-awareness, and then attempts to determine all the necessary conditions of its possibility.
- The first condition of self-awareness, according to Fichte, is an active "positing" that brings the self into existence. He argues that this self-positing depends upon the positing of a not-self, or

independent world, in contrast to which the self can experience its own freedom.

- Fichte conceives of freedom as a communal accomplishment that requires rational agents to respect each other and establish appropriate political and economic institutions.
- Fichte regards individuals as morally obliged to use their freedom to subordinate the natural world (including their own bodies) to rational purposes. Individuals can determine their specific obligations, Fichte contends, by consulting their consciences.

five

Schelling: idealism and the absolute

Friedrich Wilhelm Joseph Schelling (1775–1854) was famously prodigious, prolific and protean: he was philosophically active from a very early age, and over an extraordinarily long span, and in the course of his lifetime the nature of his philosophical projects changed repeatedly and dramatically. Consequently, Schelling is among the most forbidding and the most influential of the German Idealists: the volume and variety of his work make him exceedingly difficult to encapsulate or summarize, but at the same time have inspired a remarkable array of subsequent thinkers and movements.

Schelling entered the theological seminary at Tübingen when he was only fifteen. His close friends at the seminary included Hegel and Hölderlin, both of whom would ultimately become more prominent than Schelling, but who were initially overshadowed by the brilliance of their younger companion. Together the three studied Kant, celebrated the French Revolution, and aspired to employ philosophy and poetry to disseminate and deepen the spirit of freedom in Germany.

Schelling began to publish while still in his teens, quickly attracted the attention and admiration of the great Goethe, and in 1798, at the age of twenty-three, was appointed to a professorship of philosophy at Jena. Joining Fichte on the faculty, Schelling was widely presumed to be the incipient and rightful heir to the Kantian tradition, and his ascension was further accelerated when Fichte was suddenly dismissed from the university the following year. While in Jena, Schelling participated in and benefited from an intellectual circle that included a number of the key figures in the birth of Romanticism. The conversations and works generated by this circle played an important role in stimulating and shaping Schelling's own developing views. Schelling remained in Jena only until 1803, but between 1795 and 1805 he published an astonishing number of works that secured his reputation as the pre-eminent German philosopher.

Over the next decade, however, Schelling's professional and personal circumstances changed markedly. Hegel's *Phenomenology of Spirit* appeared in 1807, and its Preface contained a thinly disguised attack on Schelling's philosophy that contributed to a rapid deterioration of the friendship and collaboration between the two men. In 1809 Schelling was devastated by the sudden death of his wife, and although he continued to write for another four decades, he never published again after this pivotal year. Hegel's *Science of Logic* appeared in 1812, and soon thereafter Schelling found himself eclipsed by his former friend, who was offered professorships in Heidelberg and then Berlin in quick succession.

Schelling did enjoy a brief renaissance late in life. In 1841, at the age of sixty-six, he was invited by the King of Prussia to assume Hegel's old chair in Berlin, for the express purpose of combating the progressive political influence that continued to linger ten years after Hegel's death. Schelling's lectures were initially a great sensation, drawing large and enthusiastic crowds, and through these Schelling had a significant impact on Kierkegaard and Marx. The enthusiasm wore off quickly, however, and Schelling died in 1854, leaving as his legacy not a single definitive system, but rather a series of related philosophical endeavours, many elements of which have played an important role in European philosophy ever since.

The serial evolution of Schelling's views was a source of amusement to Hegel, who mocked his one-time colleague for "conducting his philosophical education in public". But a more charitable and accurate judgement is that Schelling was fiercely committed to the truth, and remarkably willing to forsake an opinion, or even an entire philosophical approach, when he concluded it was flawed. As already noted, this makes Schelling particularly challenging to grasp or present. Kant, Fichte and Hegel, difficult as they are, each established a mature philosophical position that remained essentially unchanged after its initial development. To understand Kant is to understand the transcendental idealism that emerged with the *Critique of Pure Reason* and unfolded over the next twenty years. To understand Fichte is to understand the systematic transformation of transcendental idealism presented in *The Science of Knowledge* and its practical extensions. And to understand Hegel is to understand the critique of transcendental philosophy developed in the *Phenomenology of Spirit*, and the subsequent ontolo-gical project encapsulated in his *Encyclopedia of Philosophical Sciences*. But there is no single Schelling to understand, and thus any attempt to grasp or present his work must confront the existence of several distinct, although related, philosophical projects.

Experts divide Schelling's career into periods in a variety of ways, but for introductory purposes it is sufficient to distinguish three main stages of his philosophical development. In his earliest writings, Schelling is a self-avowed disciple of Fichte, believing that philosophy can be completed by means of a successful execution of the task set forth in *The Science of Knowledge*. He aims to produce a transcendental demonstration that the definitive characteristics of our natural and social worlds are in fact necessary conditions of the possibility of self-conscious experience.

Very quickly, however, Schelling reached the conclusion that tran-scendental idealism needed to be not only completed, but also comple-mented by a distinctive endeavour that he called the philosophy of nature. Whereas transcendental philosophy takes subjectivity as given, and attempts to explain certain features of the natural world as neces-sary conditions of its possibility, the philosophy of nature begins with the objective world and attempts to explain why subjectivity must necessarily emerge from it. In this second phase of his development, Schelling believed that philosophy demands the completion of both of these distinctive "sciences", as well as their successful reconciliation with each other. These projects are often referred to collectively as the "philosophy of identity", because in this period Schelling shared Spinoza's conviction that subjectivity and objectivity are not absolutely different, but rather two modes in which a single underlying substance manifests itself. Schelling rejected Spinoza's determinism, however, and therefore strove to demonstrate that monism and human freedom are in fact compatible.

Schelling was never fully satisfied, however, with his own attempts to complete either transcendental philosophy or the philosophy of nature, and he eventually grew sceptical of the possibility and value of these *a priori* projects. In his third and final phase, then, Schelling rejected the goal of articulating the logically necessary features of con-sciousness and nature (which he had shared with Hegel, and which Hegel never abandoned) in favour of a return to empiricism and an emphasis on temporality and existential freedom.

Which of these three phases one chooses to emphasize, and how one interprets them, is likely to depend as much upon how one views Hegel as upon how one views Schelling. Hegelians often consider Schelling to be a mere way station on the road from Fichte to the *Phenomenology of Spirit* and the *Science of Logic*. They agree with Schelling's own assessment that his *a priori* projects failed, but reject his conclusion that these failures indicate the impossibility of *a priori* philosophy. They therefore regard the early and middle Schelling as an important precursor to Hegel, and the late Schelling as posing important challenges that Hegel's system is ultimately able to meet. Critics of Hegel, however, are much more likely to value Schelling's philosophy for its own sake, and to celebrate his final rejection of metaphysics as paving the way for Kierkegaard, Marx, Heidegger and postmodernism.

This chapter will focus on the initial two phases of Schelling's development. The first section will explore Schelling's early works, in which he sets out to complete Fichte's transcendental idealism but quickly becomes persuaded of the need to develop a philosophy of nature. The second section will examine Schelling's middle period, in which he works on the philosophy of nature and attempts to reconcile it with transcendental idealism and its commitment to human freedom. Schelling's late rejection of *a priori* philosophy will be discussed in the conclusion of the book, where it most naturally belongs, since this rejection functions conceptually and historically as the beginning of the end of German Idealism and the transition to the radically different philosophical ambitions that defined European philosophy after 1840.

Early Schelling: from Fichte to Spinoza

Schelling's elaboration and transformation of Fichte's project is presented in two essays published in 1795: "Of the I as the Principle of Philosophy, or, On the Unconditional in Human Knowledge", and "Philosophical Letters on Dogmatism and Criticism". In the first of these essays Schelling is expressly committed to Fichte's project, and makes extensive use of Fichte's terminology, but signs of his imminent shift to the philosophy of identity are already evident. In the second essay Schelling continues to regard himself as a critical philosopher, but now calls directly for an expansion of Kantian and Fichtean criticism to include consideration of the relationship between the absolute substance underlying all things and the emergence of conscious subjectivity. Two years later Schelling would respond to this call with his first publication on the philosophy of nature, and with this open embrace of metaphysics his break with critical philosophy in favour of what would soon become the philosophy of identity became transparent.

"The Unconditional in Human Knowledge" opens by seconding Fichte's two central criticisms of Kant: the *Critique of Pure Reason* is insufficiently scientific, because it presupposes principles that it does not demonstrate; and Kant's critical philosophy as a whole is insufficiently systematic, because no common principle unites its theoretical and practical components. The Preface to this essay also embraces Fichte's goal of remedying these deficiencies by establishing the principles that Kant assumes, and strictly deriving the content of both theoretical and practical philosophy from them. Schelling concurs with Fichte that philosophy must be scientific and systematic, and that systematic science must begin from a single first principle, knowledge of which is immediate and unconditional. All other knowledge must derive from this principle, and will therefore be mediated and conditioned by it.

Schelling quickly deviates from Fichte, however, by conflating the unconditional knowledge of a principle with the unconditional existence of an ontological absolute. In the span of a single sentence, Schelling moves from the Fichtean assumption that philosophy must begin with a principle that is known immediately, unconditionally, or absolutely, to the quite distinct assumption that there must be something that exists unconditionally or absolutely: "as soon as philosophy begins to be a science, it must at least *assume* an ultimate principle and, with it, something unconditional" ("UHK": 72). This shift from the quest for an epistemological absolute to the quest for an ontological absolute is the first sign of Schelling's incipient abandonment of the Kantian critical project in favour of a wholehearted embrace of rationalist metaphysics in the tradition of Spinoza.

Having claimed that philosophy must begin by assuming the existence of something unconditional, Schelling immediately begins to consider the necessary characteristics of this unconditional something. The unconditional, he reasons, can be neither a subject nor an object, since each of these is what it is only in virtue of its distinction from the other: every subject is dependent upon or conditioned by the objects from which it is distinct; and every object is equally conditioned by the subjects that distinguish themselves from it. More generally, Schelling concludes, the unconditional cannot be a thing at all. His argument for this claim initially appears to be linguistic, depending upon the fact that in German a thing is "*ein Ding*" and unconditional is "*unbedingt*", or "un-thingly". Behind these linguistic relations, however, lies the conceptual point that every thing owes its existence and initial character to other things and forces that serve as the cause of its coming into being as the particular thing that it is. To be a thing is thus, by definition, to be conditioned, and so to be ruled out as a candidate for the ontological absolute that Schelling seeks to identify.

If the unconditional cannot be a thing, Schelling concludes, then it must be a thought, and if it cannot be the effect of prior causes, then it must be responsible for its own existence. The unconditional must therefore be a self-causing thought, which Schelling refers to as the "absolute I". Schelling is careful to distinguish the absolute I from empirical subjects, the existence and characteristics of which are conditioned by other subjects and objects. But he claims that we can infer the existence of such an absolute subject from the existence of conditioned subjects and objects, since it serves as the ultimate condition without which they would not be. This inference relies implicitly upon the principle of sufficient reason; Schelling assumes, like the rationalists who preceded him, that there must be an explanation sufficient to account for the existence and characteristics of the contingent things that constitute the world, which only an absolutely necessary being could provide.

Schelling also claims that this ontological absolute must serve as an epistemological absolute, as "that which furnishes validity in the entire system of my knowledge" ("UHK": 76). Consequently, a bidirectional "regress must be possible; that is, I must be able to *ascend* from the lowest conditioned proposition to the unconditioned, just as I can *descend* from the unconditional principle to the lowest proposition in the conditional sequence" (*ibid.*).

Schelling has clearly, even at this earliest point in his career, already abandoned Kant's critical insistence that we must avoid the temptation to treat ideas of reason (including the idea of an ontological absolute) as if they could inform us about the world. Kant had warned that such ideas could be employed legitimately only as regulative hypotheses for our theoretical and practical enquiries, but Schelling is engaged in *a priori* metaphysics of precisely the sort that Kant sought to render obsolete. Having claimed to establish the existence of an ontological absolute, Schelling proceeds to devote a substantial portion of his essay to a specification of the features of the unconditional I. His manner of proceeding, and the conclusions he draws, are both highly reminiscent of Spinoza. Schelling contends that the absolute I must be fully responsible for its own being ("UHK": §7), and therefore purely free (§8). It must be absolutely unified (§9), and must contain all being within itself (§10). It must therefore be infinite (§11) and singular (§12), the only substance and the immanent cause of all that is (§13).

Schelling claims, however, that he is in fact innocent of transcending the limits of reason established by Kant. Because the absolute I is not a thing, it is not the hypostatized subject of rational psychology that Kant attacked in his paralogisms as the chimerical result of a logical fallacy. Moreover, because the absolute I is not a thing, it is not the thing-in-itself that Kant insisted we cannot know. The absolute I, Schelling emphasizes, "is neither a merely formal principle, nor an idea, nor an object, but pure I determined by intellectual intuition as absolute reality" ("UHK": 104).

Schelling is willing to grant that this characterization of the absolute I may not be entirely clear, and admits to wishing that he had "Plato's gift of language, or that of his kindred spirit, Jacobi, in order to be able to differentiate between the absolute, immutable being and every kind of conditional, changeable existence" (*ibid.*: 109). In the very next sentence, however, Schelling declares that the fault lies not with him, but with language itself, for the "absolute in us cannot be captured by a mere word . . . [and] only the self-attained insight into the intellectual in us can come to the rescue of the patchwork of our language" (*ibid.*: 109–10).

Despite the acknowledged difficulty in making his point, Schelling resolutely insists that he remains within the bounds of legitimate philosophical enquiry as defined by Kant. He even claims that the question with which Kant's critical philosophy begins is identical to the central question of his own enterprise: "How are synthetic judgements *a priori* possible? . . . This question in its highest abstraction is none other than: How is it possible for the absolute I to step out of itself and oppose to itself a not-I?" ("UHK": 81). Schelling's equation of these quite different questions is made possible by the conflation of the epistemological and the ontological that underlies this entire essay. Kant asked an epistemological question (how is it possible to *know* anything to be necessarily and universally true that is not an analytic conceptual relation?) to which Schelling gives an ontological transformation (how is it possible for there to *be* differentiated subjects and objects, without which there would be no need for cognitive synthesis?).

"The Unconditional in Human Knowledge" thus sets out from an explicit commitment to completing Fichte's transcendental project, but concludes with an implicit commitment to completing Spinoza's metaphysical project. Schelling writes: "the perfect system of science proceeds from the absolute I, excluding everything that stands in contrast to it" ("UHK": 81). The twofold task of philosophy, as he understands it in this essay, is to explain how anything at all emerges from the absolute, undifferentiated I, and to reconcile the existence of this all-encompassing I with the freedom of the particular empirical subjects to which it gives rise. This task, the reconciliation of Spinozistic pantheism with human freedom, guided Schelling's reflections throughout his early and middle periods, until he eventually abandoned *a priori* metaphysics altogether.

Schelling's second essay of 1795, "Philosophical Letters on Dogmatism and Criticism", is more explicit about breaking with Kant and Fichte. The essay is constructed as a series of "letters", written by an advocate of the "critical" position to an advocate of "dogmatism". Schelling uses the term "dogmatism", as Fichte did, to indicate a commitment to materialism and determinism, in contrast to the Kantian commitment to self-consciousness and freedom. He uses the term "criticism", however, in a way that clearly and deliberately distinguishes his own project and position from those of Kant and Fichte.

In the second letter, Schelling writes that the aim of "criticism" must not be limited to proving the inability of reason to prove "dogmatism", but instead should encompass the positive assertion and defence of human freedom. The aspirations of criticism have been overly narrow, Schelling contends, because critique has been based upon an analysis of our cognitive faculty rather than upon an assessment of our entire being or essence. The third letter makes explicit that the target of this complaint is Kant: because the *Critique of Pure Reason* criticizes only our cognitive faculty, Schelling reasons, it is able to establish only the negative result that we cannot know whether determinism is true. Kant regarded this result as a triumph, because it opened up the possibility of free agency and morality by undermining Hume's assertion of determinism. But Schelling is unsatisfied with merely refuting dogmatism, and is undeterred by Kant's insistence that we cannot positively know that we are free. Schelling calls upon philosophy to establish human freedom by undertaking a more comprehensive investigation of human being, within which the critique of our cognitive capacities functions as merely one part among others, rather than as the foundation of the whole.

Schelling criticizes Kant and Fichte for basing philosophy upon a critique of cognition not only because this basis cannot support the claim of human freedom, but also because he regards the given fact of experience from which such critique proceeds as in need of further explanation. In the sixth letter, Schelling remarks that although the critique of cognition explains why synthetic propositions are necessary conditions of the possibility of experience, it fails to explain why there is experience at all. Kantian critique, that is, explains the epistemological function of synthesis, but fails to give an ontological account of how there come to be differentiated subjects and objects in the first place. Without such differentiation cognitive synthesis would be neither necessary nor possible, and Schelling therefore regards its presence as the ultimate condition of experience that calls out for explanation.

Because he is concerned with the ultimate condition of the possibility of experience, Schelling continues to regard himself as carrying out the Kantian project, despite the fact that in shifting from the epistemological to the ontological he has clearly overstepped the limits of reason proposed by Kant. Echoing a claim that he made in "The Unconditional in Human Knowledge", Schelling reiterates in the third letter that his own question is really the same as Kant's, although it is expressed in different terms. Asking, "How do I ever come to egress from the absolute, and to progress toward an opposite?" Schelling insists, is simply to rephrase Kant's fundamental question: "How did we ever come to judge synthetically?" In the sixth letter, Schelling describes his own formulation of this question as "the riddle of the world, the question of how the absolute could come out of itself and oppose to itself a world?" ("PL": 173–4). He concludes that "the main task of all philosophy consists of solving the problem of the existence of the world" (*ibid.*: 177).

Schelling's basic objection is thus that Kant takes as his starting point the existence of a manifold of experience, without ever asking how this manifold itself has come to be. Schelling believes that a truly systematic philosophy must begin by attempting to explain how a differentiated manifold could emerge from an absolutely self-identical unity. Because Kant neglects to do this, Schelling declares in the fifth letter, his critical philosophy amounts to a successful science of knowledge that falls short of being a complete and adequately grounded philosophical system.

Attempting to answer how differentiation could emerge from unity is equivalent, Schelling suggests, to attempting to answer how finite entities could emerge from infinitude. Almost as soon as he insists that this transition is the most important thing for systematic philosophy to comprehend, however, Schelling suddenly and surprisingly asserts that it cannot in fact be comprehended by any philosophical system. This transition, and the fact of experience that depends upon it, Schelling declares to be theoretically unintelligible, on the ground that reason cannot possibly discover a middle term that would connect the infinite and the finite.

Schelling also holds, however, that it is equally impossible for rational beings to surrender the aspiration to make the connection between their finitude and the infinite from which they have emerged. Schelling concludes that because "a dissolution of the question can no longer be theoretical, it necessarily becomes *practical*" ("PL": 175). Philosophy must "make the absolute, which could not be an object of *knowledge*, an object of *action*, or . . . *demand the action* by which the absolute is realized" (*ibid*.: 190–91). This practical demand on the finite subject to realize the absolute by reuniting itself with the infinite requires, according to Schelling, that "I must leave the realm of experience myself, that is, I must do away, for myself, with the bound of the world of experience; I must cease to be a finite being" (*ibid*.: 175).

In the ninth letter, Schelling recognizes and describes two paths by which finite subjects could renounce their finitude, reunite with the infinite, and thereby realize the absolute. Either the finite subject could dissolve itself in objectivity, which would thereby become absolute; or the finite subject could seek to become absolute, by dissolving all finite objects within itself. The former path is that of "dogmatism", which holds that all reality is ultimately reducible to the material, and the latter is that of "criticism", which regards subjectivity and freedom as absolutes that cannot be reduced to anything else.

Dogmatism demands, according to Schelling, that the finite subject strive to annihilate its own free causality and become a purely passive vehicle for the emanations of the absolute. Schelling regards this as a possible path, but one that amounts to the subject's own moral extinction. Criticism, by contrast, demands that the subject strive to make all finite objects into means to the accomplishment of its own ends, and thus into extensions of itself. By making objectivity into an extension of subjectivity, criticism no less than dogmatism annihilates the finite subject, which depends for its existence upon a contrast with a world of objects. But this particular form of annihilation, because it is accomplished by an absolutely active subject, rather than an absolutely passive one, is not equivalent to moral extinction. Indeed, criticism issues the moral demand that we finite subjects come to "*know* that there is an objective power which threatens our freedom with annihilation, and, with this firm and certain conviction in our heart, to fight *against* it exerting our whole freedom, and thus to go down" ("PL": 192). Schelling concludes: "In criticism, my vocation is to strive for immutable selfhood, unconditional freedom, unconditional activity. Be! is the supreme demand of criticism" (*ibid.*).

With this identification of the "supreme demand" of critical philosophy, Schelling's early period reached its culmination. Having set out to contribute to Fichte's attempt to complete Kant's transcendental idealism, Schelling quickly concluded that a truly systematic philosophy also requires the development of an entirely new and complementary science. Transcendental idealism takes the fact of subjective experience as given, and enquires into the necessary conditions of its possibility. Schelling regarded this critique of cognition as philosophically indispensable, but concluded that it leaves unanswered the even more fundamental question of how subjective experience arises at all. How is it, Schelling asked, that finite subjects and finite objects emerge from an infinite absolute and come to stand in relation to each other? This ontological question, which transcendental idealism does not address (because, Kant would emphasize, it lies beyond the limits of rational enquiry), Schelling declared to be theoretically unanswerable yet nonetheless unavoidable. Reason cannot comprehend, he believed, the self-differentiation of the infinite into a manifold of finite beings, but at the same time finite subjects cannot help feeling, and desiring to overcome, their alienation from the absolute. One possible response to this condition is the adoption of a Stoic or mystical passivity that strives to eliminate all desires and intentions, and thereby to renounce selfhood. At this point in his career, however, Schelling advocated a practical declaration of freedom that commits finite subjects to making the objective world a means to the accomplishment of their aims, and thereby to bringing about a reconciliation with it.

Middle Schelling: the philosophy of identity

Schelling's middle period began with, and is largely defined by, a commitment to develop the philosophy of nature as the necessary complement to transcendental idealism. Whereas transcendental idealism begins with subjective experience, and infers that certain features of objectivity are necessary conditions of its possibility, the philosophy of nature begins with the objective, natural world, and attempts to determine why it must have certain features, and especially why it must give rise to self-conscious subjects. Each of these complementary philosophical sciences thus takes as given one of the two modes in which the absolute manifests itself, and attempts to use this given as an explanatory ground for the other mode of manifestation: transcendental idealism explains objectivity in terms of subjectivity, and the philosophy of nature explains subjectivity in terms of objectivity. Taken together, the two sciences comprise a single, larger endeavour known as the philosophy of identity, because Schelling regards subjectivity and objectivity as distinct manifestations of the same underlying absolute. The third and final aspect of the philosophy of identity is a reconciliation of its two constitutive parts: the explanations offered by transcendental idealism and the philosophy of nature must be compatible with each other, and in particular the assertion of human freedom must somehow be compatible with the assertion of natural necessity. The challenge of reconciling freedom and necessity proved to be the greatest obstacle to Schelling's philosophy of identity, and his dissatisfaction with his own attempted solutions was a primary factor in his ultimate abandonment of *a priori* systematic philosophy.

Philosophy of nature

Only two years after the appearance of "The Unconditional in Human Knowledge" and "Letters on Dogmatism and Criticism", Schelling published the first of a series of works on the philosophy of nature that quickly won him fame and prestige. *Ideas for a Philosophy of Nature* appeared in 1797, and was followed in 1798 by *On the World Soul*, which earned Goethe's admiration and support for Schelling's appointment to a professorship at Jena. In preparation for, and as a companion to, his first lectures at Jena, Schelling published the *First Outline of a System of the Philosophy of Nature* in 1799. In 1803 Schelling published a second edition of *Ideas for a Philosophy of Nature*, adding substantial supplements to the introduction and each of the chapters, which served largely to efface the residual Fichtean language in which Schelling had originally expressed himself.

Schelling reports that the *Ideas* and the *Outline* represent the two different ways in which the philosophy of nature may be approached. The *Ideas* proceeds from particular phenomena toward general principles, whereas the *Outline* works from *a priori* principles toward particular phenomena. The latter mode of presentation is more strictly scientific, but Schelling regards the two modes as compatible with each other, since he holds that *a priori* knowledge is simply experiential knowledge that has been recognized to be necessarily true. The *Ideas* takes particular experiences as its starting point, and from them derives principles that must hold true of the natural world. The *Outline*, conversely, begins with first principles of nature, and from them derives phenomena that must emerge and be available to experience.

The introduction to the *Outline* defines the philosophy of nature by distinguishing it from transcendental philosophy, on the one hand, and empirical science, on the other. Philosophy, according to the introduction, is a single science that assumes, and seeks to explain, the identity of the real and the ideal, the objective and the subjective. An adequate account of this identity must incorporate two equally necessary orientations, one of which explains the real in terms of the ideal, and one of which explains the ideal in terms of the real. Scientific philosophy must therefore incorporate two equally necessary sub-sciences: transcendental philosophy explains the characteristics of objectivity as necessary conditions of the possibility of subjective experience; and the philosophy of nature explains the characteristics of subjective experience as necessary manifestations of the objective world. Transcendental philosophy is thus idealistic, but the philosophy of nature is realistic because it regards the natural world as self-subsistent, and not merely as a condition of the possibility of experience. Schelling therefore regards his philosophy of nature as "speculative physics", an *a priori* account of the essential features of the natural world itself.

In the introduction to the second edition of the *Ideas*, Schelling criticizes Fichte for mistakenly believing that *The Science of Knowledge*, which provides only a transcendental philosophy, has completed philosophy itself. Schelling refers to Fichte's philosophy as a "relative idealism" (*IPN*: 51), which makes claims that have validity only in relation to the conscious subject. Schelling acknowledges that in the first edition of the *Ideas* he made this very same mistake, but in the second edition he now insists that the philosophy of nature must and can provide absolute knowledge of objectivity itself. He explains the concept of absolute knowledge by means of an analogy to mathematics, in which "what is valid of [the] construction as form is also eternally and necessarily valid of the object" (*ibid*.: 45). The mathematician, that is, determines not merely how we must think of triangles, but how triangles themselves must be. Schelling thus takes mathematics to be a paradigm case of the identity of subjective thinking and objective being, of the ideal and the real, and it is this same identity that he aims to achieve in his philosophy of nature.

Schelling anticipates, and quickly dispatches, the critical objection that our knowledge of objects is necessarily limited to how they appear to us:

> If anybody wishes to remind the philosopher ... that the absolute-ideal is once again only *for him* and only *his thinking* ... then we bid such a one, for his part, just to heed the quite simple consideration that indeed this very reflection, by which he makes this thinking *his* thinking, and consequently subjective, is again only *his* reflection, and thus a merely subjective affair, so that here one subjectivity is corrected and removed by another. (*Ibid.*: 45–6)

The critical idealist, in other words, is limited, by his own position, to claiming that it *appears to us* that we can only know things as they appear. But, Schelling retorts, this means that the critical idealist cannot definitively demonstrate that we do not in fact know things as they actually are. Schelling does not claim that such knowledge has already been produced, but does insist that if there is to be a truly scientific philosophy, then it must know its objects not "in a conditioned but only in an unconditioned and absolute way, and thus also know only the absolute of these objects themselves" (*ibid.*: 44). By declaring his aspiration to know nature absolutely, Schelling sharply distinguishes his own philosophy of nature from the transcendental treatments that nature received in Kant and Fichte.

The philosophy of nature, or speculative physics, must also be carefully distinguished from empirical physics, according to Schelling. In the introduction to the *Outline*, Schelling distinguishes speculative physics from empirical physics in virtue of the central problems it raises, the methodology it employs to solve them, and the resulting conception of nature that emerges.

The first problem of speculative physics, Schelling reports, is to determine the absolute cause of motion (*OSPN*: 195). This problem does not, he argues, allow of a mechanical solution. A particular motion (that of a billiard ball, for example) might be explained in terms of a preceding mechanism (that of a second billiard ball striking the first), but this account generates the need to explain the initial motion itself. Another mechanical explanation might be offered (the second ball was struck by yet a third ball), but this generates the need for yet another explanation (what caused the third ball to move?). The problem recurs *ad infinitum*, for no matter how far back a mechanical explanation is traced, there always stands at its head an initial motive force that remains unexplained. It follows that mechanistic physics can never provide a sufficient account of the absolute cause of motion, and Schelling therefore concludes that speculative physics cannot be mechanistic.

Speculative physics cannot assume, in other words, that the natural world is composed of inert particles that depend for their motion upon the impact and influence of other particles and forces. Instead, speculative physics must be dynamic physics: it must assume that nature itself is composed, at the most fundamental level, of motive forces, and that all mechanical interactions between particular things are derivative of these more primary sources of motion. Whereas empirical, atomistic physics is interested in the mechanical motion of elementary particles, Schelling's speculative physics is concerned solely with the constitutive forces upon which all motion ultimately depends.

Schelling reformulates this point by characterizing the object of mechanistic physics as "being", in distinction from the object of dynamic physics, which is "becoming" (*OSPN*: 201). Empirical, mechanistic physics observes particular things, or beings, and on the basis of these observations develops generalized descriptions and predictions of the properties and behaviour of entities of the same type. Dynamic physics, by contrast, is solely concerned with nature as a whole, and has no interest in the particular things that have come to be. Nature as a whole is the productive totality that constantly gives rise to and destroys the particular products or objects that are the concern of empirical physics. Dynamic physics is the science of this infinite and continuous process of production, whereas mechanistic or atomistic physics is the science of the finite and discrete products that the process creates.

In the second edition of the *Ideas*, Schelling refers to the productive process that creates and destroys natural beings as the self-differentiation of the absolute. He writes that "the birth of things" takes place "through the eternal self-division of the absolute into subject and object, whereby its subjectivity, and the unknowable infinitude hidden therein, is made known in objectivity and finitude, and turned into something" (*IPN*: 150). Another way of putting this is that "the individualized thing is only one moment of the eternal act of transformation of the essence into the form; for this reason the form is distinguished as particular, for example as the embodiment of the infinite into the finite; but that which becomes objective through this form is still only the absolute unity itself " (*ibid.*: 48). In these terms, the first problem of the philosophy of nature is that of showing why it is that the originally unified and infinite absolute must differentiate itself into finite subjects and objects at all. Schelling concludes the *Ideas* by declaring, "the final goal of all consideration and science of nature can only be knowledge of the absolute unity which embraces the whole . . . that which combines the infinite possibility of all things with the reality of the particular, and hence is the eternal urge and primal ground of all creation" (*ibid.*: 272–3).

Schelling grants that we cannot perceive the productive forces that are the fundamental and simple elements of a dynamic physics of the absolute, but rather must infer their existence and influence from our perceptions of the objects that they create, influence, and ultimately destroy. Dynamic physics thus relies upon ordinary observation and empirical physics to provide the evidence of the forces that are its concern. Once the existence of these fundamental forces is assumed, however, it then becomes mysterious how the existence of observable, static objects that persist over time is possible at all. Given that the whole of nature is constantly in motion, constantly becoming something other than it currently is, it appears difficult to explain how a particular being could assume a relatively permanent form. If the first problem of the philosophy of nature is to explain why the absolute must set itself in motion, the second problem is to explain how it could ever come to rest.

Schelling responds to this challenge by suggesting that particular beings subsist only in virtue of being continually re-produced by the fundamental forces of nature. He introduces the phenomenon of the whirlpool as a paradigm for all objects: the whirlpool persists over time only in virtue of the fact that a continual stream of water sustains its form. Were the flow of water to cease, the whirlpool would quickly disintegrate. Schelling sees this as a model for understanding the persistence of objects, which he attributes to the constant action of the invisible forces that sustain their visible forms. Dynamic physics is concerned with determining the essential characteristics that these fundamental forces of nature must have in order to explain the emergence and persistence of the world of objects and conscious subjects with which we are familiar.

Schelling distinguishes speculative physics from empirical physics not only in virtue of its dynamic conception of nature, and its concern with fundamental productive forces rather than the particular objects that they produce, but also in virtue of its *a priori* methodology. Schelling remarks in the *Outline* that "physics, as empiricism, is nothing but a collection of facts, of accounts of what has been observed, what has happened under natural or artificial circumstances", from which he concludes that "what is pure empiricism is not science, and conversely, what is science is not empiricism" (*OSPN*: 201). To contemporary ears this sounds patently false, since "science" and "empiricism" have become nearly synonymous. But Schelling's claim makes sense in light of the fact that he uses "science", like Fichte before him, to indicate a discipline based upon unconditional principles, which cannot be derived from empirical observation, since such observation can yield only inductive generalizations. Speculative physics aims to be scientific in this sense, and thus aims to produce an *a priori* derivation of the principles that provide the ultimate ground of observable phenomena. In the introduction to the second edition of the *Ideas*, Schelling again presents mathematics as the model for his science: "In the philosophy of nature, explanations take place as little as they do in mathematics; it proceeds from principles certain in themselves, without any direction prescribed to it, as it were, by the phenomena" (*IPN*: 53).

Schelling acknowledges the concern that such an *a priori* science of the natural world, however desirable, might not be possible. He recognizes the worry that *a priori* principles could prove to be mere presuppositions or hypotheses foisted upon nature, which would therefore distort rather than enhance our understanding. Schelling responds by offering a twofold test: first, genuine *a priori* principles of nature must be experienced as absolutely necessary, in the sense that our minds are involuntarily compelled to adopt them; and, second, it must be possible to recognize all natural phenomena as absolutely necessitated by these principles. This second criterion implies that the principles of speculative physics must be rejected or revised not only if an exception to them can be identified, but also if there are empirical phenomena that cannot be explained as necessary consequences of them. Speculative physics must therefore remain open and responsive to developments in empirical physics, since such developments will call for demonstrations showing that the newly observed phenomena follow necessarily from the fundamental principles of dynamics.

The first of these tests is yet another indication of Schelling's abandonment of the critical perspective on the limitations of knowledge. Kant and Fichte, like Schelling, seek to identify necessary principles of thinking, but unlike Schelling they scrupulously refuse to assume that these principles governing all of our experience of nature can inform us about the natural world itself. Even if the validity of the test is granted, however, the prospects of passing it might seem rather bleak. The test requires us to be able to distinguish sharply and accurately between those principles that we are absolutely compelled to adopt, and those that we adopt voluntarily. Fichte also drew this distinction, but he admitted quite candidly that our judgements regarding the status of particular principles must always be provisional, because there is no criterion other than experimental trial-and-error to enable us to sort those that are necessary from those that are voluntary.

Schelling, however, has no qualms about either our ability to draw this distinction or the validity of the test itself. In the introduction to the *Ideas*, he insists, "you can very easily distinguish what is arbitrary and what is necessary in the conjunction of your concepts" (*IPN*: 32). And he immediately pronounces this to be equivalent to being able to distinguish what is merely a feature of our thinking and what is a feature of the natural world:

> Whenever you conjoin things which are separated in space in a *single* aggregate, you act quite freely; the unity which you bestow on them you transfer to them simply from your thoughts; there is no reason residing in the *things themselves* which required you to think of them as one. But when . . . you must seek the reason for that [unity] in the *thing outside you*: you feel yourself constrained in your judgment; you must therefore confess that the unity with which you think it is not merely *logical* (in your thoughts), but *real* (actually outside you). (*Ibid.*: 32)

Schelling thus claims that we are able to determine *a priori*, constitutive principles of nature by attending to the judgements that we necessarily make. But he also claims that necessary judgements can be recognized as such only in distinction from arbitrary judgements, and so he holds that nature must have features that cannot be determined *a priori*. This conclusion places an important restriction on Schelling's second test for a successful and complete philosophy of nature, because it means that such a science need not demonstrate the necessity of *all* of the features of every natural phenomenon. Instead, speculative physics is charged with demonstrating the necessity of the essential features of nature, and the innumerable contingent properties of natural phenomena are left to empirical observation and experimentation. Although the aim of speculative physics remains ambitious, Schelling's distinction between the necessary and contingent features of nature saves the enterprise from seeming immediately preposterous.

In the two Books that comprise the *Ideas*, Schelling introduces the dynamic conception of matter, and discusses many of the mechanical and chemical processes that create, destroy and affect material objects, including combustion, electricity, and magnetism. Schelling also promised, but never delivered, a third Book, which was to have given an account of organic nature. This topic therefore became the central focus of the *Outline*, which appeared two years later.

The *Outline* comprises three divisions, the first devoted to organic nature, the second to inorganic nature, and the third to the relationship between the two. The particular aim of the first division is to prove "that nature is *organic* in its most original products" (*OSPN*: 5). In adopting this aim, Schelling intends to mount a direct assault on mechanistic conceptions of nature, which claim that the distinction commonly drawn between organic and inorganic entities cannot be sustained, because all the things that we regard as organisms are in fact merely complicated machines. At the same time, Schelling also intends an assault on Kant's view, which contends that the concept of organism may be legitimately employed in our judgements of nature, but concedes to the mechanist that we cannot in fact know whether any of the things we judge to be organisms are in fact truly organic rather than mechanical. Schelling aims to establish not only that nature contains organisms – beings that cannot be reduced to complicated mechanisms – but also that organisms are the most fundamental natural entities, and thus that all mechanistic processes are ultimately reducible to the organic.

Schelling's argument for these claims begins with the contention that nature itself is an organic whole, a self-moving totality that cannot be reduced to, or explained in terms of, the interactions of its parts. Schelling then seems to infer, without ever stating so explicitly, that the most fundamental products of this constructive activity must be analogous to the natural totality that is their source. Because this totality is organic, Schelling reasons, the most basic natural entities must be organisms.

Schelling himself ultimately acknowledged that his philosophy of nature failed to fulfil the extraordinary aims he set for it. His *a priori* construction of natural principles never yielded a compelling account of the necessary emergence of self-conscious beings, much less one of all of the essential characteristics of the natural world. Moreover, many of the specific principles that Schelling did construct, and use to account for particular phenomena, are no longer compatible with, or credible in light of, contemporary science.

Nonetheless, Schelling provides an important corrective to Fichte's conception of nature as a purely passive collection of material objects that we have a moral obligation to subordinate to our own aims. By conceiving of nature holistically, and placing an emphasis on dynamic processes, Schelling prefigures ecological understandings of the world. And by stressing that rational beings like ourselves emerge from nature, and that natural processes themselves exhibit rational structure, Schelling offers a basis for rethinking the relationship of human beings to the world we inhabit.

Transcendental idealism

After devoting three years and as many books to the philosophy of nature, Schelling turned his attention to the other branch of philosophical science, and in 1800 published his *System of Transcendental Idealism*. The *System* is Schelling's most comprehensive and polished work, important for its own sake, for the influence it had on Hegel's early development, and for the way it anticipates Schelling's later rejection of systematic philosophy.

Schelling declares in the Foreword that "the purpose of the present work is simply this, to enlarge transcendental idealism into what it really should be, namely a system of all knowledge" (*STI*: 1). Schelling aims, in other words, to complete and perfect Fichte's project: in a single volume the *System* canvasses not only the theoretical and practical topics that Fichte addressed in *The Science of Knowledge*, *Foundations of Natural Right* and *The System of Ethics*, but also develops and integrates a philosophy of history and a philosophy of art.

Although he thinks the scope of Fichte's project was overly restricted, Schelling admires and seconds his predecessor's insistence that transcendental idealism must be strictly systematic. Schelling's transcendental idealism thus begins, as Fichte's did, with the incorrigible fact of self-consciousness, the self-awareness of the "I", and attempts to develop everything that follows from this foundational principle alone. Whereas Fichte's system develops, however, by means of a successive identification of the necessary conditions of the possibility of selfhood, Schelling's system is driven by his introduction of the novel conception of a "progressive history of self-consciousness":

> The means, furthermore, whereby the author has sought to achieve his aim of setting forth idealism in its fullest extent,

consist in presenting every part of philosophy in a single continuum, and the whole of philosophy as what in fact it is, namely a progressive history of self-consciousness, for which what is laid down in experience serves merely, so to speak, as a memorial and document. In order to trace this history with precision and completeness, it was chiefly a matter, not only of separating exactly the individual stages thereof, and within these again the individual moments, but also of presenting them in a sequence, whereby one can be certain, thanks to the very method employed in its discovery, that no necessary intervening step has been omitted. (*STI*: 2)

Schelling's idea, which is explored in greater detail below, is that there are different levels or "epochs" of self-consciousness, through which conscious subjects must pass in order to become fully or adequately self-aware. The *System* attempts not only to identify each of these epochs of self-consciousness, but also to show how each successive stage in the philosophical reconstruction of the history of consciousness follows necessarily from, by representing an advance upon, the preceding stage.

Part One of the *System* offers a deduction of the "I" as the first principle of transcendental philosophy. Schelling follows Fichte in assuming that knowledge must rest on an unconditional principle, and that only the activity of thinking is unconditionally known, since we are immediately acquainted with this activity through intellectual intuition. The first principle of transcendental philosophy must therefore be self-consciousness, expressed in the proposition, "I am". Part Two of the *System* then explains that the truth of transcendental idealism – of the thesis that the objective world must conform to the conditions that make experience of it possible – will be demonstrated "in the very process of actually deducing the entire system of knowledge from the principle in question" (*STI*: 34).

Transcendental philosophy therefore proceeds, according to Schelling, on the basis of nothing but the existence of self-consciousness, to overcome its initial scepticism regarding objectivity and demonstratively vindicate our most important ordinary convictions about the world and our relationship to it. First, it proves "that there not only exists a world of things outside and independent of us, but also that our representations are so far coincident with it that there is *nothing else* in things save what we attribute to them" (*STI*: 10). Second, it proves "that representations, arising *freely and without necessity* in us, pass over from the world of thought into the real world, and can attain objective reality" (*ibid*.: 11). Transcendental idealism must then confront, however, the apparent contradiction between these two convictions: "The first assumes that objects are *unalterably determined*, and thereby also our own representations; the second assumes that objects are *alterable*, and are so, in fact, through the causality of representations in us" (*ibid*.). The third and highest task of transcendental philosophy is thus to overcome the contradiction, and reconcile the two convictions, by explaining how "*we can think both of representations as conforming to objects, and objects as conforming to representations*" (*ibid*.). This bidirectional conformity "is unintelligible", Schelling continues, "unless between the two worlds, the ideal and the real, there exists a *pre-determined harmony*. But this latter is itself unthinkable unless the activity, whereby the objective world is produced, is at bottom identical with that which expresses itself in volition, and *vice versa*" (*ibid*.: 11–12).

Transcendental philosophy thus has three primary tasks, which Schelling tackles, respectively, in Parts Three, Four and Five of the *System*. Part Three provides a theoretical philosophy, intended to account for the experience of an independent and objective world, in the course of which Schelling introduces the concept of "epochs" of consciousness. Part Four provides a practical philosophy, intended to account for the experience of freely willed action, in the course of which Schelling develops his concept of history. And Part Five is intended to reconcile theoretical and practical philosophy, by ascribing a pre-established harmony between the mechanisms that determine the course of the objective world and the actions freely undertaken by conscious subjects. It is in this final Part of the *System* that Schelling develops his concept of art as the making visible of this harmony between, or identity of, subjectivity and objectivity.

Theoretical philosophy begins with the given fact of conscious experience, and attempts to determine the necessary conditions of its possibility. Schelling, like Fichte before him, regards empirical consciousness as the result of an absolutely spontaneous "activity, which, since it is the condition of all limitation and consciousness, does not itself come to consciousness" (*STI*: 47). Because this act cannot be an object of consciousness, there is no direct evidence of its occurrence, so the philosophical claim that it must have taken place rests upon the inference that only through such an act can the undeniable fact of experience be explained.

Once the necessity of such a free act of self-creation has been inferred, the immediate task faced by the transcendental philosopher is to explain how the empirical self could find itself limited by the objective world from which it is distinguished. It *must* find itself so limited, since experience is defined by the distinction between the subject and its object, but the question Schelling poses is *how* an infinitely spontaneous self could be limited at all. He reasons that it could not be limited by something other than itself, for then it would not be infinitely spontaneous, so it must be limited by itself. Experience is thus constituted by a primary act of self-limitation, which literally brings the distinction between self and world into existence.

If the very existence of the world is due to the self, then so are its essential features, and the rest of Schelling's theoretical philosophy consists of an attempt to determine how these features result from the acts of the self that are necessary to the constitution of its own experience. The task of philosophy, according to Schelling, is to freely reconstruct these necessary acts. Were this task ever to be completed, Schelling claims, "the whole structure of the objective world, and every determination of nature down to the infinitely small, would have to be revealed to us" (*STI*: 50). Because, however, "the one absolute act we start from contains – united and condensed – an infinity of actions whose total enumeration forms the content of an infinite task ... philosophy can enumerate only those actions which constitute epochs, as it were, in the history of self-consciousness" (*ibid.*).

The "epochs" of consciousness, which it is the task of philosophy to identify and reconstruct, are the essential stages in a journey from the simple awareness of oneself in distinction from the world, to the ultimate destination of full-fledged self-comprehension. "Transcendental philosophy", Schelling writes, "is nothing else but a constant raising of the self to a higher power; its whole method consists in leading the self from one level of self-intuition to another, until it is posited with all the determinations that are contained in the free and conscious act of self-consciousness" (*STI*: 90).

The first and lowest form of self-consciousness Schelling refers to as "sensation", which involves the subject distinguishing itself from the objective world that it senses. The subject is here aware only of the fact that it is a limited being, confronted by a realm of otherness. In this epoch, the self senses the world, which immediately provides it with the awareness of its own limitation, but the self is not yet aware of sensation as its own activity. The second level of self-consciousness thus involves the development of what Schelling refers to as a second-order intuition: "This intuition is an intuiting of intuition, for it is an intuiting of sensation [and] sensing is already itself an intuiting, but an intuiting of the *first order*" (*STI*: 72). Schelling refers to this second-order intuition as "productive intuition", which is therefore the starting point for the second level or epoch of self-consciousness.

The derivation of all of the successive epochs in Schelling's history of self-consciousness proceeds in precisely the same way. The beginning of each epoch is defined by a particular activity, in which the self is engaged without explicit awareness. The transition to the next epoch of self-consciousness takes place when the self engages in a new, higher-order activity that makes it explicitly aware of its prior, lower-order activity. The task of the transcendental philosopher is to explain how each successive higher-order activity is necessary to the subject becoming aware of the activity in which it is already engaged, and thereby progressing towards fully adequate self-consciousness.

Schelling's theoretical philosophy identifies three epochs of self-consciousness: productive intuition makes the self aware of sensation; reflection makes the self aware of productive intuition; and willing makes the self aware of reflection. With the introduction of willing, theoretical philosophy gives way to practical philosophy, but for Schelling this nominal transition does not disrupt the single, comprehensive system of transcendental idealism. Part Four of the *System* continues where Part Three left off, and proceeds to explicate the stages of the subject's increasingly adequate awareness of its own free activity. And Part Five concludes the *System* by identifying art as the activity that completes self-consciousness by making the subject aware of the pre-established harmony that exists between its own free activities and the mechanistic transformations of the objective world. In a concluding "General Observation on the Whole System", Schelling emphasizes this continuity between the parts of his enterprise: "The whole sequence of transcendental philosophy is based merely upon a continual raising of self-intuition to increasingly higher powers, from the first and simplest exercise of self-consciousness, to the highest, namely the aesthetic" (*STI*: 233).

The first stages of Schelling's practical philosophy largely mirror the opening moves in Fichte's *Foundations of Natural Right*, arguing that self-awareness depends upon free activity, and that free activity depends upon the catalysing summons of another free being. Schelling's subsequent accounts of politics and morality are not nearly as rich as those of Fichte, but the *System* extends the scope of practical philosophy by developing an account of history, which Schelling understands as the process by which the institutions constitutive of freedom are brought into being. Schelling contends that this process must be conceived as being both necessitated, in virtue of being essential to the full actualization of self-consciousness subjectivity, and brought about by freely chosen human actions. He therefore understands history as "a necessity which choice itself is compelled to serve" (*STI*: 199), a description that he goes on to characterize as "a mere transcendental expression of the generally accepted and assumed relationship between freedom and a hidden necessity, at times called fate and at times providence" (*ibid*.: 204).

Schelling's conclusion that we must regard history as aiming at the realization of freedom echoes the position developed by Kant in the *Critique of the Power of Judgment*. But Schelling's innovation (which Kant would consider a violation of the limits of reason) is to attribute the providential harmony between subjectivity and objectivity to the absolute identity that is the underlying source of them both: "Such a pre-established harmony of the objective (or law-governed) and the determinant (or free) is conceivable only through some higher thing, set *over* them both . . . This higher thing itself can be neither subject nor object, nor both at once, but only the *absolute identity*" (*STI*: 208–9). Schelling goes on to claim that this absolute identity cannot have any predicates, or be an object of knowledge, since it precedes the subject–object distinction that is the ground of all predication and knowing. Nonetheless, because this identity underlies all objective and subjective change, Schelling concludes that "history as a whole is a progressive, gradually self-disclosing revelation of the absolute" (*ibid*.: 211).

The final problem transcendental philosophy must solve is to explain how conscious subjects complete their self-awareness by coming to realize that their own actions are in fact providentially coincident with the law-governed historical actualization of freedom. "This coincidence of conscious and unconscious activity", Schelling contends, "can evidence itself only in a product that is purposive, without being purposively brought about" (*ibid*.: 214). Such a product could either be something known to be the result of natural laws, but which nonetheless appears to be a purposive whole, or something known to be the result of purposive activity, but which nonetheless appears to present unconscious insights.

Following Kant, Schelling regards organisms as instances of the first type. But Schelling joins his Romantic friends, and anticipates Heidegger, in breaking new ground by regarding artworks as evidence of the second sort. The artistic genius, according to Schelling, "is conscious in respect of production, unconscious in regard to the product" (*STI*: 219). The product or content of true art must be unconscious because it is the absolute identity itself, which precedes and is not available to consciousness, since the latter is defined by the distinction between subjectivity and objectivity. Consequently, "the work of art . . . reflects to me what is otherwise not reflected by anything, namely [the] absolutely identical" (*ibid.*: 230). Art is therefore the pinnacle of human activity, since it accomplishes the ultimate stage in the elevation of self-consciousness by "speak[ing] to us of what philosophy cannot depict in external form, namely the unconscious element in acting and producing, and its original identity with the conscious" (*ibid.*: 231).

Schelling's account of art returns transcendental philosophy to the point from which it set out – the intellectual intuition of the unity of subjectivity and objectivity – and thereby brings his *System* to a close by completing the progressive history of self-consciousness. Schelling seconds Fichte's view that "a system is completed when it is led back to its starting point", and declares:

> This is precisely the case with our own. The ultimate ground of all harmony between subjective and objective could be exhibited in its original identity only through intellectual intuition; and it is precisely this ground which, by means of the work of art, has been brought forth entirely from the subjective, and rendered wholly objective, in such wise, that we have gradually led our object, the self itself, up to the very point where we ourselves were standing when we began to philosophize. (*STI*: 232)

Human freedom and absolute necessity

From his earliest works, Schelling aspired to reconcile the Spinozistic view that the necessary manifestations of an absolute substance determine the course of the world with the Kantian and Fichtean commitment to the freedom of the conscious subject. The *System of Transcendental Idealism* concludes by declaring that this challenge has been met, but Schelling quickly grew dissatisfied with the resolution provided in this work. He therefore returned to the issue yet again, and made it the central focus of what would prove to be his last significant publication, the *Philosophical Inquiries into the Nature of Human Freedom*, which appeared in 1809, when Schelling was still only thirty-four years old.

The Foreword to the *Inquiries* reiterates that "the innermost centre of philosophy comes to view" only in "the contrast between necessity and freedom" (*INHF*: 3). The *Inquiries* itself, which forms a single unbroken essay, then begins by rejecting the common assumption (prominently espoused by Jacobi, although he is not mentioned here by name) that the very enterprise of systematic philosophy necessarily results in determinism and a denial of freedom. Schelling continues to aspire to develop a systematic philosophy within which the belief in human freedom can be justified and preserved.

Schelling grants in the *Inquiries*, however, that the strategy adopted in his *System of Transcendental Idealism* cannot fulfil this aspiration. Schelling's earlier transcendental idealism functioned as a complement to his philosophy of nature, and although the former presupposed free subjectivity as its starting point, the latter never succeeded in demonstrating the emergence of freedom in the objective world. In the *Inquiries*, Schelling writes that "it would by no means suffice to declare [as transcendental idealism does] that 'Activity, life, and freedom are alone true reality' . . . Rather it is required that the reverse be proved too – that all reality (nature, the world of things) is based upon activity, life and freedom" (*INHF*: 24).

Schelling has not yet abandoned hope that *a priori* philosophy can provide such a demonstration, but the *Inquiries* acknowledges from the outset that the existence of human freedom does seem incompatible with the existence of an omnipotent and benevolent God. Human freedom implies the real possibility of evil, which an omnipotent and benevolent God would never allow. So there appear to be only two options: "either real evil is admitted, in which case it is unavoidable to include evil itself in the infinite substance or in the primal will, and thus totally disrupt the conception of an all-perfect being; or the reality of evil must in some way or other be denied, in which case the real conception of freedom disappears at the same time" (*INHF*: 26). Schelling thus links the problem of human freedom, in classic fashion, to the need for a theodicy, a justification of the presence of evil in a world fashioned by an omnipotent and benevolent God.

Having posed the problem of theodicy, Schelling rejects both the solution favoured by Spinoza, and the solution toward which his own *System of Transcendental Idealism* points. Spinoza responded to the problem of theodicy by choosing the second option presented above: he denied the reality of human freedom, and of real evil, contending that everything that occurs follows necessarily from the nature of the substance underlying all particular things, and that the occurrences that seem evil from our perspective cannot be judged to be evil from the perspective of the whole, to the perfection of which they must contribute. Schelling's own *System*, he now concludes, also implicitly denies the existence of freedom, by postulating a pre-established harmony between natural law and human action, which ultimately means that the purported freedom is reduced to "nothing but a force of nature, a mainspring which like all others is subordinate to mechanism" (*INHF*: 14).

The approach to theodicy that Schelling takes in the *Inquiries* proceeds from the distinction, introduced in his writings on the philosophy of nature, between being as a whole and the particular beings that it continually creates and destroys. Here he reformulates the distinction as that between "being insofar as it exists, and being insofar as it is the mere basis of existence" (*ibid*.: 31). The value of this distinction for theodicy is that it enables our existence to be dependent upon God ("being insofar as it is the mere basis of existence"), while allowing for the possibility that our essence is not determined by this dependence. Schelling argues: "Dependence does not exclude autonomy or even freedom. Dependence does not determine the nature of the dependent, and merely declares that the dependent entity, whatever else it may be, can only be as a consequence of that upon which it is dependent; it does not declare what this dependent entity is or not" (*ibid*.: 18). Indeed, Schelling continues, it would "be contradictory if that which is dependent or consequent were not autonomous. There would be dependence without something being dependent . . . that is, the whole conception would vitiate itself " (*ibid*.: 18–19). Schelling's point is that a dependent existence must be genuinely distinct from that upon which it is dependent, otherwise it is merely a part of that from which it emerges. Taking seriously the distinction between being as a whole and particular beings, then, requires attributing genuine autonomy to those particular beings.

Schelling concludes that pantheism, a species of which he is explicitly advocating, is compatible with human freedom. Spinoza must not have been led to determinism by his pantheism, but rather by an independent mistake, Schelling reasons: "The error of his system is by no means due to the fact that he posits all *things in God*, but to the fact that they are *things* . . . He treats the will, too, as a thing, and then proves, very naturally, that in every case of its operation it must be determined by some other thing, which in turn is determined by another, and so forth endlessly" (*INHF*: 22). Schelling holds, however, that "God is not a God of the dead but of the living. It is incomprehensible that an all-perfect being could rejoice in even the most perfect mechanism possible. No matter how one pictures to oneself the procession of creatures from God, it can never be a mechanical production, no mere construction or setting up, in which the construct is naught in itself " (*ibid*.: 19). Again drawing upon his earlier philosophy of nature, Schelling concludes, "the concept of becoming is the only one adequate to the nature of things" (*ibid*.: 33).

Having rejuvenated the possibility of a reconciliation between the existence of God and the existence of freedom, Schelling infers freedom's actuality from what he takes to be the undeniable reality of evil. Evil is possible only in virtue of human freedom, which leads Schelling to declare, famously:

> Man has been placed on that summit where he contains within him the source of self-impulsion toward good and evil in equal measure; the nexus of the principles within him is not a bond of necessity but of freedom. He stands at the dividing line; whatever he chooses will be his act, but he cannot remain in indecision because God must necessarily reveal himself and because nothing at all in creation can remain ambiguous.
>
> (*INHF*: 50)

Schelling summarizes the point in another proto-existentialist formulation: "man's being is essentially *his own deed* " (*ibid*.: 63).

Schelling emphasizes that freedom cannot be understood as mere indeterminism, which would make human action the result of accident or chance. Schelling contends that "accident is impossible and contradicts reason as well as the necessary unity of the whole; and if freedom cannot be saved except by making actions totally accidental, then it cannot be saved at all" (*ibid*.: 60). Indeed, Schelling regards determinism as philosophically preferable to indeterminism, but he criticizes both for being "ignorant of that higher necessity which is equally far removed from accident and from compulsion or external determination but which is, rather, an inner necessity which springs from the essence of the active agent itself " (*ibid*.: 61).

Schelling owes this conception of freedom – "that is free which acts according to the laws of its own inner being and is not determined by anything else either within it or outside it" (*ibid*.: 62) – to Spinoza. Unlike Spinoza, however, Schelling attributes such self-determination to individual human beings, and not merely to being as a whole. The immediate objection, of course, is that if we necessarily act according to the laws of our inner being, but are not responsible for those laws themselves, then we continue to be externally determined rather than free. Schelling parries this objection by contending that each human being determines his or her own essence, from which all subsequent acts necessarily follow, by means of an initial and eternal selection of character.

This device, which Schelling acknowledges having borrowed from Kant, who resorted to it in his writings on religion, locates the initial determination of character outside of time (since everything temporal is determined by the conditions that precede it). Nonetheless, Schelling claims, "it is not at all an act of which no consciousness remains to man. Thus someone, who perhaps to excuse a wrong act, says: 'Well, that's the way I am' – is himself well aware that he is so because of his own fault, however correct he may be in thinking that it would have been impossible for him to act differently" (*INHF*: 64–5).

Despite the implausibility of the metaphysical hypothesis involved in this account of human freedom, Schelling bravely claims that "there seems to be only one reason that could be raised in objection to this view: namely that it cuts out all conversions from good to evil and *vice versa* for man, at least in this life" (*ibid*.: 67). To preserve the possibility of conversion, Schelling refines the view to accommodate the possibility that after the initial determination of character people might remain open to external influence, divine or human, that would help them change for the better. Whether or not one accepts such influence, however, must itself be determined by the initial act of self-definition, so that being open or closed to conversion is pre-ordained from this definitive moment.

Towards the end of the *Inquiries*, Schelling grants that he has yet to answer the central question of theodicy: "The chief problem of this whole inquiry is still ahead of us. Up to now God has merely been viewed as being revealing itself . . . [But] what is God's relation as a moral being to evil, the possibility and reality of which depend upon his self-revelation?" (*INHF*: 73). In other words, Schelling has claimed to demonstrate that there is real evil in the world, that such evil can result only from human freedom, and that human freedom must, like everything else, emerge from being as a whole, which is equivalent to being an aspect of God's self-revelation. The inescapable conclusion, however, is that evil is a necessary consequence of God's self-revelation, which leaves the problem of theodicy looming as large as ever.

Schelling acknowledges, but is unwilling to take, the option of declaring that God might not have foreseen the consequences of revealing himself, and thus might be exculpated from responsibility for evil. Schelling's God is omniscient as well as omnipotent. The pressing question, therefore, is how God can continue to be regarded as benevolent.

Schelling takes one final stab at preserving divine benevolence, asserting that "in the fact that God brought the disorderly spawn of chaos into order and pronounced his eternal unity in nature, he really opposed darkness and set up the Word as a constant centre and eternal beacon against the unruly movement of the irrational principle. The will to creation was thus directly only a will to bring light to birth and, therein, goodness" (*INHF*: 82). Of course, the indirect result of this will to goodness was the inevitable emergence of evil, which God, by Schelling's own admission, must have foreseen. But at this point Schelling has exhausted his resources, and declares that "the question why God did not prefer not to reveal himself at all, since he necessarily foresaw that evil would at least follow as an accompaniment of self-revelation, this question really deserves no reply" (*ibid.*: 82–3).

Schelling concludes the *Inquiries* in remarkable fashion, by returning briefly to reconsider, and in so doing to undermine, the distinction with which the entire investigation began. "What", he asks, "is to be gained by that initial distinction between being insofar as it is basis, and being insofar as it exists? For either there is no common ground for the two – in which case we must declare ourselves in favour of absolute dualism; or there is such common ground – and in that case in the last analysis, the two coincide again" (*INHF*: 86–7). If the latter of these alternatives is the case, then "we have one being in all opposites, an absolute identity of light and darkness, good and evil" (*ibid.*: 87). And this is, indeed, the view to which Schelling's *Inquiries* have ultimately led him: "There must be a being *before* all basis and before all existence, that is, before any duality at all; how can we designate it except as 'primal ground' or, rather, as the 'groundless'? As it precedes all antitheses these cannot be distinguishable in it or be present in any way at all. It cannot then be called the identity of both, but only the absolute indifference as to both" (*ibid.*). Schelling's attempt at theodicy has thus brought an end to his philosophy of identity, and deposited itself in a negative theology, in the postulation of a groundless primal ground that is "naught else than [the] non-being [of all distinctions], and therefore has no predicates except lack of predicates, without its being naught or a non-entity" (*ibid.*).

Conclusion

By 1809, at the age of thirty-four, Schelling had scaled the heights of German philosophy and published his last work. In the span of fifteen years, his relentless commitment to the truth had transformed Schelling from a transcendental idealist in the mould of Fichte, to a metaphysician in the mould of Spinoza, to a thinker increasingly sceptical about the possibility and promise of *a priori* philosophy.

Schelling's abandonment of strictly Kantian criticism, in favour of a return to more traditional metaphysics, was driven by his insistence that philosophy cannot begin with the given fact of experience, but must explain how it is that a world of differentiated subjectivity and objectivity comes to be. Schelling's desire to understand the emergence of finite objects and conscious subjects led him to develop the philosophy of nature, an *a priori* ontology that conceives of the natural world holistically and dynamically. Nature is presented as an organic, self-moving whole, comprising fundamental forces that establish and destroy particular entities over time. This conception of nature stands in stark contrast to that of atomistic, mechanistic physics, and offers a basis for resisting Fichte's view that the natural world is a collection of purely passive, material objects that we are morally obliged to subordinate to the purposes of reason.

Schelling did not simply replace transcendental idealism with the philosophy of nature, but rather joined the two, giving each a necessary place as one half of the philosophy of identity, which aimed to explain both why subjectivity must emerge from objectivity, and why objectivity must be experienced by subjects in the way that it is. In the *System of Transcendental Idealism*, Schelling aimed to complete and perfect Fichte's project, and in the course of doing so contributed the novel conception of "epochs of consciousness", historical stages through which subjectivity must pass in order to achieve fully adequate self-understanding. Schelling identified the last of these stages as the aesthetic appreciation of the identity or providential harmony that he claimed to obtain between the law-governed course of the objective world and the actions freely produced by conscious subjects in the course of history. Schelling joined his Romantic friends and colleagues in regarding art as being able to show what philosophy cannot say, and in so doing placed it at the pinnacle of human development and achievement.

Schelling's attempt to reconcile freedom and necessity, a constant throughout his early and middle periods, culminated in the *Philosophical Inquires into the Nature of Human Freedom*. In this last of his significant publications, Schelling's reflections upon the classic problem of theodicy lead him to transform Kant's distinction between intelligible and empirical selfhood into a proto-existentialist distinction between essence and existence, and to claim that each of us is ultimately responsible for our original free choice of a good or evil character. The end of the *Inquiries*, however, reveals Schelling's increasing concern that *a priori* philosophy cannot solve the tasks to which it has been appointed. Schelling attempts to reconcile being as a whole with the becoming of particular entities by means of a groundless, primal ground, about which literally nothing can be said. This move anticipates Schelling's later rejection of *a priori* philosophy, which he would declare to be "negative", in favour of a "positive" philosophy concerned with empirical existence rather than eternal essence.

Although Schelling ultimately rejected many of the philosophical positions that he explored in his early and middle periods, the work he produced in these years had a significant impact on many other thinkers. His conceptions of nature and art were important to Romanticism (indeed, Josiah Royce, the eminent American pragmatist, dubbed Schelling "the prince of the Romantics"). His insistence that our essence is not predetermined by our existence, and his exhortation to choose a good character, were important to Kierkegaard and other existentialists. And his distinction between being and beings, as well as his theory of aesthetic intuition, would prove important to Heidegger. The most immediate and profound impact of these works, however, was upon Hegel, who was working closely with Schelling as he began to develop his own, distinctive philosophical position in the first years of the nineteenth century.

Summary of key points

- Schelling's early work expands Fichte's search for an unconditional first principle of knowledge into the search for an unconditional or absolute ground of the existence of all particular things. This transforms the critical idealism of Kant and Fichte into "absolute idealism".
- In Schelling's middle period, he develops absolute idealism into a philosophy of identity composed of two complementary disciplines: transcendental idealism and the philosophy of nature.
- Schelling's *a priori* philosophy of nature argues that the world is fundamentally dynamic and organic, and thus encourages an ecological understanding of the cosmos.
- Schelling's transcendental idealism presents a systematic examination of the "epochs" through which conscious subjects must

pass in order to become fully self-aware, and concludes that the highest stage of self-awareness is reached through art.

- In his final publication, Schelling attempts to reconcile human freedom with the claim that everything emerges necessarily from the absolute.

six

Hegel: systematic philosophy without foundations

Georg Wilhelm Friedrich Hegel (1770–1831) came of age as a person and an author at the same time that the triumphant proclamations of the arrival of the age of reason promised revolutionary transformations of human thought and action. In 1787, when Hegel was seventeen years old, Kant declared his own philosophy to be the epistemological equivalent of the Copernican revolution: arguing that the possibility of metaphysical knowledge cannot be explained if one assumes that the cognizing subject must conform to the object of cognition, Kant inverted this assumption. The result was transcendental idealism, with which Kant claimed to have determined the means, extent and limits of truly rational cognition. Only two years later, in 1789, when Hegel was a student in Tübingen, the practical equivalent of this theoretical development manifested itself in France: arguing that freedom is impossible if one assumes that political subjects must conform to the will of the ruling authority, the revolutionaries inverted this assumption and promised to establish a truly rational system of government.

Hegel celebrated both the Kantian and the French revolutions, but not uncritically. Hegel's enthusiasm stemmed from his agreement with the revolutionary insistence on the right of reason: modern theoretical claims and practical arrangements must be, above all and by definition, rational. Hegel's criticism, however, stemmed from his view that the age of reason failed to live up to its name: neither Kantian philosophy nor the French Revolution was truly rational, because both rested on a misconception of rationality itself. Hegel's own concern, from his first publication to his last, thus became the development of a truly rational philosophy, one that could determine and thereby help to sustain the conditions of a truly rational life.

Hegel's emergence as a significant thinker, however, was not nearly as rapid as that of Schelling. Hegel completed his studies in Tübingen in 1793, but it would be another twenty-three years before he finally became a salaried professor of philosophy, joining the faculty in Heidelberg in 1816. Upon leaving Tübingen, Hegel found employment as a private tutor, and he worked in this capacity in Bern and Frankfurt for the next seven years. During this period Hegel wrote a number of essays, most of which concerned religious and political themes, but his writing went unpublished and he had no prospects of an academic career. In 1800, at the age of thirty, Hegel resolved to write to Schelling, with whom he had had no contact for several years, to state his intention to pursue systematic philosophy, and to seek advice from his already successful and celebrated friend. Schelling encouraged Hegel to move to Jena, and even offered temporary lodging, which Hegel quickly and gratefully accepted.

For the next six years, from 1801 to 1807, Hegel scratched out a living in Jena as an unsalaried lecturer, dependent upon the fees that students paid to attend his lectures. Although this position offered Hegel neither professional nor financial security, the intellectual community in Jena – which included not only Schelling, but also some of the most important early Romantics – proved invaluable to his philosophical development. In 1801 Hegel published his first book, *The Difference between Fichte's and Schelling's System of Philosophy*. The book aided Schelling, who at that time was commonly regarded as a disciple of the recently departed and still revered Fichte, by making it clear that he had in fact developed his own distinctive philosophical position. At the same time, however, the book also gave Hegel a reputation as Schelling's follower, despite the fact that it contains important hints of Hegel's own emerging views.

In 1802 Schelling founded the *Critical Journal of Philosophy*, and invited Hegel to join him as a co-editor. Schelling intended the journal to be a vehicle for the dissemination of his philosophical programme, and Hegel's participation further cemented his reputation as a mere labourer working in the service of his brilliant friend. During the brief existence of the journal, however, Hegel contributed a number of pieces in which his own philosophical position became, to Schelling's displeasure, increasingly evident. The most important of these essays are: "On the Relationship of Skepticism to Philosophy", "Faith and Knowledge" and "On the Scientific Treatment of Natural Law". The collaboration came to a quick end when Schelling, following in the footsteps of the most interesting members of the Romantic circle, moved away from Jena in 1803, leaving Hegel with no journal, no real job, and a greatly diminished intellectual community. Hegel remained in Jena for another four years, where he eventually earned the "distinction" of being the oldest unsalaried lecturer in town.

In 1807, with his financial situation increasingly precarious, Hegel gave up lecturing and took a position in Bamberg as a newspaper editor. This move, which could easily have put an end to Hegel's philosophical aspirations, coincided ironically with the publication of the *Phenomenology of Spirit*, his first fully mature work, which serves as the introduction to his systematic philosophy.

Hegel's career as a journalist was short-lived, however, and in 1808 he became the rector of a *Gymnasium*, or high school, in Nuremberg. For the next seven years Hegel ran the school, bravely tried to teach his developing ideas to teenage boys, and worked feverishly on his next great work, the *Science of Logic*. The *Logic*, which constitutes the first part of Hegel's system, appeared in three volumes, published in 1812, 1813 and 1816, and the last of these coincided with Hegel finally being offered, at the age of forty-six, a salaried academic position at the University of Heidelberg.

In the final fifteen years of his life, Hegel enjoyed the public success and recognition that had eluded him over the preceding two decades. Shortly after arriving in Heidelberg, in 1817, he published the first edition of his *Encyclopedia of Philosophical Sciences* (revised editions of which would appear in 1827 and 1830). The *Encyclopedia* provides a comprehensive overview of the entirety of Hegel's system, the three main parts of which are logic, the philosophy of nature and the philosophy of spirit. In 1818 Hegel accepted a prestigious professorship in Berlin, and in 1820 he published *Elements of the Philosophy of Right*, which elaborates on the social and political aspects of the philosophy of spirit. For the next eleven years Hegel lectured on various elements of his system, including the philosophy of history, aesthetics and religion. His sudden death in 1831, exactly fifty years after Kant's publication of the *Critique of Pure Reason*, brought to a close the great era of German Idealism.

The systematic significance of the pre-systematic writings

Hegel's early writings, including those he published in Schelling's *Critical Journal*, are pre-systematic in the sense that they are largely polemical analyses of contemporary positions that make no pretence to establish or develop Hegel's own philosophical system. *The Difference* offers critical expositions of Fichte, Schelling and Reinhold. "On the Relation of Skepticism to Philosophy" is a withering treatment of Gottlob Schulze (the author of *Aenesidemus*) and of modern scepticism in general, which Hegel regards as dogmatic in comparison with the ancient variety. "Faith and Knowledge" devotes its three sections to Kant, Jacobi and Fichte. And the "Natural Law" essay aims to explain why neither empiricism nor critical idealism can provide an adequate political philosophy.

These pre-systematic works have systematic significance, however, because they contribute to Hegel's attempt to fulfil the promise of German Idealism by developing a truly rational philosophy. This attempt consists of three steps: first, an identification of the not-fully-rational in Hegel's most important philosophical contemporaries and predecessors, in the service of a positive specification of the criteria of a fully rational philosophy; second, a critique of philosophical approaches falsely claiming to have met those criteria; and third, the development of a philosophy that does in fact meet the criteria of rationality.

Hegel's *Phenomenology of Spirit* and three-part *Encyclopedia* represent, respectively, his attempts to carry out the second and third steps of his task. The *Phenomenology* exposes philosophical approaches that claim, falsely in Hegel's view, to have delivered truly rational cognition but attends to these philosophical failures in a way designed to reveal that and how truly rational cognition can be delivered. The *Encyclopedia* then claims to deliver truly rational cognition by developing a complete system of knowledge in accordance with the only philosophical approach left open by the *Phenomenology*. Both of these steps, however, employ the conception of rational cognition developed in the pre-systematic writings. Beginning with *The Difference*, his very first publication, Hegel undertook a relentless critical examination of the age of reason and its pre-eminent philosophical representatives, which ultimately led him to the project of the *Phenomenology* and the concept of rationality that informs it. It is therefore the Jena writings that accomplish the first step of Hegel's task and prepare the way for the systematic philosophy he later developed.

The leitmotif of Hegel's early critique of the so-called age of reason, or the Enlightenment, is that it in fact defaults on the modern promise of rationality and freedom, because, as he puts it in the opening pages of *Faith and Knowledge*, "Enlightened reason . . . is no longer reason . . . [It is] mere understanding, [which] acknowledges its own nothingness by placing that which is better than it in a *faith outside and above* itself, as a *beyond*. This is what has happened in the *philosophies of Kant, Jacobi, and Fichte*. Philosophy has made itself the handmaid of faith once more" (*FK*: 55–6). Making sense of Hegel's critique thus requires making sense of the distinction he draws between reason and understanding.

In the Preface to *The Difference*, Hegel characterizes "reason" as "the identity of subject and object" (*D*: 80). What Hegel means by the "identity of subject and object" becomes evident when one attends to the fact that his use of this formulation occurs in the course of a direct engagement with Kant, and in particular with Kant's transcendental deduction. The deduction aims to show that the categories necessarily used by the thinking subject must also apply to the objects of thinking, which in Hegel's terms amounts to showing that there is an "identity of subject and object". If Kant's deduction is successful, then the thinking subject and the object of thought are identical in the sense that they share the same constitutive features or "determinations": the categories, or necessary conceptual determinations, that the subject uses to think its object are also the determinations of the object that it thinks.

Although the signification of the "identity of subject and object" of which Hegel speaks derives from Kant, the identity Kant claims to have established with the transcendental deduction is not itself what Hegel refers to as "reason". For if Kant is right, the deduction demonstrates an identity between the subject and its object *qua* phenomenon, or as it appears, but is powerless to demonstrate an identity between the subject and the object-in-itself. According to Kant, that is, we can know that all objects of experience must have the categorial determinations that make it possible for them to be experienced as objects by thinking subjects, but about the determinations of beings themselves we can know nothing at all. Hegel thus joins Schelling in characterizing the identity established by Kant (and seconded by Fichte) as a merely "subjective subject–object" (*D*: 81) that is tantamount to being no true identity at all. Indeed, Kant not only fails to demonstrate the identity of subject and object, but actually claims to have demonstrated the necessity of an unbridgeable gap between them: according to Kant the conceptual determinations of the thinking subject can never be known to be those of beings themselves.

The "identity of subject and object" that Hegel calls "reason" therefore refers to precisely the state of affairs denied by Kant: the determinations constitutive of thinking are the determinations constitutive of beings themselves. Hegel makes this explicit in *The Difference*: "the true identity of subject and object" means "the ideal determinations nature receives in [philosophical] science are also immanent in it" (D: 160).

Hegel refers to the identity of subject and object as "reason" because it is the necessary condition of actuality – that which truly is – being amenable to rational cognition or comprehension; actuality can be comprehended only if the determinations of being can be revealed and grasped by the determinations of thought. Were the opposite state of affairs to obtain, actuality would be "irrational" in the sense that it could not be known or grasped by rational cognition, and so would have to be regarded as "a fixed realm of the incomprehensible, and of a faith which is in itself non-rational" (FK: 61). In this case, actuality would be "an absolutely unthought, unrecognized, and incomprehensible beyond" (ibid.: 94) inaccessible to human experience, which is precisely the conclusion reached by the critical philosophy of Kant and Fichte.

Hegel credits Descartes, the empiricists and Kant with raising the modern demand for a justification of the claim that the determinations of thinking and being are identical. This demand makes these thinkers representatives of what Hegel refers to as the standpoint of "understanding", which separates the thinking subject from the objects of its experience and refuses to concede the identity of their determinations unless and until it has been demonstrated.

The standpoint of understanding is thus defined by the rejection of traditional metaphysics and the consequent granting of priority to epistemology. Hegel makes this point with respect to Kant in *Faith and Knowledge*, where he writes, echoing Schelling, that "the whole task and content of this philosophy is not the cognition of the absolute, but the cognition of . . . subjectivity. In other words, it is a critique of the cognitive faculties" (FK: 68).

Hegel grants that Hume and Kant successfully deduce the epistemological consequences of the dualism they take for granted, but emphasizes that the assumption of this dualism fails to meet the standards of rational justification established by Kant himself. From the assumption of an essential difference in kind between subject and object, between the pure universality of concepts and the brute particularity of beings, the impossibility of rational cognition does in fact follow. Given this assumption, in other words, the belief in the incomprehensibility of actuality is justified. But, Hegel contends, this assumption is expressly undermined by Kant's own philosophy, which rightly insists that rational justification demands the complete abnegation of conditional presuppositions. By presupposing a dualism of subject and object, the standpoint of understanding fails to meet its own critical test.

Kant's self-undermining of the standpoint of understanding reopens the possibility that the standpoint of reason might be attained. For if the dualism upon which empiricism and transcendental idealism rest constitutes a conditional presupposition, then the impossibility of rational cognition that they announce constitutes an unjustified conclusion. Hegel is fully aware, however, that empiricists and Kantians will not be quick to abandon their presuppositions and embrace the standpoint of reason. Bringing such dualists to the standpoint of reason is the project of the *Phenomenology*, which aims to justify the claim that the determinations constitutive of thinking are in fact the determinations constitutive of being by demonstrating that the distinction between constitutive determinations of thinking and being cannot justifiably be sustained. This demonstration culminates in what the final chapter of the *Phenomenology* refers to as "absolute knowing", which is another name for the standpoint of reason, the standpoint at which it is known that to work out the determinations constitutive of thinking would at the same time be to work out the determinations constitutive of being, and thus to provide rational cognition of the constitution of actuality.

The *Phenomenology* claims to demonstrate that rational cognition is possible, but such cognition can be achieved only if the determinations constitutive of thinking and being can be articulated. The chief task of philosophy is therefore the articulation of these determinations, to which Hegel devotes his entire system, beginning with the *Science of Logic* and continuing throughout the *Encyclopedia*.

Hegel's claim that his philosophical system articulates the constitution of actuality makes him post-Kantian in the sense that he rejects and moves beyond Kant's conclusion that philosophy is incapable of rational cognition; Hegel joins Schelling in restoring metaphysics to its pre-Kantian place as the queen of the philosophical sciences. But Hegel remains at the same time firmly post-Kantian in the sense that his encyclopedic system does not constitute a reversion to pre-critical metaphysics; Hegel's philosophical enterprise is a thoroughly critical one, governed by the insistence that rationality demands the avoidance of all conditional presuppositions. The lesson Hegel learns from Kant's critical inspiration is that philosophy must be more thoroughly critical than Kant's own transcendental idealism managed to be.

Hegel argues that a radically critical philosophy must return to metaphysics because it cannot accept the Kantian presuppositions that lead to the conclusion that thinking cannot determine the truth of being. The particular metaphysical project to which Hegel returns, and the way in which he attempts to execute it, are also governed by his resolutely critical stance.

Because a truly critical philosophy cannot presume the existence of any particular thing as the object of its concern, Hegel's project is an ontology – an account of what it is to be – rather than an investigation of any supposedly supersensible entity. Hegel thus breaks with Schelling in not regarding philosophy as the science of a transcendent absolute. Hegel makes this point explicitly in the "Skepticism" essay, where he accuses Schulze of falsely understanding speculative philosophy to be "the science of the *highest and most unconditioned causes of all conditioned things*" ("S": 317). Hegel uses "the absolute" not in reference to a special entity, but rather as a synonym for the set of determinations that are the basis of the identity of subjectivity and objectivity in virtue of being constitutive of both the thinking of subjects and the being of objects. It is the articulation of the determinate constitution of actuality, rather than the proof of any supersensible existence, that Hegel considers the task of philosophy.

Hegel's execution of this ontological task is also guided by his critical insistence that rationality demands the strict avoidance of all presuppositions. He argues, first, that philosophy must not ground itself upon, by taking for granted, any particular conceptual determination. Second, philosophy must subsequently incorporate only those conceptual determinations that prove to unfold with immanent necessity from its unconditional beginning. The introduction of an extraneous or contingent conceptual determination at any point would undermine philosophy's claim to articulate the absolute truth of being by making the articulation conditional upon, or relative to, the validity of the introduced concept. Together, these two conditions entail that philosophy must form a single, self-contained set of conceptual determinations, all of which amount to the explication of the truth implicit in the initial, non-arbitrary determination. Only if philosophy can be made systematic in this sense, Hegel concluded in Jena before he sat down to write the *Phenomenology*, can it also be the science of rational cognition.

Introduction to systematic philosophy: the *Phenomenology of Spirit*

The *Phenomenology of Spirit* is Hegel's most famous and influential book, although not necessarily for the right reasons. The *Phenomenology* is best known for particular sections that have intrigued and inspired readers both within and beyond philosophy over the last two hundred years. These include the discussions of desire, recognition, the master and slave, unhappy consciousness, Antigone, absolute freedom and terror, conscience, and the beautiful soul. As fascinating and fruitful as these individual sections have proved to be, however, their philosophical significance lies in the larger project to which they contribute.

"The goal" of the *Phenomenology*, Hegel writes in the Preface, is "spirit's insight into what knowing is" (*PhenS*: 17). Bringing about such insight requires "the *education* of consciousness itself to the standpoint of science" (*ibid.*: 50). "Consciousness" is another name for the standpoint of understanding, defined by the dualistic assumption that knowledge requires a thinking subject to represent truthfully the realm of objectivity with which it is confronted, and from which it distinguishes itself: "*consciousness* contains the two moments of knowing and the objectivity negative to knowing" (*ibid.*: 21). The "standpoint of science" is another name for the standpoint of reason, defined by the suspension of epistemological dualism and the awareness that in philosophy the thinking subject achieves "absolute knowing" by revealing the actual truth of being, to which it has access in its own thought. Consequently, "the standpoint of consciousness which knows objects in their antithesis to itself, and itself in antithesis to them, is for science the antithesis of its own standpoint" (*ibid.*: 15). The philosopher at the standpoint of reason, however, cannot simply dismiss the individual at the standpoint of consciousness, for this "individual has the right to demand that science should at least provide him with a ladder to this standpoint, should show him this standpoint within himself" (*ibid.*: 14–15). The *Phenomenology* responds to this demand by attempting to show the individual at the standpoint of consciousness that his own assumptions, considered carefully on their own terms, undermine themselves and lead to the standpoint of reason or absolute knowing, from which systematic philosophy can then commence with the *Science of Logic*.

The *Phenomenology* thus cannot be regarded as Hegel's version of Fichte's *Science of Knowledge* or Schelling's *System of Transcendental Idealism*. Despite the fact that all three books are concerned with consciousness, each has a quite distinctive aim and procedure. Fichte aims to provide a transcendental account of the conditions of the possibility of consciousness; he takes selfhood as a given fact, and argues it is possible only in virtue of the experience of an external world and various forms of interaction with other self-conscious agents. Schelling also begins with the immediate fact of selfhood, and then aims to provide an account of the historical epochs through which he claims that self-conscious beings must pass in order to achieve fully adequate self-understanding. Hegel's *Phenomenology*, however, offers neither a transcendental nor a historical account of consciousness. In fact, the *Phenomenology* does not present Hegel's own account of consciousness at all; that account is to be found in the *Philosophy of Spirit*, the part of his *Encyclopedia* devoted to articulating what it is to be a thinking being.

The *Phenomenology*, as its title suggests, is an account of how consciousness *appears* or seems to be from its own standpoint, rather than an account of what consciousness truly *is* (which Hegel contends can only be determined from the standpoint of reason or philosophical science). Hegel claims that the phenomenological examination forces consciousness to revise its initial assumptions about itself and its object, so that it gradually comes to understand itself as being also self-conscious, rational, spiritual, religious and, finally, philosophical: capable of determining from within its own thinking the necessary or constitutive features of actuality. This sequence of progressively revised assumptions, which Hegel characterizes as a series of "shapes of consciousness", thus presents the coming-to-be or *appearance*, for consciousness itself, of the standpoint of reason: "It is this coming-to-be of *science as such* or of *knowledge* that is described in the *Phenomenology of Spirit*" (*PhenS*: 15).

The "shapes of consciousness" that emerge in the course of the *Phenomenology* are related to each other logically, not transcendentally or historically. Hegel is not arguing, transcendentally, that the later shapes of consciousness are necessary conditions of the possibility of their predecessors. He does not hold, for example, that religious experience is a necessary condition of the possibility of self-consciousness. Nor is he arguing, historically, that human beings must have passed through each of the stages of consciousness in order finally to arrive at the standpoint of reason. Hegel's claim is that the succession is logically necessary, in the sense that each shape of consciousness proves to be internally contradictory and each particular contradiction that emerges can be resolved only by the new shape of consciousness that follows it. The *Phenomenology* thus constitutes an extremely long argument for the claim that if consciousness is to understand itself in a non-contradictory way, then it must adopt the standpoint of reason.

But Hegel is well aware that people are entirely capable of developing and retaining contradictory self-understandings, and thus of never achieving the standpoint from which the philosophical science of actuality is possible. Indeed, in the course of the *Phenomenology* he sometimes remarks that certain historical individuals and cultures have understood themselves in ways that correspond to the logical stages he describes.

The *Phenomenology* is written to show readers who inhabit any of these self-contradictory perspectives that the implications of their own assumptions about themselves and the world require them to adopt the standpoint of reason. The book is not necessary reading, therefore, for those who already feel the full force of the modern demand for rationality, and are consequently willing to suspend their assumptions about subjectivity and objectivity in order to engage in a presuppositionless examination of the actual truth of being. Hegel believes that radical self-criticism is by itself sufficient to attain the standpoint of reason, and that those already at this standpoint may skip the *Phenomenology* and proceed directly to systematic philosophy, propelled simply by "the resolve . . . to consider thought as such" (*SL*: 70). "To enter into philosophy," Hegel continues, "calls for no other preparations, no further reflections or points of connection" (*ibid.*: 72). The *Phenomenology* is intended for those who remain at the standpoint of consciousness, and therefore fail to recognize either the need for, or the possibility of, systematic philosophy.

The most basic assumption of the standpoint of consciousness, which is common to all of the shapes of consciousness explored in the *Phenomenology*, is that knowing is a relationship between a conscious subject and an object other than itself. Hegel believes this assumption to be mistaken, but he does not confront it with alternative assumptions about knowing. Hegel recognizes, like Socrates before him, that such a confrontation would require a third party, armed with a neutral criterion of adjudication, to settle the dispute. Instead of developing such an external critique, therefore, Hegel inhabits the standpoint of consciousness at the outset of the *Phenomenology*, and then attempts to show that, and precisely how, it fails to meet its *own* criterion of knowing, and is thus *self*-undermining. In virtue of this method of immanent critique, Hegel reasons, "we do not need to import criteria, or to make use of our own bright ideas and thoughts during the course of the inquiry; it is precisely when we leave these aside that we succeed in contemplating the matter in hand as it is *in and for itself*" (*PhenS*: 54). This enables the *Phenomenology* to qualify as the "Science of the

Experience of Consciousness", rather than being merely Hegel's particular reflections upon the subject.

The phenomenological examination of consciousness is driven forward, at each stage, by comparing what consciousness claims to be true of its object with the way in which the object appears to consciousness. The achievement of knowledge requires these two characterizations of the object to coincide, for if they do not then the object-as-experienced by consciousness does not represent the truth of the object-itself. The revelation of a gap between the two characterizations thus contradicts the claim of consciousness to have attained knowledge, and the resolution of this contradiction requires a revision of the assumptions consciousness holds about itself and its object. In Hegel's terminology, these revisions amount to a "negation" of the shape of consciousness under consideration, which is shown *not* to be the truth of knowing after all. This negation is "determinate" because it results in a new shape of consciousness that resolves the specific contradictions implicit in the assumptions of its predecessor.

The examination continues in the same fashion for the duration of the *Phenomenology*: a shape of consciousness is defined; its experience of the object is compared to its conception of the object; if there is a discrepancy between the two, then the prevailing assumptions are revised accordingly, giving rise to a new shape of consciousness. The process is then repeated, until there is no longer any contradiction: "The goal . . . is the point where knowledge no longer needs to go beyond itself, where knowledge finds itself, where concept corresponds to object and object to concept" (*PhenS*: 51). When consciousness reaches this goal, as Hegel claims it does at the end of the *Phenomenology*, it finally understands itself properly, and in so doing it attains the standpoint of reason, from which philosophy proper can finally begin. Hegel anticipates this development in the closing lines of the Introduction to the *Phenomenology*:

> In pressing forward to its true existence, consciousness will arrive at a point at which it gets rid of its semblance of being burdened with something alien, with what is only for it, and some sort of 'other', at a point where appearance becomes identical with essence, so that its exposition will coincide at just this point with the authentic science of spirit. And finally, when consciousness itself grasps this its own essence, it will signify the nature of absolute knowledge itself.
>
> (*Ibid.*: 56–7)

The initial shape of consciousness, which Hegel refers to as "sense-certainty", is defined in the first paragraph of the body of the *Phenomenology*:

> The knowledge or knowing which is at the start or is immediately our object cannot be anything else but immediate knowledge itself, a knowledge of the immediate or of what simply *is*. Our approach to the object must also be *immediate* or *receptive*; we must alter nothing in the object as it presents itself. In *ap*prehending it, we must refrain from trying to *com*prehend it. (*Ibid.*: 58)

Consciousness initially conceives of its knowing as immediate, and of itself as purely passive, because it assumes that any activity or mediation would inevitably compromise knowledge by distorting the appearance of the object.

Hegel then raises the question that propels the entire phenomenological investigation: "The question . . . [is] whether in sense-certainty itself the object is in fact the kind of essence that sense-certainty proclaims it to be" (*ibid.*: 59). Continuing, he reiterates that the properly scientific approach to this question is "not to reflect on [the object] and ponder what it might be in truth, but only to consider the way in which it is present in sense-certainty" (*ibid.*).

Sense-certainty claims to know its object immediately. According to Hegel, however, the immediacy with which it claims to know is incompatible with its claim to know a particular object; there is a contradiction between *what* consciousness claims to experience, and *how* it claims to experience it. All that consciousness can experience immediately is "This", which is "Here" "Now". To experience anything more complex as a single object, the complexity would have to be unified, but such unification would require a process of mediation. Universal terms such as "This", "Here" and "Now", which apply equally to every experience consciousness could have, are insufficient, however, to enable consciousness to experience any particular object as distinct from any other. Sense-certainty cannot, therefore, know particular objects immediately.

The certainties of this initial form of consciousness, Hegel concludes, prove to be false. Neither consciousness nor its object is in truth as sense-certainty initially assumed them to be. The particular object experienced by consciousness cannot be an irreducibly simple "This", because all irreducible simples are indistinguishable from each other, and thus lack particularity. The object of consciousness must therefore be a complex unity or, in Hegel's terms, a mediated universal; the object is a single entity or "Thing" with a plurality of particular properties, in virtue of which consciousness can distinguish it from other objects. Consciousness cannot experience such a mediated universal immediately, however, because it must take in the variety of properties and recognize them as belonging to a single entity. Consciousness must therefore play a more active role in the experience of its object than sense-certainty assumed, by correctly picking out the features that belong to this object, in distinction from other objects. The active identification of a thing that manifests a multiplicity of properties Hegel refers to as "Perception", which is therefore the second shape of consciousness.

"Perception" begins, as "sense-certainty" began before it, by defining the assumptions that this shape of consciousness holds regarding itself and its object. The object of knowledge is now assumed to be a "*thing with many properties*" (*PhenS*: 67). For example, "salt is a simple 'Here', and at the same time manifold; it is white and *also* tart, *also* cubical in shape, of a specific gravity, etc. All these many properties are in a single simple 'Here', in which, therefore, they interpenetrate; none has a different 'Here' from the others, but each is everywhere, in the same 'Here' in which the others are" (*ibid*.: 68). Consciousness is now assumed to be "percipient in so far as this 'Thing' is its object. It has only to *take* it, to confine itself to a pure apprehension of it, and what is thus yielded is the true. If consciousness itself did anything in taking what is given, it would by such adding or subtraction alter the truth" (*ibid*.: 70). Perception thus involves an active taking of the object into consciousness, whereas sense-certainty claimed to be purely passive in the reception of its object, but the perceiving consciousness must ensure that its activity does not distort the object and thereby result in deception rather than knowledge.

The subsequent examination of "perception" proceeds just as the examination of "sense-certainty" did. "Let us see now", Hegel suggests, "what consciousness experiences in its actual perceiving . . . It is only a matter of developing the contradictions that are present therein" (*ibid*.).

Consciousness claims to perceive the thing that is its object. But again, according to Hegel, there proves to be a contradiction between what consciousness claims to know and how it claims to know it. The thing is a single entity with a multiplicity of properties; in Hegel's terms, it is both a "One" and an "Also". Consciousness can perceive both the oneness of the object and the multiplicity of properties, but it cannot perceive whatever it is that unites them, whatever it is that accounts for the fact that these particular properties belong to this singular object. Since the thing is the unity of the oneness and the multiplicity, however, this means that the thing cannot be fully known through perception. Essential to the thing is an imperceptible source of the unity of the perceived oneness and multiplicity. Consciousness cannot, therefore, perceive the whole truth of the thing.

The certainties of consciousness have proven false, Hegel concludes, once more. Neither consciousness nor its object is in truth as perception initially assumed them to be. The thing is not merely a perceptibly unified set of perceptible properties, but is also constituted in part by imperceptible forces that account for the unification of this particular multiplicity. Consciousness cannot perceive such imperceptible forces, and therefore must contribute more to its experience of things than the act of perception. Knowledge requires not only perception, but also understanding the imperceptible forces that express themselves in the perceptible qualities of things. The third shape of consciousness identified by Hegel is therefore discussed in a section entitled "Force and Understanding".

"Force and Understanding" unfolds in precisely the same way as "Sense-Certainty" and "Perception": the constitutive assumptions of the shape of consciousness under consideration are identified; examination of those assumptions makes explicit their implicit contradictions; and these contradictions are then resolved by the transition to yet another shape of consciousness.

At this stage, consciousness claims to know its objects in virtue of understanding the imperceptible forces that explain appearances. The central contradiction that emerges is that the positing of imperceptible forces serves only to redescribe, rather than truly to explain, that which appears in perception. Positing "the force of gravity", for example, does not help consciousness understand *why* massive bodies are attracted to each other, but simply gives a name to this observable fact. Yet again, Hegel concludes, consciousness proves not to know that which it claims to know in the way that it claims to know it.

The move from "Force and Understanding" to the next shape of consciousness marks an important transition from the first major section of the *Phenomenology*, entitled "Consciousness", to the second, which is called "Self-Consciousness". "Consciousness" includes the first three shapes of consciousness: "Sense-Certainty", "Perception" and

"Force and Understanding". These three shapes of consciousness fall under the same general heading because, despite their differences, they all share the same basic assumption that knowing depends upon the subject accurately representing the object as it truly is in-itself. In the course of "Force and Understanding", however, it becomes evident that the object in-itself cannot be meaningfully distinguished from what the subject understands the object to be. With this realization, consciousness comes to regard its object as a reflection of itself, and thus experiences itself in and through its experience of its object. This reflexive form of experience is examined in "Self-Consciousness".

"Self-Consciousness" contains well-known analyses of desire, recognition, the master and slave, Stoicism, scepticism, and unhappy consciousness. All of these are "shapes of consciousness" in the sense that they retain the fundamental assumption, which is operative throughout the *Phenomenology* until the standpoint of reason is attained in the final chapter, that knowing is a relation of a conscious subject to an object other than itself. They belong to "Self-Consciousness" rather than to "Consciousness", however, because they all assume that the subject does not depend upon objects to determine the contents of its thinking, but rather determines independently its own thoughts and what objects are to be for it.

At the outset of "Self-Consciousness", the subject tries to demonstrate its independence from objects, and its capacity to determine what they are, by literally destroying them; consciousness consumes things in order to satisfy its own desires. By eating a piece of cake, for example, it reveals that the confection is not merely a perceptible thing with properties governed by imperceptible forces, but also a means to satisfy the hunger of consciousness itself. In consuming objects, however, desiring consciousness ultimately demonstrates that it is in fact dependent upon them, because without an object to consume the subject cannot experience its own independence, which is what it claims to know to be the truth. Desiring consciousness thus literally needs to have its cake and eat it too, because it can see its independence reflected only in the presence of the object, but as long as the object remains present, consciousness has failed to demonstrate that it is truly independent. The result is a consumptive frenzy in which consciousness repeatedly destroys one object only to replace it with another, and thus succeeds only in reiterating and reinforcing its dependence upon things other than itself. Relief from this performative contradiction requires consciousness to experience an object that confirms, rather than threatens, its own independence, and which therefore need not be destroyed. Such an object must itself manifest the independence that consciousness attributes to itself, and therefore "Desire" gives way to "Recognition", in which the self-conscious subject receives acknowledgement of its independence from another self-conscious subject.

"Self-Consciousness" proceeds – via the same sort of logical necessitation that drives the developments within "Consciousness" – from "Desire" and "Recognition" through a series of stages that culminates in "Unhappy Consciousness", which then gives way to "Reason", the third and final major section of the *Phenomenology*. Throughout "Consciousness", the prevailing assumption is that the subject seeks knowledge by conforming its thinking to the truth of an independent object. In "Self-Consciousness", this assumption is overturned and replaced by the assumption that the object is what the independent subject determines it to be. "Reason" is defined by the replacement of this assumption with the certainty that what the subject determines the object to be is also what the object itself truly is.

"Reason" begins with a shape of consciousness that is recognizably Kantian, described in terms of its claim that thinking and objectivity are both structured by the same categories. This claim is contradicted, however, by the assumption of consciousness that the objects of its experience must be given to it empirically, which limits the validity of the categories to appearances and precludes any knowledge of objects themselves. The examination of "Reason" therefore continues – it ultimately comprises a full two-thirds of the text of the *Phenomenology* – describing a series of increasingly complex shapes of consciousness that emerge from the attempt to uphold without contradiction the subject's claim to know the rational structure of the object itself. This series of shapes arrives at "Spirit" (a major subsection within "Reason") when consciousness takes its object to be other self-consciously rational agents like itself. "Spirit" – which contains the famous discussions of Antigone, absolute freedom and terror, conscience, and the beautiful soul – then gives way to "Religion" (another major sub-section within "Reason") when consciousness becomes certain that rationality is embodied not only in self-conscious agents, but also in being itself. Finally, "Religion" becomes "Absolute Knowing" when consciousness no longer imagines being as a transcendent entity, but instead recognizes that the rational structure of being is immanent in, and accessible to, the thinking of the self-consciousness agent.

"Absolute Knowing" does not describe a new shape of consciousness because, for the first time in the *Phenomenology*, the dualistic assumption that defines consciousness is no longer operative. The contradictions implicit in that assumption have, Hegel claims, led with logical necessity to the standpoint of reason. Having achieved this standpoint, the subject finally knows that knowing does not involve the attempt to gain access to an external object, but rather involves articulating the rational structure of its own thought, which is at the same time the rational structure of being. The subject at this standpoint, in other words, is prepared to undertake systematic philosophy, which Hegel commences to do in his next work, *Science of Logic*.

Hegel's *Phenomenology* is an immense and infuriatingly complicated work, and we have only skimmed its barest outline. The success of the work depends entirely, however, on the details, for Hegel's claim that the internal contradictions of consciousness lead inexorably to the standpoint of reason is true only if *all* of the transitions in the *Phenomenology* have the logical necessity that Hegel attributes to them. If even a single one of these transitions is driven by anything other than logical necessity (and cannot be made good by appropriate revisions), then the *Phenomenology* fails to demonstrate that consciousness can avoid self-contradiction only by adopting the standpoint of reason. Although many readers have found the *Phenomenology* to be a rich and rewarding text, relatively few have been convinced that the project succeeds on its own terms at every moment.

Even if it should prove, however, that the *Phenomenology* is not sufficient to bring consciousness to reason, it is important to remember that Hegel himself does not regard the *Phenomenology* as a prerequisite for this achievement. The standpoint of reason, he holds, can be reached by anyone who is willing to suspend his own assumptions about the relation of thinking to objectivity. And the *Phenomenology* may, even if it fails to be completely convincing, prove useful in encouraging this willingness: "For it brings about a state of despair about all the so-called natural ideas, thoughts, and opinions, regardless of whether they are called one's own or someone else's, ideas with which the consciousness that sets about the examination [of truth] *straight away* is still filled and hampered, so that it is, in fact, incapable of carrying out what it wants to undertake" (*PhenS*: 50). By subjecting the assumptions of ordinary consciousness to rigorous sceptical scrutiny, that is, the *Phenomenology* aims to weaken the reader's confidence in them, and in so doing make him increasingly open to joining Hegel in the attempt to determine the truth by means of systematic philosophy.

Systematic philosophy

In the very first sentence of the Introduction to the *Encyclopedia*, Hegel writes: "Philosophy lacks the advantage, which the other sciences enjoy, of being able to *presuppose* its *objects* as given immediately by representation. And, with regard to its beginning and advance, it cannot *presuppose* the *method* of cognition as one that is already accepted" (*EL*: 24). The requirement that philosophy not presuppose a particular subject matter, conceptual scheme or method follows from the dual awareness that the truth claims philosophy advances are only as secure as the assumptions from which they follow, and that any foundational assumption is always subject to challenge. The attempt to justify such an assumption necessarily leads to either an infinite regress, a vicious circle, or an exhausted admission that no further justification is available (this is the Agrippan trilemma, posed by the ancient sceptics for whom Hegel has such deep respect). Since these alternatives can provide at best conditional assurance that the conclusions advanced are indeed true, they are inadequate bases for philosophy, which is a distinctive discipline or science in virtue of its quest for the unconditional or necessary truth that defines rational cognition.

A truly modern, rational, self-critical philosophy must begin, then, without any foundational presuppositions. At the outset it is impossible to say what philosophy will prove to be about, or how it will proceed. Hegel insists, in quasi-Cartesian fashion, that philosophy can begin only with the immediate and incorrigible fact of thinking itself. Unlike Descartes, however, Hegel neither infers his own existence from the fact of thinking, nor asserts that his mind is innately furnished with any particular ideas. Instead, as he puts in the *Encyclopedia Logic*: "When thinking is to begin, we have nothing but thought in its pure lack of determination" (*EL*: 137).

Philosophy is thus, Hegel contends, an examination of the indeterminate immediacy – or "being" – of thought. In order for this examination to be strictly rational, philosophers conducting it must set aside their own particular interests and opinions in order to let the objective nature of thought emerge. Hegel therefore understands philosophy to be thought's *self*-determination, a determination necessarily free from the influence of objects external to thought, and from the influence of subjective thinkers. As such, philosophy must be the self-development of a self-contained totality of thoughts, for if it failed to be self-developing and self-contained, philosophy would be externally influenced and so would fail to be self-determining. A self-developing and self-contained totality is what Hegel calls a system, and thus he concludes that "systematic derivation . . . [is] the very thing that is indispensable for a scientific philosophy" (*EL*: 1).

For Hegel, then, philosophy is systematic philosophy, and systematic philosophy is the self-development of thought. It begins with completely indeterminate thought, and then follows this thought as it develops into other, more determinate thoughts. As he writes in *Introduction to the Lectures on the History of Philosophy*: "This process involves making distinctions, and by looking more closely at the character of the distinctions which arise – and in a process something different necessarily arises – we can visualize the movement as development" (*ILHP*: 70–71). As long as the philosophers who record the self-development of thought successfully abstain from incorporating any extraneous distinctions of their own devising, the process results in the articulation of the determinations necessary to thought itself, those constitutive of its own being, which Hegel refers to, collectively, as "the concept".

Following Aristotle and Kant, Hegel calls the necessary determinations of thought that systematic philosophy articulates *categories*; as the form of thought itself, they are the concepts that make possible all conceptual activity whatsoever. The categories are assumed and used in everything we think and do, but typically without our being aware of them. Hegel describes the totality of categories as

> the net which holds together all the concrete material which occupies us in our action and endeavor. But this net and its knots are sunk in our ordinary consciousness beneath numerous layers of stuff. This stuff comprises our known interests and the objects that are before our minds, while the universal threads of the net remain out of sight and are not explicitly made the subject of our reflection. (*ILHP*: 28)

He also gives several examples of the categories and their everyday, implicit use: "Everyone possesses and uses the wholly abstract category of *being*. The sun *is* in the sky; these grapes *are* ripe, and so on *ad infinitum*. Or, in a higher sphere of education, we proceed to the relation of cause and effect, force and its manifestation, etc. All our knowledge and ideas are entwined with metaphysics like this" (*ibid.*: 27). Hegel concludes that "the task and business of philosophy [is] . . . to display . . . the thought-out and known necessity of the specific categories" (*ibid.*: 21–2).

Hegel's own philosophical system is the result of his efforts to complete this task that he understands to define philosophy. The *Logic* begins with the simplest thought – that of indeterminate immediacy, or "being" – and attempts to develop all, and only, those determinations that it implicitly contains. The course of this development generates an increasingly refined understanding of what it is to be, and Hegel claims that it ultimately leads to the knowledge that to be is to exist in a form other than that of thought, which is to be a spatiotemporal or natural being. The *Philosophy of Nature* then begins with the simplest conception of spatiotemporal being, and attempts to develop all, and only, those determinations that it implicitly contains. The course of this development generates an increasingly refined understanding of what it is to be natural, and Hegel claims that it ultimately leads to the knowledge that to actualize all of the capacities inherent in nature is to be capable of thinking, which is to be what Hegel refers to as a "spiritual" being. The *Philosophy of Spirit* then begins with the simplest conception of thinking being, and attempts to develop all, and only, those determinations that it implicitly contains. The course of this development generates an increasingly refined understanding of what spiritual being involves, and Hegel claims that it ultimately leads to the knowledge that to be fully spiritual is to be a cognitive, moral, social, political, aesthetic, religious and philosophical being.

Hegel's insistence that scientific philosophy cannot tolerate the introduction of extra-systematic elements of any kind applies not only to the *Logic*, but also to the *Philosophy of Nature* and the *Philosophy of Spirit*. Indeed, Hegel emphasizes that although it might seem that "the title *Encyclopedia* could leave room for a lesser degree of rigor in the scientific method, and for the compilation of external parts . . . the nature of the matter entails that logical coherence must remain fundamental" (*EL*: 4). The preservation of strict systematicity is precisely what distinguishes the *philosophical* consideration of nature and spirit from the treatment they receive in other disciplines. Consequently, "the whole of philosophy genuinely forms *one* science" (*ibid.*: 39), and this single "science is the self-development of the concept", which requires one "to take up the development of the concept, and submit one's thinking, indeed, one's whole heart and mind, to the logical necessity of the concept" (*ibid.*: 16–17).

Figure 6.1 provides a map of Hegel's philosophical system.

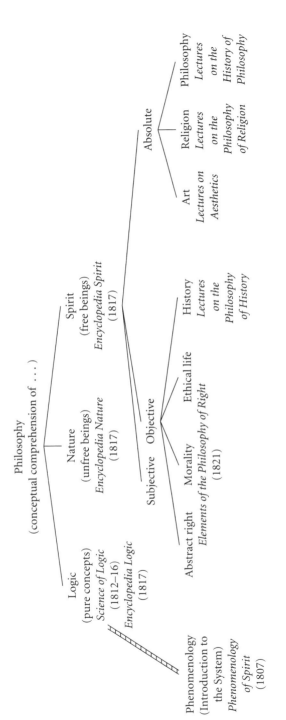

Figure 6.1 Hegel's philosophical system

The structure of being: the Science of Logic

Hegel's *Science of Logic* is an entirely different enterprise from the formal analysis of arguments with which most philosophy students are familiar. Hegel calls the first part of his system "logic" because it articulates the being of *thought*. At the same time, he conceives of it as ontology because it articulates the *being* of thought. The *Science of Logic* claims to articulate, at one and the same time, the necessary determinations that are constitutive of both thought and actuality. Hegel thus unabashedly shares Spinoza's view that "the order and coherence of ideas (the subjective) is the same as the coherence and order of things (the objective)" (*D*: 166). "*Logic*", he writes, "coincides with *metaphysics*, with the science of *things* grasped in *thoughts*" (*EL*: 56).

Hegel is unabashed about holding this view because he regards it as more fully critical, and therefore rational, than the alternative position that sceptically distinguishes between our representations of being and being itself. Although this sceptical position, referred to by Hegel as the standpoint of the understanding, prides itself on its critical restraint, Hegel insists that it uncritically assumes more than does his own presuppositionless philosophy. The standpoint of the understanding presupposes that there is a gap between the thinking subject and the object of his thoughts, and thus that being might in truth be other than the subject thinks it to be. Presuppositionless philosophy, however, assumes nothing whatsoever about subjectivity or objectivity, and thus assumes neither that there is a gap between them that must be bridged, nor that being might be other than the being of which thought is immediately aware. Presuppositionless philosophy begins with the indeterminate being of thought, and nothing else, and its unfolding of the determinations implicit in this thought is therefore necessarily logical (an account of how being must be thought) and ontological (an account of what being must be).

Although Hegel regards Spinozistic ontology as more genuinely critical than Kantian epistemology, he breaks with Spinoza by refusing to presuppose a determinate conception of being or substance as the foundation of philosophy: "No philosophical beginning could look worse than to begin with a definition as Spinoza does" (*D*: 105). Kant was right, Hegel believes, to demand that philosophy determine the categories of thinking scientifically, by means of an investigation of the nature of thinking itself, rather than "rhapsodically" (after the fashion of Aristotle) or by stipulation (after the fashion of Spinoza). Hegel also believes, however, that Kant himself uncritically assumed not only the existence of a gap between thinking and being, but also that the categories of thought can be derived from a consideration of the forms of judgement. Presuppositionless philosophy cannot assume that thinking is equivalent to judging, but rather must allow the nature of thought to emerge from the consideration of nothing but the indeterminate immediacy of thinking itself.

When philosophy does allow thought to determine itself without presuppositions, Hegel argues, it reveals the falsity of yet another uncritical assumption made by Kant and the other representatives of the standpoint of the understanding. This standpoint is characterized, according to Hegel, by the drawing of sharp and fixed distinctions between not only subjectivity and objectivity but also many particular conceptual pairs. Understanding assumes, for example, that to be infinite is not to be finite. Hegel believes, however, that the development of thought within presuppositionless philosophy reveals that this conceptual distinction (and many others) should not be regarded as absolute: the infinite proves to be inseparable from, and manifested only within, the finite.

Hegel's point is not that philosophy cannot make distinctions (indeed, he regards the task of philosophy as nothing but the making of distinctions), but rather that careful examination reveals the distinctions that are necessarily implicit in the being of thought to be self-overcoming, or dialectical, in nature: "Dialectic . . . is the *immanent* transcending, in which the one-sidedness and restrictedness of the determinations of the understanding displays itself as what it is, i.e., as their negation" (*EL*: 128). It is only in virtue of this dialectical character that thought can be *self*-determining, developing of its own accord from one determination to the subsequent determinations that are implicit in it, rather than being dependent upon the thinking subject to define, distinguish, and relate particular concepts. "Hence", Hegel concludes, "the dialectical constitutes the moving soul of scientific progression, and it is the principle through which alone *immanent coherence and necessity* enter into the content of science" (*ibid.*).

Hegel does not presuppose that thought and being are dialectical. But he refuses to join the standpoint of the understanding in presupposing that they are not. He begins his *Science of Logic*, and with it his philosophical system, with only the indeterminate immediacy of thought and an open mind. Hegel resolves to consider only being itself, in order to determine what, if anything, it necessarily is to be.

The *Science of Logic* opens with a sentence fragment that reflects the paucity of the only beginning available to presuppositionless philosophy:

"Being, pure being, without any further determination" (*SL*: 82). Hegel then elaborates: "If any determination or content were posited, which could be distinguished within being or distinguish it from an other, being would not be held fast in its purity. It is pure indeterminacy and emptiness" (*ibid*.). Immediate being must be indeterminate because any determination would violate its immediacy. As indeterminate, however, "being . . . is in fact *nothing*, and neither more nor less than *nothing*" (*ibid*.). The pure indeterminacy of nothing itself immediately *is*, however, otherwise it would not *be* indeterminate: "Nothing is, therefore, the same determination, or rather absence of determination, and thus altogether the same as, pure *being*" (*ibid*.).

In the span of one short paragraph, Hegel concludes that pure immediacy and pure indeterminacy, being and nothing, are logically inseparable: neither can be what it is without the other. The attempt to think *only* immediate being is a failure, because to think immediate being is also, necessarily, to think the indeterminacy that is nothing. But the attempt to think *only* indeterminate nothingness is equally hopeless, because to think indeterminate nothingness is also, necessarily, to think the immediacy that is being. The first result of systematic philosophy is thus the realization that neither being nor nothing is self-sufficient: each is what it is only in virtue of vanishing into the other. Being is the movement from immediacy to indeterminate nothingness, and nothing is the movement from indeterminacy to immediate being: "Their truth is", Hegel concludes, "this movement of the immediate vanishing of the one in the other: *becoming*" (*SL*: 83).

The failure to think immediate being, because being necessarily involves nothing and becoming, can also be construed as a success, however, for it provides the first instance of the dialectical self-determination of thought. Immediate, indeterminate being has proven itself to be mediated and determinate.

Although this initial result might seem underwhelming, it has significant implications. First, it demonstrates that presuppositionless, philosophical science is possible, because starting with immediate being and refraining from the incorporation of extraneous determinations does not consign philosophy to repetition of the same empty term. Second, it shows that scientific philosophy does not proceed by means of a formulaic positing of thesis, antithesis and synthesis. This method, which was practised by Fichte, is often falsely attributed to Hegel, but in fact it has nothing to do with the development of his philosophical system. Third, it repudiates Schelling's insistence that the absolute, by definition, excludes all mediation and determination, and therefore lies beyond the reach of articulate thought. The opening of Hegel's *Logic* constitutes an argument that a purely immediate and indeterminate absolute is logically impossible, because being itself is necessarily determinate. In the Preface to the *Phenomenology* Hegel chastises Schelling (without mentioning him by name) for failing to grasp this point, writing that "it is just this that is rejected [by Schelling] with horror, as if absolute cognition were being surrendered when more is made of mediation than in simply saying [as Schelling does] that it is nothing absolute, and is completely absent in the absolute" (*PhenS*: 11). The initial moves in the self-development of thought thus establish, according to Hegel, both the impossibility of an absolute that transcends all determination, and the actuality of absolute cognition that delivers a determinate conception of being.

It is nonetheless true, however, that saying only that to be is necessarily to be determinate is not to say very much. Hegel's *Science of Logic* goes on, not surprisingly, to say quite a bit more. From the initial determinations of "being", "nothing" and "becoming", the *Logic* follows the immanent dialectic of thought to demonstrate, according to Hegel, that to be is necessarily to be (among other things) qualitative and quantitative, to have an essence that manifests itself in a variety of appearances, and to have a conceptual or rational structure. The *Logic* finally concludes that rationally structured being necessarily exists in a form other than that of pure thought, and is therefore spatiotemporal or natural being. With this result the *Logic* gives way to the *Philosophy of Nature*.

The structure of spatiotemporal being: the Philosophy of Nature

The *Philosophy of Nature* is the second of the three main parts of Hegel's system. Because the entire system forms a single science, defined by a strictly immanent conceptual development that permits no recourse to any extra-systematic elements, the *Philosophy of Nature* is not absolutely distinct from the *Logic*, but rather necessarily an outgrowth of it: the *Philosophy of Nature* simply picks up the dialectic of being where the *Logic* leaves off, and goes on to determine what it is to be natural.

The transition from the *Logic* to the *Philosophy of Nature* reveals that Hegel is a realist about the natural world. The *Logic* culminates by claiming that being has a rational conceptual structure, and that rationally structured being must exist in extra-conceptual form. Hegel believes, in other words, "that the so-called mere concept is no such thing, but rather essentially its own actualization" (note appended to the first paragraph of the *Elements of the Philosophy of Right* in 1822). Hegel holds that the determinate content of the concept is actualized in the extra-conceptual realm of space and time; he is thus committed to the realistic position that the natural world exists in a form other than thought and independently of thinking subjects.

Hegel is also, however, an absolute idealist, because he believes that nature has a conceptual structure that thinking can comprehend. He refers to the actualized concept as the "absolute idea" because the determinations it includes are ab-solved from the distinction between pure thought and actuality in virtue of being constitutive of them both. He therefore takes the transition from the *Logic* to the *Philosophy of Nature* to demonstrate not only that the rational is actual, but also that the actual is rational. The *Philosophy of Nature* provides absolute knowledge of the natural world, Hegel claims, because the necessary determinations implicit in the concept of nature are also the necessary determinations of nature itself.

Hegel's position – which might be called "realistic absolute idealism" – must be sharply distinguished from those of Kant and Fichte. Kant, like Hegel, acknowledges the existence of an extra-conceptual realm of objectivity, but denies that the concepts we necessarily employ in our experience of this realm can be known to structure nature itself. Transcendental idealism holds, for example, that space and time are forms through which *we* intuit the world, and that cause and effect are concepts by means of which *we* understand the world. Hegel, by contrast, holds that nature itself is spatiotemporal, and that spatiotemporal beings themselves interact causally. Fichte is even more remote from Hegel, since he regards objectivity as having been posited by the conscious subject, and therefore denies the existence of a realm independent of thought.

Hegel's *Philosophy of Nature* must also be sharply distinguished from empirical natural science. As a part of the presuppositionless articulation of the truth of being, the *Philosophy of Nature* is a strictly *a priori* enterprise. It cannot proceed by means of observing and reflecting upon the natural world, nor can it incorporate the results of the observations and reflections carried out by empirical scientists. The *Philosophy of Nature* must, if it is to meet the standard of rational cognition, restrict itself to articulating all and only those determinations that are implicit in the concept of natural being.

Hegel acknowledges that attention to empirical phenomena, and a desire to understand them, are what lead us to philosophy in the first place. He also emphasizes that "in the progress of philosophical knowledge, we must not only give an account of the object *as determined by its concept*, but we must also name the *empirical* appearance corresponding to it, and we must show that the appearance does, in fact, correspond to its concept" (*PN*: 6–7). So it is not surprising, and even to be expected, that Hegel introduces numerous empirical terms and examples throughout the *Philosophy of Nature*, as he seeks to ascertain the extent of the correspondence between various observed phenomena and the necessary determinations of natural being. What Hegel cannot do, and claims he does not do, is allow the introduction of such empirical terms and examples to affect the further conceptual unfolding of the system.

Hegel's *a priori* account of nature is not intended to be a substitute for the work of empirical natural science. Indeed, Hegel's systematic philosophy leads to the conclusion that empirical science is irreplaceable, because natural beings are necessarily subject to contingency. This means that no empirical phenomenon can be purely rational. All empirical phenomena have contingent features that are opaque to systematic philosophy and can only be determined by the careful observation and reflection that characterize the best empirical science.

Hegel is thus quite clear about the fact that there is a limit to what systematic philosophy can tell us about the natural world. Systematic philosophy provides rational cognition, or knowledge of the determinations that are constitutive of nature. Because one of these determinations is contingency, however, every natural phenomenon necessarily exceeds philosophy's grasp to some degree. Hegel writes, "nature in its manifestations does not hold fast to the concept. Its wealth of forms is an absence of definiteness and the play of contingency" (*PN*: 299), and this "sets limits to philosophy and [makes it] quite improper to expect the concept to comprehend – or as it is said, construe or deduce – these contingent products of nature" (*ibid.*: 23).

For example, Hegel believes that systematic philosophy can determine that natural being is necessarily material, but cannot predict the particular forms matter will take. Matter contingently takes all kinds of forms, the determination of which lies entirely outside the scope of systematic philosophy. Hegel makes this particular point explicitly in an early response to the criticism of one of his contemporaries, Wilhelm Krug, who challenged Hegel to deduce his pen, and thereby demonstrated a complete misunderstanding of the limited aspirations of *a priori* reason: "He cannot help understanding [philosophy] like the most vulgar man in the street, and demanding that every dog and cat shall be deduced – yes and why not his own pen too . . . If Mr. Krug had even the vaguest notion of the [task of reason], how could it occur to him to demand from philosophy the deduction of his pen?" ("How the Ordinary Human Understanding Takes Philosophy", 298–9).

Hegel's philosophy is thus not "totalizing" in any of the ways that it is sometimes taken to be. His system is complete in the sense that it claims to fully articulate the determinations inherent to the initial thought of indeterminacy. Being complete in this sense does not imply, however, that there is no extra-conceptual form of existence, or even that the system includes all conceptual determinations. The system includes only those determinations that are necessary to the comprehension of being, and explicitly excludes those contingencies that exceed the determinacy of the concept. The system claims to comprehend the rational aspects of empirical phenomena, but remains resolutely and necessarily mute about their contingent features.

Hegel's philosophical aspirations are therefore significantly more limited than those of Fichte and Schelling, both of whom thought that a perfected philosophy should, at least in principle, be able to provide an exhaustive account of every feature of our experience. Hegel rejects this view on the ground that rational cognition is intrinsically limited to necessary truths and the natural world is intrinsically full of contingent matters of fact.

The limitations of systematic philosophy and the irreplaceability of empirical science do not mean, however, that there is no place for an *a priori* account of nature. Hegel's position is that such a philosophical approach is indispensable to providing rational cognition of the natural world, by determining the characteristics that are constitutive of its very being. This is something that empirical science cannot do, because observation and induction can reveal only what happens to be the case, but not what necessarily must be the case. Hegel therefore regards the philosophy of nature and empirical natural science as complementary. Systematic philosophy determines, for example, that nature is necessarily material, mechanical, chemical and organic, and empirical science studies the particular entities, mechanisms, chemical reactions and organisms that happen to exist.

The *a priori* investigation of the natural world conducted in the *Philosophy of Nature* ultimately leads, Hegel argues, to the conclusion that being that actualizes all of the capacities inherent in nature is not only mechanical, chemical and organic, but also thinking and free. Such being remains natural, but it is not *merely* natural, because the merely natural is that which "exhibits no freedom in its existence, but only *necessity* and *contingency*" (*PN*: 17). Natural beings that are also free, in virtue of their capacity to think, Hegel refers to as "spiritual", and thus the third and final part of his system is the *Philosophy of Spirit*.

The structure of free being: the Philosophy of Spirit

The *Philosophy of Spirit* takes up where the *Philosophy of Nature* leaves off, and proceeds to determine what it means to be spiritual or free. It begins by conceiving of spiritual beings as those that are not merely natural. This should not be taken to mean that spiritual beings are supernatural, for on Hegel's account everything spiritual is also natural. For example, human beings (which are spiritual in Hegel's sense) are also animals (which are natural). But our animality cannot account for our freedom. On the contrary, in Hegel's view it is the fact that humans are not merely natural, but also spiritual, or capable of thinking, that gives us a freedom that animals lack.

Hegel finds a conceptual contradiction in this initial understanding of the spiritual, however: spiritual beings are conceived as free in virtue of being not merely natural, but as long as spiritual beings are conceived as merely not-natural they cannot be free, because to be not-natural is to relate to nature as something external, alien and restrictive. Hegel thus rejects Kant's belief that freedom involves the transcendence of nature. Even if such transcendence were possible, Hegel argues, it would not in fact be truly liberating. True freedom, he concludes, depends upon thinking beings achieving a reconciliation with the merely natural world from which they differ.

The entire *Philosophy of Spirit* is devoted to revising the conception of spiritual beings until they are understood to be reconciled with, or at home in, the natural world while preserving their difference from it. At each stage in this process, spiritual beings are conceived in a way that is thought to be adequate to their freedom. But, Hegel argues, each of these conceptions, except for the last, proves to be self-contradictory: spiritual beings are thought both to be free, and to be subject to external limitations on their freedom. Such contradictions force further revisions that overcome the specific externalities to which spiritual beings have been shown to be subject. This process, and with it the *Philosophy of Spirit*, ends only when a conception of spiritual beings has been developed in which they are truly self-determining and free.

The conceptual development that comprises the *Philosophy of Spirit* takes place in three parts, which Hegel calls subjective, objective and absolute spirit. All three are presented in condensed form in the final third of the *Encyclopedia*. More detailed expositions of the last two are also available. Objective spirit is presented in the *Philosophy of Right* and the lectures on the philosophy of history. Absolute spirit is presented in the lectures on aesthetics, religion and the history of philosophy. "Subjective spirit", "objective spirit" and "absolute spirit" do not refer to mysterious entities, but rather to a sequence of progressively adequate conceptions of the freedom of thinking beings.

In subjective spirit, thinking beings are conceived as seeking to overcome their alienation from nature by coming to know the objective world. Through knowing, Hegel claims, the subject is able to "liberate the intrinsically rational object from the form of contingency, singleness, and externality which at first clings to it, and thereby free *itself* from the connection with something which is for it an other" (*PhilS*: 182). This is accomplished, for example, when it is demonstrated that certain natural phenomena behave in such a way that they can be subsumed under scientific laws. In this accomplishment, rational subjects recognize that the objects of their cognition – the law-like natural phenomena – are rational too, and thereby achieve a degree of reconciliation with them.

But the reconciliation with the natural world that the activity of knowing provides is only partial, Hegel argues, so in this activity the subject remains incompletely free. The reconciliation is partial because the natural phenomena that the subject experiences are fundamentally independent of the mental activity for which they supply the content. Consequently, nature remains alien to the subject, even when thinking successfully represents the objective world with which it is confronted.

Since freedom is compromised by the dependence of knowing on an externally given content, spiritual beings must be reconceived as the source of the contents of their own activities. The subject that is understood to set "only itself for its goal, becomes *will* which . . . does not begin with an isolated object externally given, but with something it knows to be its own" (*PhilS*: 28). This transition from knowing to willing initiates the transition from subjective to objective spirit.

The *Philosophy of Right* is an account of the freedom available through willing. It develops a series of four main conceptions of the will, which are presented in the four main sections of the book: the introduction, abstract right, morality and ethical life. Each conception is initially thought to be adequate to the freedom of the willing subject, but upon examination is shown to suffer from limitations built into the very features that define it. This forces the will to be reconceived in a way that preserves the freedom established in the prior conception while overcoming its limitations.

In the introduction to the *Philosophy of Right*, the will is conceived as the faculty of choice. As such, it is understood to have three basic moments or aspects. First, there is the moment of abstraction, or indeterminacy: the will is free because it can abstract from any particular choice, because it is not bound to pursue any particular interest. Second, there is the moment of determination: the will is free because it can determine itself to a particular choice, because it can choose to pursue a particular interest. Third, there is the moment of remaining abstract in determination: the will is free because even when it has determined itself to a particular choice, it can again abstract from it. This last moment means that even though every determination or choice the will makes belongs to it, the will is never defined by any particular choice it makes; an important part of this freedom is the realization that the will has an identity that persists through an ongoing temporal process of determining itself to, and abstracting itself from, particular choices and interests. Thus freedom of the will, understood as freedom of choice, is essentially freedom as possibility: the will is free because it is possible for it to pursue or not to pursue any of its chosen interests.

But the willing subject, as initially conceived, suffers from two significant limitations. First, even though the subject is free to pursue its chosen interests, it is not responsible for what those interests are. Its interests are merely "the *drives, desires, and inclinations* by which the will finds itself naturally determined" (*PR*: 45). Freedom of choice consists in the will's ability to resolve itself to satisfy a particular drive in a particular way, but does not entail that it satisfy one drive rather than another. As a result, the "free" choices of the will are actually determined by the relative strengths of natural inclinations, over which the will has no control. Second, the willing subject is still confronted by nature as by an independent, external world that may or may not conform to its drives, desires and inclinations. This remains the case as long as "that which is willed . . . is still only a content belonging to self-consciousness, an unaccomplished end" (*ibid.*: 55). To become free, the subject must overcome both of these limitations: it must take responsibility for the purposes it chooses to adopt, and it must accomplish those purposes in the natural world.

In abstract right, therefore, the willing subject is conceived as being committed to willing not simply whatever it happens naturally to desire, but its own freedom. The first step in willing its own freedom is overcoming its alienation from the natural world, which the subject seeks to do by claiming some aspect of the world as its own. The first stage of its effort is the acquisition of property, in which the subject identifies itself not only with its ability to choose, but with an object of its choice as well. Property objectifies the will by subordinating a concrete thing in the world to the purposes of the willing subject.

Hegel thus holds that property ownership is a necessary condition of freedom and, as such, must be established and secured as a universal right. But property remains an inadequate form of freedom because the choice to own *this* piece of property is still not a product of the will. It is essential to the free will that it own property, but it is not essential that it own any particular piece of property, so the preference for one piece of property over another cannot come from the will itself, and therefore no piece of property with which the will happens to identify can be a truly sufficient objectification of its freedom. Freedom therefore requires that the willing subject sometimes alienate and exchange its property. Failing to do so, it would become permanently identified with decisions that did not stem from its will, and would not be fully free.

The establishment of the universal right to own and exchange property depends upon willing subjects reciprocally recognizing each other as free beings entitled to all the rights that freedom entails. Hegel thus concludes that, paradoxically, increased freedom requires increased interdependence. The freedom of a person is now understood to reside not only in the property he owns, but also in the contracts he enters into, and in his respect for and performance of the obligations contained in those contracts.

The great significance of this development is that it is now possible for an individual's pursuit of his chosen interests to conflict with the requirements of his freedom. For example, a person might get the property he wants by violating the mutual respect of rights that contracts require (perhaps by defrauding his counterpart). Freedom thus depends upon willing subjects placing the upholding of universal rights above the satisfaction of their own particular interests. Such subjects display what Hegel refers to as a moral will, which is considered in the next main section of the *Philosophy of Right*, entitled "Morality".

Morality examines the conception of the will that emerges logically from the contradictions implicit in abstract right, but Hegel regards this conception as having been represented in the history of philosophy by Kant and Fichte. According to this conception, freedom requires the willing subject to abstract from all its particular interests, in order to strive to fulfil its universal duties for their own sake. The subject must therefore be able to determine the specific duties that have an unconditional claim on all free beings, which it tries to do on the basis of the principle that intentional maxims are permissible only if they can be universally adopted without self-contradiction. Hegel argues, however, that this Kantian criterion is insufficient to determine the particular duties that are in fact required by freedom; he concludes that the moral will ultimately has recourse only to its own conscience to distinguish between right and wrong. This is Fichte's position, which Hegel regards as reducible to "the assertion that what [the particular moral will] knows and wills is *truly* right and duty" (*PR*: 164). This self-righteous certainty that it knows the good makes the moral will capable of evil, Hegel contends, because it entails an absolute commitment to acting upon the dictates of conscience while lacking an objective standard by means of which to evaluate them. The moral will is therefore not the objectification of freedom, but rather a perversion of it in which the universal content of the good is subjectively determined via the judgements of an individual.

Ethical life, the final main section of the *Philosophy of Right*, attempts to resolve the contradictions of morality by uniting the dispositions of the individual subject with that which is objectively right. In ethical life, freedom is objectified in communal customs and institutions "that are not something *alien* to the subject. On the contrary, the subject bears *spiritual witness* to them as to *its own essence*, in which it has its *self-awareness* and lives as in its element which is not distinct from itself" (*PR*: 191).

Hegel's point is not that all customs and institutions are automatically liberating. He is well aware that the conditions that happen to prevail in a particular time and place can be irrational, unjustified and oppressive. Precisely for this reason, his account of ethical life, which comprises fully half of the *Philosophy of Right*, is devoted to a determination of the specific customs and institutions that are essential to freedom.

Hegel attempts to discriminate between those customs and institutions that are necessary to liberation, those that are inessential yet harmless, and those that are positively unjust. Such discrimination depends upon the ability to specify the determinate content of freedom in order to be able to make competent evaluations of current conditions. And such determinate specification of the content of freedom depends, Hegel argues, upon a systematic exposition that takes nothing for granted, which is precisely his philosophical project. It is therefore that project, and only that project, Hegel contends, that enables philosophy to be "*its own time comprehended in thoughts*" (*PR*: 21), which it is in virtue of grasping both the extent to which contemporary institutions are rational, and the particular contemporary conditions that are intolerable. Presuppositionless systematic philosophy thus does not serve the uncritical rationalization of the status quo, but is rather the necessary presupposition of a genuinely rational critical theory of historical and contemporary institutions.

The three main sections of ethical life treat the family, civil society and the state, providing analyses of the social, economic and political conditions of liberation. Hegel claims to establish, among other things, universal rights to marry, to work, and to be represented by a government that is concerned with the common good.

The ultimate conclusion of the *Philosophy of Right* is that willing subjects are free to the extent that they live in societies that succeed in establishing and securing truly rational laws, customs and institutions. Such societies result from the efforts of thinking beings to transform the initially independent objectivity of nature into a world that reflects the demands of freedom, and in which they are therefore at home. As Hegel puts it: "in the *ethical realm* . . . the principle of freedom has penetrated into the worldly realm itself, and . . . the worldly, because it has been thus conformed to the concept, reason, and eternal truth, is freedom that has become concrete and will that is rational" (*LPR*: III, 341–2). He therefore concludes that ethical life is "the perfection of objective spirit" (*PhilS*: 253).

But Hegel does not regard the perfection of objective spirit as the perfection or truth of spirit *simpliciter*. He argues that spiritual beings remain burdened, even as they are conceived in ethical life, with two limitations that prevent them from being fully free.

The first limitation of spiritual beings at the end of objective spirit stems from what Hegel calls the contradiction of willing. On the one hand, the willing subject is certain that it has the ability to transform the immediate and insignificant shape of the natural world through the realization of its purposes; but on the other hand, the willing subject also presupposes that natural world as fundamentally independent of itself, and therefore understands its purpose of realizing its freedom to be only *its* purpose, to be merely subjective. The willing subject does not regard nature itself as aiming at the construction of a rational state, but rather as having this form imposed upon it. This means that even at the culmination of objective spirit spiritual beings remain alienated from the natural world, and therefore incompletely free.

The second limitation of willing subjects stems from the fact that their conception of freedom may not accord with the objective requirements of freedom itself. Willing therefore can and does manifest itself in a wide variety of social and political arrangements. As long as these arrangements fairly reflect the willing subject's self-understanding, it will feel at home and free in them; ethical life becomes literally second nature for the willing subject. But a particular shape of ethical life can become natural to its citizens without being in accordance with all the conceptual requirements of freedom. And this means that the feeling of a people that they are free, which manifests itself in their patriotic obedience to the state, cannot in fact guarantee that they are.

Consequently, willing is unable to forge a fully satisfying reconciliation with the natural world. The ultimate reconciliation and satisfaction must be sought, Hegel argues, not through willing, but through the activities presented in absolute spirit, those of art, religion and philosophy.

Hegel thinks all three activities considered in absolute spirit overcome the first limitation of willing: all of them overcome the presupposition (common to both subjective and objective spirit) that spiritual beings and the natural world, subject and object, are fundamentally alien to each other. In the theoretical activity of knowing, the contents of the natural world are understood to be imposed on a receptive spiritual subject. And in the practical activity of willing, spiritual contents are understood to be imposed on an indifferent natural world. The activities of absolute spirit, however, are precisely those in which spiritual subjects come to understand that the theoretical and practical presumption of the mutual alienation of the spiritual and the natural must be false, for only if the spiritual subject and the natural world are already reconciled is it possible for successful knowing and willing to take place. Art, religion and philosophy, that is, show that the very condition of the possibility of the theoretical and practical activities that strive to unify the determinations of thought and being is that the determinations of thought and being must always already have been unified. In all three activities, then, spiritual beings know themselves to be truly free, for they know that they have no absolute other. The activities of absolute spirit thus finally overcome the alienation of the spiritual subject from the natural world.

Hegel locates the principal difference among the three activities of absolute spirit in the form in which each grasps and manifests the truth of human freedom. Art creates beautiful objects that present the truth to our senses. In the best Greek sculpture, for example, we can actually see human freedom: the harmony of mind and body, the satisfied repose in the present, and the potential for purposive action are all immediately apparent in the stone figures. Religion develops symbolic myths and rituals that represent and enable us to feel the truth. Hegel regards "God", for example, as "a representation of the philosophical idea that we make for ourselves" (*LPR*: I, 122), a powerful pictorial symbol that helps us to feel at home in the natural world. Philosophy generates conceptual comprehension of the truth. The *Philosophy of Spirit*, for example, systematically articulates the constitutive determinations of our freedom.

This difference is important, because it means that only philosophy is able to overcome the second limitation of willing by developing a justified account of the specific conditions of freedom. Philosophy is thus, according to Hegel, "the highest, the freest, and the wisest configuration" of spirit (*IPH*: 52). In art and religion, as in philosophy, spiritual beings achieve an adequate understanding of themselves as thinking beings who comprehend and thus complete the unity of thinking and being. Only in philosophy, however, is this self-understanding raised to self-knowledge, through being demonstrated by thinking beings to themselves in the form of systematic thought.

With this philosophical comprehension of philosophy, Hegel's system comes to an end. The systematic philosopher finally comprehends his philosophical practice as the activity of coming to comprehend himself as a free spiritual being, and he comprehends that it is through this philosophical self-comprehension that he becomes a fully free spiritual being by completing his reconciliation with the natural world. He thus realizes in retrospect that ever since he adopted the standpoint of systematic philosophy at the beginning of the *Logic* he has not only been thinking about the meaning of freedom, but has been participating in his own liberation.

Hegel's claim that art, religion and philosophy are necessary conditions of freedom does not imply that he thinks they are sufficient. In Hegel's view, freedom involves all the essential determinations developed in subjective, objective and absolute spirit: to be a free being is to be an aesthetic, religious and philosophical being, but it is also to be a cognitive, legal, moral, familial, economic and political being. The degree to which one is free is determined by the degree to which one enjoys the various types of reconciliation that contribute to liberation. A person at home in his social and political situation (one who enjoys ethical life) is more free than one who is not. Given two people who enjoy ethical life, one is more free than the other if his social and political situation more closely accords with the concept of objective freedom. Given two people with roughly equal degrees of objective freedom, one is more free than the other if he also has the kind of awareness of himself as a free being that Hegel thinks is developed in art, religion and philosophy. And, finally, given two people who have such an awareness, one is more free than the other to the extent that his self-understanding is more explicit and complete, which is why Hegel claims that philosophy offers a degree of freedom not available through other activities.

So the most complete freedom requires both the theoretical comprehension of the world, and its practical transformation. Moreover, Hegel believes that art, religion and philosophy sustain and direct our striving for social and political freedom by providing the self-understanding of ourselves as free beings that guides our efforts to transform the world. He insists that "the way in which the subject determines its goals in worldly life depends on the consciousness of its own essential truth . . . Morality and the political constitution are governed wholly by whether a people grasps only a limited representation of the freedom of spirit, or has the true consciousness of freedom" (*LPR*, one-volume edition: 69–70).

Hegel's point is that the social and political conditions we strive to bring about, and in which we are able to feel at home, depend upon the details of our self-understanding: we strive to realize the social and political conditions that we take to be most appropriate for beings like us, and thus our theoretical understanding of the sort of beings we are plays a crucial role in determining the direction of our practical undertakings. Of course, what we are, most basically, is free. But to say that is not to say very much, and thus, as Hegel emphasizes in the passage just cited, everything depends on exactly how we understand our freedom: people with different understandings of freedom develop very different social and political arrangements.

This insight regarding the relationship between theoretical comprehension of ourselves and practical transformation of the world is, Hegel believes, nothing less than the key to understanding human history, in which he finds a development toward an increasingly adequate consciousness and realization of freedom. Hegel's discussion of history also makes clear, however, that he does not claim that the practical realization of freedom depends upon distinctly *philosophical* self-knowledge spreading far and wide. All human beings must come to know that all human beings are free, but certainly not all, nor even very many, need be philosophers. Hegel considers religion, rather than philosophy, to be the primary means by which the self-consciousness of human freedom is disseminated broadly enough that it can become an increasingly powerful practical force.

But Hegel also believes that religion is ultimately incapable of discharging the very demand to which its consciousness of freedom gives rise, the modern demand that all knowledge claims, as well as all social and political institutions, dispense with reliance on authority and be justified to free thinking. The inability of religion to satisfy its own demand results from the fundamental contradiction at its core: on the one hand, the truth that religion presents (its content), according to Hegel, is the fact of human freedom, the fact that we are self-determining and therefore should reject all unjustified authority; but on the other hand, religion asks us to accept this truth on faith (its form), and so it asks us to accept an unjustified authority as the basis for our belief that no unjustified authority should be accepted.

The modern response to this situation must be an attempt to produce a non-arbitrary justification of the truth, one that appeals to reason alone and is therefore justifiable to all rational beings. Failing this, there will be no choice but to acknowledge that theoretical and practical commitments are relative to whichever presuppositions or authorities one happens to take as a starting point. As Hegel puts it in the Preface to the *Philosophy of Right*:

> The *truth* concerning *right, ethics, and the state* is at any rate *as old* as its *exposition and promulgation* in *public laws and in public morality and religion* . . . [But] it needs to be *comprehended* as well, so that the content which is already rational in itself may also gain a rational form and thereby appear justified to free thinking. For such thinking does not stop at what is *given*, whether the latter is supported by the external positive authority of the state or of mutual agreement among human beings, or by the authority of inner feeling and the heart and by the testimony of the spirit which immediately concurs with this, but starts out from itself and thereby demands to know itself as united in its innermost being with the truth. (*PR*: 11)

In other words, although religion can give people an awareness of, and a desire to live in accordance with, the truth that humans are free, only systematic philosophy can provide a non-arbitrary justification of the truth that the religious person deeply feels.

Hegel's conclusion is that philosophy has an indispensable role to play in guiding the realization of freedom in the social and political world by striving to educate people about the conditions of their liberation. The philosopher cannot force people to be free, nor does he have any expertise in designing or implementing plans for social and political change, nor will the intricate details of his arguments motivate people to pursue freedom. But for those who already desire to be free, the dissemination of the philosophical knowledge of the conditions of freedom can help to ensure that they are in fact aiming at the right target. If philosophers can teach people, for example, that freedom demands the establishment of a truly universal right to marry, then all people can make use of this knowledge in their pursuit of social and political liberation. Consequently, philosophical knowledge, when coupled with education, harbours transformative and even revolutionary potential:

> Philosophy in general has, as philosophy, other categories than those of ordinary consciousness: all education reduces to the distinction of categories. All revolutions, in the scientific disciplines no less than in world history, arise only on account of the fact that spirit, to understand and comprehend itself, in order to possess itself, has changed its categories, and so has grasped itself more truly, more deeply, more intimately, and more in unity with itself. (*PN*: 11)

Hegel thus identifies philosophy as the capstone of the most comprehensive freedom. Freedom certainly requires the practical transformation of the world, such that we come to be increasingly at home in our social and political situation. But freedom also requires the theoretical consciousness that we are free, and once people develop this consciousness they cannot be fully at home in their social and political situation unless they know that it is in accordance with the concept of freedom. Although people attain self-consciousness of their freedom through art, religion and philosophy, only philosophy can determine the content of the conception of freedom that all three of these activities present. Modern practical freedom therefore depends upon philosophy to comprehend the conditions of freedom against which the existing social and political situation must be measured, and towards the realization of which all people must work if they are to enjoy the fullest liberation. In the absence of such a worldly realization people's freedom will be incomplete, but in the absence of philosophy such a worldly realization will be not only less likely to occur, but also impossible to recognize if it does, and therefore harder to sustain.

Conclusion

Hegel's conception of philosophy, and the projects of the *Phenomenology* and the *Encyclopedia* that aim to realize that conception, follow from his conception of rational cognition as unconditionally justified true belief regarding the constitution of actuality. Many either do or would object, however, that this conception sets the standard of rationality absurdly high. If this is the case, then rather than attempting to pursue Hegel's projects, philosophers would be better off working to develop a more suitable conception of rational cognition. From this perspective, Hegel demonstrates not the need for a *Phenomenology* or a *Science of Logic*, but rather the need for a retreat from metaphysical ambition to the epistemological drawing board. Hegel may well have defined the standpoint of reason, in other words, in a way that makes evident the superior sensibility of the standpoint of understanding.

Hegel must admit, or else violate his own standard of rationality, that his standard of rationality itself cannot be presupposed but rather must be justified. And this justification cannot be accomplished simply by noting that Kant too associated reason with the refusal to be contented with conditional justifications, for such a justification would itself be conditional, in virtue of presupposing that Kant had a proper appreciation of rationality. Instead, Hegel's standard of rationality must be justified on the basis of an argument that it is only if we meet this standard that we do in fact have knowledge of the constitution of actuality.

Such an argument for Hegel's standard of rationality can be reconstructed, although only one of its two essential parts is provided by Hegel. The first half of the argument is provided by the ancient sceptics, whom Hegel regards as having developed the most devastating critique of the possibility of knowledge. The ancient sceptics successfully undermine, Hegel believes, all knowledge claims that rest on conditional presuppositions. Because the ancient sceptics did not recognize the possibility of a knowledge claim that did not rest on conditional presuppositions, they concluded that knowledge, and therefore philosophy *qua* science of knowledge, are impossible. Hegel, however, refuses to presuppose even the impossibility of a presuppositionless knowledge claim, and thus turns the sceptics' negative critique into a positive standard: if and only if philosophy can proceed without incorporating any conditional presuppositions can it resist the force of the ancient sceptical attack and justifiably claim to have knowledge of the constitution of actuality, or rational cognition.

Hegel thus responds to those who object that his standard of rationality is too high by objecting that their appreciation of ancient scepticism is too low. Hegel raised this objection against a variety of his contemporaries, including those who engaged in dogmatic metaphysics, and those who dogmatically asserted that metaphysics is impossible. His objection to the metaphysicians and epistemologists of today would be precisely the same: an appreciation of the force of ancient scepticism requires us to suspend the subject–object dualism of modern philosophy, or at least to subject it to sceptical examination by undertaking the project of the *Phenomenology*. If that project is successful, then it is known that the constitutive determinations of thought and being are identical, but an appreciation of the force of ancient scepticism requires us not to presuppose that any particular determinations are members of the constitutive set, and hence to undertake the project of the *Encyclopedia*.

Of course, even if one does appreciate the force of ancient scepticism, the projects of the *Phenomenology* and the *Encyclopedia* are not apodictically necessary. It is possible to grant that one has no answer to the ancient sceptics, and yet to pursue a variety of theoretical projects, including empirical science and philosophy in all its contemporary diversity. We do not need an answer to the ancient sceptics to carry on with our careful observation of the world and our enquiries into what it is reasonable to believe on the basis of our observations. Moreover, even if one has no answer to the ancient sceptics, there is no choice but to pursue the practical project of living one's life. We do not need an answer to the ancient sceptics to get on with the business of making our way in the world as best we can.

Because we can pursue almost all our theoretical and practical projects, and often with tremendous success, without an answer to the worries of the ancient sceptics, it is tempting to conclude that ancient scepticism is not something about which we need to be worried. Hegel would concede this to be true, if he did not believe that we need knowledge regarding the constitution of actuality. Such metaphysical knowledge cannot be had in the absence of a response to the ancient sceptics, and Hegel insists that in the absence of such metaphysical knowledge we cannot know what it is to be rational and to live accordingly. In other words, without an answer to the ancient sceptics it is possible to be premodern, or postmodern, and to live happily and perhaps even well. But without an answer to the ancient sceptics it is impossible to be modern and free. The project and promise of modernity therefore depend, Hegel concludes, upon the project and promise of rational cognition, and thus upon the project and promise of systematic philosophy without foundations.

Summary of key points

- Hegel accuses Kant's critical philosophy of not being critical enough, because it dogmatically assumes a subject–object dualism that limits knowledge to appearances.
- The *Phenomenology of Spirit* attempts to overcome subject–object dualism by exposing its internal contradictions. It examines a series of "shapes of consciousness", or ways of understanding the relationship between the knowing subject and the object of knowledge. It culminates in "absolute knowing", the standpoint at which, Hegel claims, it is known that the distinction between necessary determinations of thinking and being cannot justifiably be sustained.
- Hegel's system attempts to specify the necessary determinations of thinking and being. The *Logic* begins with the immediate being of thought, and then claims to articulate all and only those determinations that are immanent to it.
- The *Philosophy of Nature* and *Philosophy of Spirit* are continuations of the *Logic, a priori* examinations of what it is to be a spatiotemporal being and a free being, respectively.
- Hegel understands freedom as our reconciliation with the natural world and with each other. He argues that the pinnacle of such reconciliation is achieved through art, religion and philosophy, which enable us to overcome alienation by developing an adequate understanding of ourselves and the world.

seven

Conclusion: rationality, freedom and modernity?

German Idealism is best understood as the philosophical manifestation of the modern demand for rationality and freedom. It grew out of Kant's attempt to defeat the threat posed to this demand by Hume's scepticism and determinism. Fichte, Schelling and Hegel all shared Kant's aspiration to develop philosophical knowledge that could withstand the most rigorous sceptical scrutiny, and thereby to determine the conditions of a free and rational life. Despite this shared aspiration, however, these thinkers disagreed with Kant, and with each other, about how scepticism could be defeated. Their different reactions to scepticism led them to different conclusions about what it means to be rational and free, and thus to different conceptions of modernity. These methodological and substantive disagreements among the German Idealists provided the impetus for the progressive transformation of Kant's initial response to Hume into a distinctive philosophical movement.

Kant aimed to save freedom and rationality by employing what has come to be known as the transcendental method. Taking as given the fact that we experience a world of objects and events, Kant sought to determine the conditions that must obtain to make this possible. The first and most general condition he identified is that the objective world must be encountered and represented by the thinking subject. This led Kant to undertake a critical examination of the process of cognition, in order to ascertain both what thinking subjects can know and what is necessarily unknowable.

Transcendental idealism is the substantive position that resulted from Kant's critique: all objects of experience must conform to the cognitive conditions that enable us to experience them, but things-in-themselves are entirely inaccessible to us. Knowledge is therefore limited to appearances. Kant used this limitation on knowledge to rebut Hume's determinism, arguing that although we must experience all events as subject to causal necessitation, this does not preclude the possibility that some of those events, including our own actions, may be the products of freedom. Kant then argued that the exercise of freedom is a necessary condition of moral agency, and that our experience of ourselves as agents subject to moral obligation is therefore explicable only if we are in fact free.

Freedom, on Kant's view, is the capacity to transcend natural causes and act purely out of respect for our own rationality and the moral law that it imposes upon us. He held that we must ascribe this capacity to ourselves and strive to exercise it whenever morality requires. A truly modern life, according to Kant, must be organized in a way that fosters and sustains our moral striving. Education ought to teach people to think for themselves, and so to subordinate the demands of external authorities (among which he included the demands of our own natural inclinations) to the demands of reason. Politics ought to secure the liberties that are fundamental to moral agency, including the rights to think, speak and act for oneself. Religion, if it is to be modern and rational, ought to be limited to postulating the existence of God and the immortality of the human soul, in order to nurture the hope of those who strive to be moral that they will also one day be happy.

The further development of German Idealism was driven by the conviction that Kant's critical philosophy was not critical enough. Because all of Kant's conclusions depend upon his account of our cognitive faculties, and this account was regarded as insufficiently justified, transcendental idealism was immediately confronted with renewed sceptical attacks.

Reinhold and Fichte responded to the sceptical challenges of Jacobi and Schulze with methodological innovation. Their goal was to defend transcendental idealism by providing it with an unassailable foundational principle, from which all its substantive claims could be derived in strictly scientific fashion, resulting in a truly systematic philosophy.

Fichte took self-consciousness as his foundation, and attempted to demonstrate that all the essential features of experience can be explained as necessary conditions of the possibility of selfhood. The consequence was an idealism more overtly and thoroughly subjective than Kant's. Whereas Kant had argued that experience depends upon the existence of a mind-independent realm of objectivity, Fichte contended that the subject is able to encounter only that which it has posited. Because the subject must posit certain things – including the natural world – in order to become self-conscious, these necessary features of experience have a non-arbitrary or objective character.

Freedom, according to Fichte, consists of the ability to posit oneself as an active, rational agent. It depends, therefore, upon the development of the conditions that are necessary to the exercise of this ability. These include, according to Fichte, a community of human beings, the members of which recognize and respect each other's rationality and together actualize their potential for self-conscious agency. Such modern communities must, he further argued, establish the educational, economic and political institutions within which such agency can be nourished and sustained. The individuals who are raised in such communities then have the moral obligation, Fichte concluded, to subordinate the natural world to their own purposes, in the name of exercising their freedom.

Schelling shared Fichte's methodological commitment to foundational and systematic philosophy. He quickly concluded, however, that Kant and Fichte had been insufficiently ambitious, because they had attempted to account for only the relationship between, but not the ultimate origin of, subjectivity and objectivity. They had, in other words, restricted philosophy to a critique of cognition that could not answer the metaphysical question he considered most pressing: how did the world, and the rational creatures within it, come to be? Schelling therefore replaced the dualistic, subjective idealism of Fichte with his own monistic, absolute idealism, according to which the conscious subject and the objective realm it encounters are two modes in which a single underlying substance manifests itself. He regarded this substance as thoroughly indeterminate and transcending all attempts at philosophical comprehension, in virtue of being the absolute source of, and therefore prior to, all specificity and differentiation. Schelling considered art, however, to be capable of revealing to intuition the absolute identity of subjectivity and objectivity that he took to elude conceptual articulation.

Schelling insisted that human freedom is not only compatible with the monistic pantheism he espoused, but also necessary to explain the undeniable existence of evil. He was able to locate such freedom, however, only in an initial choice of character that takes place outside of time, and which determines all subsequent acts. He therefore held individuals to be responsible for their thoroughly predetermined lives. Schelling's dissatisfaction with this solution contributed to his eventual abandonment of the modern project of critical philosophy and his adoption of a traditional religious perspective.

Hegel thought critical idealism was insufficiently ambitious precisely because it was insufficiently critical. In his view, Kant, Fichte and the sceptics who challenged them all uncritically assumed a subject–object dualism that made knowledge impossible. He held that a truly modern philosophy must question even this assumption (as the ancient sceptics had) and take for granted, in quasi-Cartesian fashion, nothing more than the undeniable existence of thought.

Hegel's methodological innovation was thus based on the conviction that philosophy can respond to scepticism only by abandoning foundationalism. Philosophy cannot presuppose a substantive commitment to dualism or monism, or a purportedly self-evident principle, or a fixed method. Instead, philosophy must become scientific by restricting itself to a systematic examination of the necessary structure of thought.

Hegel's critique of foundationalism led him to embrace a very different sort of absolute idealism than that advocated by Schelling. Whereas Schelling characterized the absolute as a transcendent substance from which the world emanates, Hegel disavowed any concern with a supposedly unconditional entity that might serve as the ground of existence. Hegel's idealism was absolute in the sense that he held that the suspension of dualism precludes philosophy from assuming that there is a difference between the determinations that are necessary to think being and the determinations that are necessary to being itself. He ultimately concluded, contrary to Kant, that the categories constitutive of thought structure not only our experience but also actuality, and that philosophy can therefore give us rational cognition of that which truly is rather than mere appearances. This conclusion also amounted to a denial of Schelling's claim that the absolute truth escapes conceptual articulation and can be intuited only through art. Hegel regarded the aesthetic presentation of truth to be essential, because humans need to experience the truth in sensory as well as conceptual form, but did not believe that there is a truth available to art that philosophy cannot articulate.

The conception of freedom that emerged from Hegel's systematic philosophy was also distinctive. He conceived of freedom as the reconciliation of thinking beings with the natural world and with each other. He therefore rejected Fichte's view that rational agents must exercise their freedom by subordinating the natural world to their purposes, but shared his predecessor's understanding that freedom, rationality and modernity depend upon the establishment of legal, social, economic and political institutions within which liberating relationships can develop and be sustained. Hegel added that aesthetic, religious and philosophical experience are also essential to freedom, in virtue of enabling thinking beings to attain an adequate self-understanding.

German Idealism died with Hegel because he was the last philosopher to attempt to fulfil the promise of Kant's critical project by developing a systematic, *a priori* philosophy that could withstand the most powerful sceptical challenges. Because Hegel's foundationless ontology was widely regarded as the logical culmination of the Kantian tradition, the trajectories of German philosophy after his death were determined largely by the criticisms his enterprise received, which helped to define the alternatives that were perceived as viable and important. The most influential of these criticisms came from those who knew German Idealism the best, in virtue of having contributed to it themselves before concluding that its philosophical aspirations could not be fulfilled. These critics included the early Romantics and Schelling, who outlived his former friend by more than twenty years and enjoyed a brief return to prominence in the 1840s.

Early Romanticism: the poetic quarrel with philosophy

The group of German intellectuals who have come to be known as the early Romantics included, among others: Friedrich Hölderlin (1770– 1843), Novalis (1772–1801), Friedrich Schleiermacher (1768–1834), and Friedrich Schlegel (1772–1829), all of whom spent significant time in and around Jena during the years when Fichte, Schelling and Hegel were there. The Jena circle even briefly had its own journal, *Athenäum*, which was co-founded by Friedrich Schlegel and his brother August, and published between 1798 and 1800. The members of this circle had an important impact on the development of post-Kantian idealism, most directly through their influence on Schelling. The ultimate significance of early Romanticism, however, proved to lie in its insistence on the limitations of philosophy and the pre-eminent role that it accorded to art in revealing the truth. Hegel was fully aware of the early-Romantic position and argued against it explicitly, but it proved to have remarkable staying power, and contributed to the undermining of Hegelianism following his death.

Each of the thinkers in the Jena circle produced a substantial and complex body of work, but one of the common themes uniting them was a critical reaction to Fichte's subjective idealism, and to dualism more generally. Many of the early Romantics had initially been drawn to Fichte, but they soon grew dissatisfied with his account of the natural world and our relationship to it. Fichte treated the natural world as a mechanical totality that is necessarily posited by conscious subjects in order to experience their independence from it, which they accomplish by subordinating it to their own purposes. The early Romantics, like Schelling, regarded nature as a dynamic, rationally structured whole, of which conscious subjects are an integral part, and to which conscious subjects are called to respond attentively. This "Romantic" conception of nature envisions the natural world as a living thing that has given us our own life, rather than as a collection of impersonal particles and forces.

The early Romantics married their dynamic conception of nature to the same species of absolute idealism endorsed by Schelling. They regarded both conscious subjects and the natural world as manifestations of a single underlying substance or "absolute", which they held to be the ultimate source of all particular things. They also held this absolute to be resistant to all attempts at conceptual determination, because such attempts would violate and distort its unconditional character. As Novalis famously expressed the problem: "we seek everywhere the unconditioned and always find only the conditioned" (Novalis, 1966: 9).

The early Romantics did, however, consider it possible to experience the absolute through intellectual intuition, a direct awareness or feeling of that which transcends sensory experience and understanding. Such awareness could be induced, they contended, through art and poetic language. Artistic portrayals of the sublime – defined by Kant as that which is either so vast or so powerful as to overwhelm the capacity of the mind to understand it – convey the truth, the Romantics thought, that the absolute exceeds our ability to grasp it in concepts or words. Poetic and experimental language – including the use of metaphors, fragments, aphorisms and irony – confront the reader with the task of active and ongoing interpretation, and so embody the view that the truth always lies beyond what can be explicitly or literally said.

One practical result of the awareness of the sublime character of the absolute, according to the early Romantics, is awe and gratitude for the ultimate ground of life and thought. This is a stark contrast to Fichte's view that rational agents are morally obliged to strive for the deliberate mastery and subordination of that which is other than self-consciousness. Another practical result of the belief that the absolute truth exceeds any particular conception of it was a stance of ironic detachment –

advocated by a number of the early Romantics, but worked out most fully by Friedrich Schlegel – toward existing commitments, all of which were regarded as conditional, provisional and subject to retraction. This stance is sharply opposed to the positions of Kant, Fichte and Hegel, all of whom, despite their differences, agreed that rationality is capable of establishing the absolute validity of at least some moral and ethical commitments. Hegel was particularly scathing in his treatment of Romantic irony, which he accused in his *Philosophy of Right* of shamelessly blurring the distinction between good and evil.

The early Romantic contention that philosophy is impotent to articulate the absolute truth poses a direct challenge to Hegel's view that foundationless, systematic philosophy can specify the constitutive determinations of being. One corollary to this disagreement is the difference between the positions held by the early Romantics and Hegel on the relation between philosophy and art. Hegel conceived of art and philosophy as presenting the same truth – most importantly, the truth of human freedom – in different forms: art presents the truth in media that appeal to the senses, whereas philosophy presents it in conceptual accounts. The early Romantics, however, conceived of art as indirectly evoking a truth – that of the sublime transcendence of the absolute – of which philosophy is simply incapable of speaking.

In attempting to assess the dispute between Hegel and the early Romantics over the limitations of philosophy, it is essential to keep in mind that their understandings of absolute idealism were distinctly different. The absolute idealism of the early Romantics was concerned with the original ground that is the source of the world and all existent things. It was this ground that they held philosophy to be incapable of comprehending, and therefore sought to evoke in art and poetry. Hegel's absolute idealism, however, was unconcerned with such an original ground of existence, and therefore made no attempt to comprehend it. Hegel's aim was to articulate the constitutive determinations of actuality, not to explain the fact of existence by identifying and describing its cause. Hegel thus agreed with the early Romantic assessment that the original ground of creation is a topic inappropriate for philosophy. His disagreement was with their contention that this means that philosophy cannot comprehend the absolute truth. In Hegel's view, this contention presupposes uncritically that being must be purely indeterminate and therefore necessarily other than the way that it is presented in determinate conceptual thought.

The primary legacy of early Romanticism was the elevation of art over philosophy, in virtue of the conclusion that the literal prose of philosophy cannot tell the absolute truth and must therefore be subordinated to poetic language. Early Romanticism led to a deep suspicion of the ability of reason to be fully self-critical, and therefore to a deep suspicion of, and ironic detachment from, the philosophical aspiration to determine definitively the constitutive conditions of a free and modern life. This legacy provided one of the most influential alternatives to Hegel's idealism in the nineteenth century, and has continued to reverberate throughout the European intellectual tradition to the present day.

Schelling's late critique of Hegel

Schelling's early and middle work had much in common with that of the early Romantics, many of whom were his friends and intellectual companions during his Jena period. In that work, Schelling espoused the same absolute idealism, and held the same view about the superiority of art to philosophy, as the other members of the early Romantic circle. After 1809, however, Schelling ceased to publish, and watched Hegel rise to prominence and supplant him as the pre-eminent German philosopher.

Schelling enjoyed a renaissance in the 1840s when, almost exactly ten years after Hegel's death, he was invited to assume his rival's old chair at the university in Berlin, expressly for the purpose of combating the progressive political influence of Hegelian thought. In this final incarnation, Schelling argued (in lectures that remain largely unavailable in English) that the project of systematic, *a priori* philosophy – to which he had once been firmly committed – could not possibly succeed. He argued, in other words, that the tradition of German Idealism had exhausted itself, reaching its culmination in Hegel's system, and in so doing revealing its inability to fulfil its own aspirations or the human needs to which philosophy ought to respond.

Schelling's lectures were initially packed with enthusiastic students, many of whom went on to become leading figures in the next generation of European intellectual life. The audience included the young Friedrich Engels (1820–95) and Søren Kierkegaard (1813–55), who helped to found communism and existentialism, respectively. Although few of those who heard Schelling were persuaded to adopt his own views, which at this point were politically conservative and traditionally religious, his critique of German Idealism was widely accepted and played a decisive role in giving momentum and direction to post-Hegelian philosophy.

Schelling argued both that Hegel's system failed to succeed on its own terms, and that even if it could be made to succeed it would still fail to accomplish the most important philosophical tasks. Schelling's first criticism was that the beginning of Hegel's system was not in fact presuppositionless in the senses that it claimed to be. Pure indeterminacy, Schelling contended, simply could not contain any implicit determination within itself. Consequently, any determinacy within the system must have been surreptitiously introduced by Hegel on the basis of abstraction from his own experience. Schelling also contended, more generally, that no concepts are dialectical, and thus that all the transitions within the system must have been supplied by Hegel in order to guide the development toward a pre-ordained endpoint. Taken together, these criticisms of Hegel's beginning and procedure amounted to a denial of the possibility that philosophy could be the presuppositionless, and therefore rational, articulation of the self-determination of thought.

Schelling also argued, however, that even if systematic philosophy could succeed on its own terms, it would still be fatally flawed in virtue of failing to distinguish between the logical necessity that obtains between concepts and the existential facts that obtain in the world. *A priori* reasoning about concepts simply cannot, Schelling insisted, account for the creation and existence of the world. Nor can it, he continued, provide an ontology that reveals the truth about particular things. Both nature and history are subject to contingencies that systematic philosophy necessarily ignores and obscures. Finally, Schelling concluded, this failure to comprehend contingency makes systematic philosophy nihilistic, incapable of providing values that can guide human life.

Hegel, of course, would have responded to each of Schelling's criticisms had he lived to do so. He would have pointed out that Schelling's insistence on an absolute distinction between indeterminacy and determinacy is precisely the sort of presupposition that a properly critical philosophy cannot make. He would have reiterated that he, unlike Schelling, did not expect philosophy to give an account of the creation of the world. He would have emphasized that one of the most important conclusions of his *a priori* philosophy is that contingency is logically necessary to all existing things and processes, and that the ability of systematic ontology to determine the truth is therefore intrinsically limited. Experience and empirical science are indispensable, according to Hegel, to our theoretical and practical endeavours, our attempts to know the truth about the world and to navigate it as well as possible.

Observation and empirical science cannot, however, determine necessary truths about either the natural world or rational norms. Therefore, Hegel would have concluded, nihilism can be avoided only by means of a foundationless, systematic philosophy that can determine the absolute truth regarding the values, practices and institutions that are essential to human freedom.

Schelling's own conclusion, however, was that Hegel's "negative" philosophy (so called because Schelling took it to negate existing things in favour of an abstract account of conceptual forms or essences) needed to be replaced by a "positive" philosophy that would set out from given facts that *a priori* reason cannot establish. Philosophy must frankly acknowledge our ineliminable dependence upon givenness, and so too our dependence upon an ultimate giver. Only such a giver, or God, can account for the fact of existence, for the fact *that* there is a world at all, and that this world contains rational creatures. Schelling's positive philosophy was thus overtly religious, advocating that the truth be sought not by means of self-critical reason, but rather in the accounts of creation provided in mythology and Christian revelation. Schelling also looked to these traditional religious sources to provide the values that could avert the threat of nihilism.

Post-Hegelian alternatives

Schelling's audience was shocked and quickly disillusioned by his reactionary appeal to Christianity, but they were persuaded and inspired by his distinction between conceptual relations and empirical facts. Hegel's systematic philosophy, and the project of German Idealism more generally, were widely assumed to be demonstrable failures.

The next generation of thinkers therefore quickly set about redefining the intellectual agenda. They rejected both Hegel's *a priori* ontology and Schelling's religious dogmatism in favour of a variety of empirical investigations that would be, they believed, both more true to the facts and more valuable to the goal of human liberation. These new projects gave fresh energy and direction to the natural and the social sciences, contributing to an eventual revolution in the way that historical, economic, political and religious phenomena are understood.

Ludwig Feuerbach (1804–72) and David Strauss (1808–74) were instrumental in transforming the study of religion from a consideration of the traditional theological issues that consumed Schelling to an examination of the significance to humans of religious texts, practices and institutions. A few years after Hegel's death, but before Schelling began lecturing in Berlin, Strauss published *The Life of Jesus* (1835), which rejected the literal interpretation of scripture and advocated reading religious texts as mythological expressions of human self-understanding. Feuerbach developed and modified this anthropological approach to religion, arguing in *The Essence of Christianity* (1841) that religious myths distort rather than express the truth, and that these distortions are fundamentally pernicious. Feuerbach had a direct and important influence on Karl Marx (1818–83), who famously declared only two years later that "religion . . . is the opium of the people", a means of distracting human beings from their economic and political oppression.

Marx made this remark in an early essay, "Toward a Critique of Hegel's *Philosophy of Right*", which was written in 1843. Marx argued that Hegel's dialectical account of social and political concepts needed to be replaced by an empirical science of the dialectical development of the material forces of economic production. He agreed with Hegel that liberation depends upon the overcoming of alienation, but thought that such overcoming requires the progressive transformation of existing institutions, rather than reconciliation with them. In the last of his "Theses on Feuerbach", written in 1845, Marx summed up his critique of idealism: "Philosophers have only *interpreted* the world in various ways; the point is to *change* it" (Marx 1988: 82).

Kierkegaard, who attended Schelling's first lectures in Berlin, found both traditional theology and religious anthropology to be inadequate. Neither, he thought, could account for the individual experience of religious faith. He emphasized the inescapably personal nature of this experience, and of the choice to suspend legal, ethical and political norms when they conflict with the absolute demands of religion. Kierkegaard thus rejected the claim of systematic philosophy to be able to determine and justify the norms constitutive of modernity, and called upon individuals to respond with resolute authenticity to the choices and challenges posed by human existence. He also rejected Hegel's claim that philosophy and religion present the same truth in different forms, since Kierkegaard regarded the heart of religious experience to be a leap of faith that conceptual reasoning cannot comprehend.

In the natural sciences, the eclipse of German Idealism coincided with dramatic progress in empirical research, which made Hegel's *a priori* ontology of nature seem irrelevant and hopeless. Kant, it was thought, had a much better understanding of the relationship between philosophy and natural science; according to Kant, the contribution of philosophy is limited to establishing the necessary conditions and regulative ideals that enable and guide the acquisition of empirical knowledge. By the 1860s this conviction had developed into a full-fledged movement, known as neo-Kantianism, which adopted as its battle cry the slogan: "Back to Kant!"

It is difficult to overstate the significance of German Idealism, and of its Hegelian endpoint, for the European intellectual tradition from 1830 to the present. Because German Idealism represented the logical culmination of the philosophical attempt to defeat scepticism by developing *a priori* knowledge, and Hegel represented the logical culmination of German Idealism, many of the most important intellectuals after 1830 defined themselves and their projects in terms of their relation to Hegel.

As Bertrand Russell has pointed out, despite the widespread criticism of German Idealism, quite a few of these thinkers remained consciously indebted to Hegel:

> At the end of the 19th century, the leading academic philosophers, both in America and in Great Britain, were largely Hegelians. Outside of pure philosophy, many Protestant theologians adopted his doctrines, and his philosophy of history profoundly affected political theory. Marx, as everyone knows, was a disciple of Hegel in his youth, and retained in his own finished system some important Hegelian features. Even if (as I myself believe) almost all Hegel's doctrines are false, he still retains an importance which is not merely historical, as the best representative of a certain kind of philosophy which, in others, is less coherent and less comprehensive.
>
> (Russell 1945: 736)

Maurice Merleau-Ponty, the great French phenomenologist, has added that many other thinkers remained unconsciously indebted to Hegel, even as they rejected his methods and conclusions:

> All the great philosophical ideas of the past century – the philosophies of Marx and Nietzsche, phenomenology, German existentialism, and psychoanalysis – had their beginnings in Hegel; it was he who started the attempt to explore the irrational and integrate it into an expanded reason, which remains the task of our century . . . No task in the cultural order is more urgent than re-establishing the connection between,

on the one hand, the thankless doctrines which try to forget their Hegelian origin and, on the other, that origin itself . . . One may say without paradox that to give an interpretation of Hegel is to take a stand with respect to all the philosophical, political, and religious problems of our century.

(Merleau-Ponty 1964: 63)

And Michel Foucault, one of the leading lights of French post-modernism, has emphasized that critics of Hegel should not be too quick to assume that his philosophy is dead and buried:

For many . . . our age, whether through logic or epistemology, whether through Marx or through Nietzsche, is attempting to flee Hegel . . . But truly to escape Hegel involves an exact appreciation of the price we have to pay to detach ourselves from him. It assumes that we are aware of the extent to which Hegel, insidiously perhaps, is close to us; it implies a know-ledge, in that which permits us to think against Hegel, of that which remains Hegelian. We have to determine the extent to which our anti-Hegelianism is possibly one of his tricks directed against us, at the end of which he stands, motionless, waiting for us.

(Foucault 1972: 235)

Hegel and German Idealism do continue to wait for us. The thinkers and texts of this period are fascinating in their own right, essential to a proper appreciation of the European intellectual tradition, and rich with insights that bear directly on the conversations of contemporary philosophy. When the meaning and possibility of freedom, rationality and modernity are fiercely contested, when the interrelations of science, morality, politics, art and religion are fluid and complex, the resources of German Idealism remain indispensable to comprehending our own time in thought.

Questions for discussion and revision

two Kant: transcendental idealism

1. How does Kant justify the distinction between appearances and things-in-themselves?
2. How does Kant determine the categories that he claims structure all of our experience?
3. How does the experience of moral obligation establish our freedom, according to Kant?
4. How does Kant determine our particular moral obligations?
5. Why does Kant consider religious faith to be rational?

three Sceptical challenges and the development of transcendental idealism

1. Why does Jacobi regard Kant as a subjective idealist, despite Kant's strenuous denial that this is his position?
2. What is Jacobi's argument for the claim that only a leap of faith can overcome subjective idealism and establish belief in the external world?
3. Why does Reinhold consider Kant's transcendental idealism to be in need of a better foundation?
4. How does Schulze's criticism of transcendental idealism differ from that of Jacobi?
5. Do the objections of Jacobi and Schulze seriously threaten transcendental idealism? If so, could critical philosophy be modified to withstand their attacks?

four Fichte: towards a scientific and systematic idealism

1. What does Fichte mean by "dogmatism" and "idealism", and why does he regard "dogmatism" as an untenable philosophical position?
2. Why does Fichte reject Reinhold's "principle of consciousness" as a foundation for philosophy? How is Fichte's own first principle different from Reinhold's?
3. How does Fichte use the method of thesis–antithesis–synthesis to advance the development of his system?
4. How does Fichte arrive at his conception of freedom, and in which respects is it different from Kant's?
5. What is the relationship between politics and morality, according to Fichte? How does his understanding of this relationship differ from that of Kant?

five Schelling: idealism and the absolute

1. What objections does Schelling raise to the critical philosophy of Kant and Fichte?
2. To what extent would Kant regard Schelling as having transgressed the limits to knowledge? How does Schelling defend his expansion of Kant's project?
3. How does Schelling distinguish the philosophy of nature from empirical science?
4. How does art complete self-consciousness, according to Schelling?
5. What is Schelling's position on the problem of theodicy, and why?

six Hegel: systematic philosophy without foundations

1. How does Hegel distinguish between "understanding" and "reason", and what is the significance of this distinction?
2. In which respects does Hegel consider Kant's philosophy insufficiently critical, and why?
3. How does Hegel's attempt to make philosophy scientific and systematic differ from that of Fichte?
4. How does Hegel's absolute idealism differ from that of Schelling?
5. What is the meaning of Hegel's claim that "what is rational is actual; and what is actual is rational", and how does he justify it?

Further reading

General

Excellent studies of the development of German Idealism and its central themes include: Karl Ameriks, *Kant and the Fate of Autonomy: Problems in the Appropriation of the Critical Philosophy* (Cambridge: Cambridge University Press, 2000); Frederick Beiser, *The Fate of Reason: German Philosophy from Kant to Fichte* (Cambridge, MA: Harvard University Press, 1987); Frederick Beiser, *German Idealism: The Struggle against Subjectivism, 1781–1801* (Cambridge, MA: Harvard University Press, 2002); Paul Franks, *All or Nothing: Systematicity, Transcendental Arguments, and Skepticism in German Idealism* (Cambridge, MA: Harvard University Press, 2005); Dieter Henrich, *Between Kant and Hegel: Lectures on German Idealism* (Cambridge, MA: Harvard University Press, 2003); Terry Pinkard, *German Philosophy 1760–1860: The Legacy of Idealism* (Cambridge: Cambridge University Press, 2002).

Several valuable collections of essays are also available: Karl Ameriks (ed.), *The Cambridge Companion to German Idealism* (Cambridge: Cambridge University Press, 2000); Michael Baur and Daniel Dahlstrom (eds), *The Emergence of German Idealism* (Washington, DC: Catholic University of America Press, 1999); Sally Sedgwick (ed.), *The Reception of Kant's Critical Philosophy: Fichte, Schelling and Hegel* (Cambridge: Cambridge University Press, 2000).

Kant

For synoptic treatments of Kant's critical philosophy, readers should consult: Paul Guyer, *Kant* (London: Routledge, 2006); Susan Neiman, *The Unity of Reason: Rereading Kant* (Oxford: Oxford University Press, 1997). For a groundbreaking account of Kant's relation to the analytic tradition: Robert Hanna, *Kant and the Foundations of Analytic Philosophy* (Oxford: Oxford University Press, 2006).

Outstanding examinations of the first *Critique* include: Henry Allison, *Kant's Transcendental Idealism: An Interpretation and Defense* (New Haven, CT: Yale University Press, revised and expanded edition, 2004); Sebastian Gardner, *Kant and the Critique of Pure Reason* (London: Routledge, 1999); Paul Guyer, *Kant and the Claims of Knowledge* (Cambridge: Cambridge University Press, 2003).

For helpful investigations of Kant's practical philosophy: Henry Allison, *Kant's Theory of Freedom* (Cambridge: Cambridge University Press, 1990); Christine Korsgaard, *Creating the Kingdom of Ends* (Cambridge: Cambridge University Press, 2004); Onora O'Neill, *Constructions of Reason: Explorations of Kant's Practical Philosophy* (Cambridge: Cambridge University Press, 1990); Allen Wood, *Kant's Ethical Thought* (Cambridge: Cambridge University Press, 1999).

On the third critique: Henry Allison, *Kant's Theory of Taste: A Reading of the Critique of Aesthetic Judgment* (Cambridge: Cambridge University Press, 2005); Paul Guyer, *Kant and the Claims of Taste* (Cambridge: Cambridge University Press, second edition, 1997).

Fichte

First-rate works on Fichte include: Wayne Martin, *Idealism and Objectivity: Understanding Fichte's Jena Project* (Stanford, CA: Stanford University Press, 1997); Frederick Neuhouser, *Fichte's Theory of Subjectivity* (Cambridge: Cambridge University Press, 1990); Günter Zöller, *Fichte's Transcendental Philosophy: The Original Duplicity of Intelligence and Will* (Cambridge: Cambridge University Press, 2002).

A very useful collection of essays is Daniel Breazeale and Tom Rockmore (eds), *New Perspectives on Fichte* (Atlantic Highlands, NJ: Humanities Press, 1996).

Schelling

For insightful studies of Schelling, readers should see: Andrew Bowie, *Schelling and Modern European Philosophy* (London: Routledge, 1994); Werner Marx, *The Philosophy of F.W.J. Schelling: History, System, and Freedom* (Bloomington, IN: Indiana University Press, 1984); Dale Snow, *Schelling and the End of Idealism* (Albany, NY: SUNY Press, 1996); Alan White, *Schelling: An Introduction to the System of Freedom* (New Haven, CT: Yale University Press, 1983).

Hegel

The best and most comprehensive introduction to Hegel is Stephen Houlgate, *An Introduction to Hegel: Freedom, Truth and History* (Oxford: Blackwell, second edition, 2005). An influential, non-metaphysical interpretation of Hegel is developed in Robert Pippin, *Hegel's Idealism: The Satisfactions of Self-Consciousness* (Cambridge: Cambridge University Press, 1989).

Among the many fine works on the *Phenomenology of Spirit*, the following are highly recommended: Quentin Lauer, *A Reading of Hegel's Phenomenology of Spirit* (New York: Fordham University Press, 1976); Terry Pinkard, *Hegel's Phenomenology: The Sociality of Reason* (Cambridge: Cambridge University Press, 2004); John Russon, *Reading Hegel's Phenomenology* (Bloomington, IN: Indiana University Press, 2004).

Important treatments of Hegel's approach to foundationless ontology are provided by: Stephen Houlgate, *The Opening of Hegel's Logic: From Being to Infinity* (West Lafayette, IN: Purdue University Press, 2006); William Maker, *Philosophy without Foundations: Rethinking Hegel* (Albany, NY: SUNY Press, 1994); Alan White, *Absolute Knowledge: Hegel and the Problem of Metaphysics* (Athens, OH: Ohio University Press, 1983).

For recent, high-quality work on Hegel's philosophy of nature: Stephen Houlgate (ed.), *Hegel and the Philosophy of Nature* (Albany, NY: SUNY Press, 1998) and Alison Stone, *Petrified Intelligence: Nature in Hegel's Philosophy* (Albany, NY: SUNY Press, 2005).

The many helpful studies of Hegel's philosophy of spirit include: Will Dudley, *Hegel, Nietzsche, and Philosophy: Thinking Freedom* (Cambridge: Cambridge University Press, 2002); Frederick Neuhouser, *Foundations of Hegel's Social Theory: Actualizing Freedom* (Cambridge, MA: Harvard University Press, 2003); Allen Wood, *Hegel's Ethical Thought* (Cambridge: Cambridge University Press, 1990).

References

Fichte, J. G. 1982. *The Science of Knowledge*, Peter Heath & John Lachs (eds and trans.). Cambridge: Cambridge University Press.

Fichte, J. G. 1988. "Concerning the Concept of the *Wissenschaftslehre*". In *Early Philosophical Writings*, Daniel Breazeale (ed. and trans.). Ithaca, NY: Cornell University Press. Cited in text as "Concerning the Concept of *The Science of Knowledge*".

Fichte, J. G. 2000. *Foundations of Natural Right*, Frederick Neuhouser (ed.), Michael Baur (trans.). Cambridge: Cambridge University Press.

Fichte, J. G. 2000. "Review of *Aenesidemus*". In *Between Kant and Hegel*, George di Giovanni & H. S. Harris (eds and trans.). Indianapolis, IN: Hackett.

Fichte, J. G. 2005. *The System of Ethics*, Daniel Breazeale & Günter Zöller (eds and trans.). Cambridge: Cambridge University Press.

Foucault, Michel. 1972. "The Discourse on Language". In *The Archaeology of Knowledge*, Rupert Sawyer (trans.). New York: Pantheon.

Hegel, G. W. F. 1970. *Philosophy of Nature*, A. V. Miller (trans.). Oxford: Clarendon Press.

Hegel, G. W. F. 1971. *Philosophy of Mind*, William Wallace & A. V. Miller (trans.). Oxford: Clarendon Press. Cited in text as *Philosophy of Spirit*.

Hegel, G. W. F. 1974. *Lectures on the Philosophy of Religion I*, E. B. Speirs & J. Burdon Sanderson (trans.). New York: Humanities Press.

Hegel, G. W. F. 1977. *The Difference Between Fichte's and Schelling's System of Philosophy*, H. S. Harris & Walter Cerf (trans.). Albany, NY: SUNY Press.

Hegel, G. W. F. 1977. *Faith and Knowledge*, Walter Cerf & H. S. Harris (trans.). Albany, NY: SUNY Press.

Hegel, G. W. F. 1977. *Phenomenology of Spirit*, J. N. Findlay (ed.), A. V. Miller (trans.). Oxford: Oxford University Press.

Hegel, G. W. F. 1985. *Introduction to the Lectures on the History of Philosophy*, T. M. Knox & A. V. Miller (trans.). Oxford: Clarendon Press.

Hegel, G. W. F. 1985. *Lectures on the Philosophy of Religion III: The Consummate Religion*, Peter C. Hodgson (ed.), R. F. Brown *et al.* (trans.). Berkeley, CA: University of California Press.

Hegel, G. W. F. 1988. *Introduction to the Philosophy of History*, Leo Rauch (trans.). Indianapolis, IN: Hackett.

Hegel, G. W. F. 1988. *Lectures on the Philosophy of Religion: One Volume Edition, Lectures of 1827*, Peter C. Hodgson (ed.), R. F. Brown *et al.* (trans.). Berkeley, CA: University of California Press.

Hegel, G. W. F. 1989. *Science of Logic*, H. D. Lewis (ed.), A. V. Miller (trans.). Atlantic Highlands, NJ: Humanities Press.

Hegel, G. W. F. 1991. *Elements of the Philosophy of Right*, Allen Wood (ed.), H. B. Nisbet (trans.). Cambridge: Cambridge University Press. Cited in text as *Philosophy of Right*.

Hegel, G. W. F. 1991. *The Encyclopedia Logic*, T. F. Geraets *et al.* (trans.). Indianapolis, IN: Hackett.

Hegel, G. W. F. 2000. "How the Ordinary Understanding Takes Philosophy". In *Between Kant and Hegel*, George di Giovanni & H. S. Harris (eds and trans.). Indianapolis, IN: Hackett.

Hegel, G. W. F. 2000. "On the Relationship of Skepticism to Philosophy: Exposition of its Different Modifications and Comparison of the Latest Form with the Ancient One". In *Between Kant and Hegel*, George di Giovanni & H. S. Harris (eds and trans.). Indianapolis, IN: Hackett.

Hume, David. 2000. *A Treatise of Human Nature*, David Fate Norton & Mary J. Norton (eds). Oxford: Oxford University Press.

Jacobi, F. H. 1994. *Concerning the Doctrine of Spinoza in Letters to Herr Moses Mendelssohn*. In *The Main Philosophical Writings and the Novel Allwill*, George di Giovanni (ed. and trans.). Montreal: McGill-Queen's University Press.

Jacobi, F. H. 1994. "On Transcendental Idealism", supplement to *David Hume on Faith, or Idealism and Realism, a Dialogue*. In *The Main Philosophical Writings and the Novel Allwill*, George di Giovanni (ed. and trans.). Montreal: McGill-Queen's University Press.

Kant, Immanuel. 1996. *Critique of Practical Reason*. In *Practical Philosophy*, Allen Wood (ed.), Mary J. Gregor (trans.). Cambridge: Cambridge University Press.

Kant, Immanuel. 1996. *Groundwork of the Metaphysics of Morals*. In *Practical Philosophy*, Allen Wood (ed.), Mary J. Gregor (trans.). Cambridge: Cambridge University Press.

Kant, Immanuel. 1998. *Critique of Pure Reason*, Paul Guyer & Allen Wood (eds and trans.). Cambridge: Cambridge University Press.

Kant, Immanuel. 2000. *Critique of the Power of Judgment*, Paul Guyer (ed.), Paul Guyer & Eric Matthews (trans.). Cambridge: Cambridge University Press.

Kant, Immanuel. 2002. *Prolegomena to Any Future Metaphysics That Will Be Able to Come Forward As Science*. In *Theoretical Philosophy After 1871*, Henry Allison & Peter Heath (ed.), Gary Hatfield *et al.* (trans.). Cambridge: Cambridge University Press.

Marx, Karl. 1988. "Theses on Feuerbach". In *Selections*, Allen W. Wood (ed.). New York: Macmillan.

Marx, Karl. 1988. "Toward a Critique of Hegel's *Philosophy of Right*". In *Selections*, Allen W. Wood (ed.). New York: Macmillan.

Merleau-Ponty, Maurice. 1964. *Sense and Nonsense*, Herbert L. & Patricia Allen Dreyfus (trans.). Evanston, IL: Northwestern University Press.

Novalis. 1996. "Pollen". In *The Early Political Writings of the German Romantics*, Frederick C. Beiser (ed.). Cambridge: Cambridge University Press.

Reinhold, K. L. 2000. *The Foundation of Philosophical Knowledge*. In *Between Kant and Hegel*, George di Giovanni & H. S. Harris (eds and trans.). Indianapolis, IN: Hackett.

Russell, Bertrand. 1945. *A History of Western Philosophy*. New York: Simon & Schuster.

Schelling, F. W. J. 1936. *Philosophical Inquiries into the Nature of Human Freedom*, James Gutmann (trans.). La Salle, IL: Open Court.

Schelling, F. W. J. 1978. *System of Transcendental Idealism*, Peter Heath (trans.). Charlottesville, VA: University Press of Virginia.

Schelling, F. W. J. 1980. "Of the I as the Principle of Philosophy, or, On the Unconditional in Human Knowledge". In *The Unconditional in Human Knowledge: Four Essays*, Fritz Marti (trans.). Lewisburg, PA: Bucknell University Press.

Schelling, F. W. J. 1980. "Philosophical Letters on Dogmatism and Criticism". In *The Unconditional in Human Knowledge: Four Essays*, Fritz Martin (trans.). Lewisburg, PA: Bucknell University Press.

Schelling, F. W. J. 1988. *Ideas for a Philosophy of Nature*, Errol E. Harris & Peter Heath (trans.). Cambridge: Cambridge University Press.

Schelling, F. W. J. 2004. *First Outline of a System of the Philosophy of Nature*, Keith R. Peterson (ed. and trans.). Albany, NY: SUNY Press.

Schulze, G. E. 2000. *Aenesidemus, or, Concerning the Foundations of the Philosophy of the Elements Issued by Professor Reinhold in Jena together with a Defence of Skepticism against the Pretensions of the Critique of Reason*. In *Between Kant and Hegel*, George di Giovanni & H. S. Harris (ed. and trans.). Indianapolis, IN: Hackett.

Chronology

1724	Immanuel Kant born in Königsberg, Germany.
1739	David Hume publishes *A Treatise of Human Nature*.
1762	Johann Gottlieb Fichte born in Rammenau, Germany.
1770	Georg Wilhelm Friedrich Hegel born in Stuttgart, Germany.
1775	Friedrich Wilhelm Joseph von Schelling born in Leonberg, Germany.
1781	Kant publishes *Critique of Pure Reason*.
1787	Friedrich Jacobi publishes "On Transcendental Idealism".
1788	Kant publishes *Critique of Practical Reason*.
1789	The French Revolution begins.
1790	Kant publishes *Critique of the Power of Judgment*.
	Schelling and Hegel are room mates at the Seminary at Tübingen.
1791	Karl Leonhard Reinhold publishes *The Foundation of Philosophical Knowledge*.
1792	Gottlob Ernst Schulze publishes *Aenesidemus*.
1794	Fichte assumes Reinhold's chair as professor of philosophy at Jena.
	Fichte presents *The Science of Knowledge* in lectures at Jena.
1795	Schelling publishes his "Of the I as Principle of Philosophy, or, on the Unconditional in Human Knowledge".
	Schelling publishes "Philosophical Letters on Dogmatism and Criticism".
1797	Fichte publishes *Foundations of Natural Right*.
	Schelling publishes *Ideas for a Philosophy of Nature*.
1798	Fichte publishes *The System of Ethics*.
	Schelling joins Fichte as professor of philosophy at Jena.
1799	Fichte loses professorship at Jena on charges of atheism.
	Schelling publishes *First Outline of a System of the Philosophy of Nature*.
1800	Schelling publishes *System of Transcendental Idealism*.

1801	Hegel receives unpaid lectureship at Jena.
	Hegel publishes *The Difference Between Fichte's and Schelling's System of Philosophy*.
1802–03	Schelling and Hegel co-edit *Critical Journal of Philosophy* in Jena.
1804	Kant dies.
1807	Napoleon Bonaparte invades Prussia.
	Hegel publishes *Phenomenology of Spirit*.
1809	Schelling publishes *Philosophical Inquiries into the Nature of Human Freedom*.
1812–16	Hegel publishes *The Science of Logic*.
1814	Fichte dies.
1816	Hegel receives professorship at Heidelberg.
1817	Hegel publishes *Encyclopedia of Philosophical Sciences*.
1818	Hegel receives professorship at Berlin.
1820	Hegel publishes *Philosophy of Right*.
1831	Hegel dies.
1841	Schelling receives professorship at Berlin.
1854	Schelling dies.

Index